PEACHES &
DADDY

PEACHES & DADDY

❖

A Story of the Roaring Twenties,
the Birth of Tabloid Media,
and the Courtship That Captured
the Heart and Imagination
of the American Public

❖

MICHAEL M. GREENBURG

THE OVERLOOK PRESS
Woodstock & New York

This edition first published in the United States in 2008 by
The Overlook Press, Peter Mayer Publishers, Inc.
Woodstock & New York

WOODSTOCK:
One Overlook Drive
Woodstock, NY 12498
www.overlookpress.com
[for individual orders, bulk and special sales, contact our Woodstock office]

NEW YORK:
141 Wooster Street
New York, NY 10012

TEXT PERMISSIONS: p. 10: by permission of Esther P. Lederer Trust and Creators Syndicate, Inc.;
p. 62: from the *New York Times*, September 20, 1923, © 1923 *The New York Times*. All rights
reserved. Used by permission and protected by the Copyright Laws of the United States. The
printing, copying, redistribution, or retransmission of the material with express written permission is prohibited.

PHOTO CREDITS: p. 18: Milstein Division of United States History, Local History & Genealogy,
The New York Public Library, Astor, Lenox and Tilden Foundations; pp. 24, 27, 66, 70, 79, 82,
96, 100, 155, 166, 196, 208, 234, 252: Courtesy Daily News Archive/New York Daily News;
p. 32: Picture Collection, The Branch Libraries, The New York Public Library, Astor, Lenox
and Tilden Foundations; Courtesy of Thomas James Kearney Jr.; p. 44, 311: courtesy
NewspaperARCHIVE.com; pp. 107, 161, 163, 262, 292: Corbis; p. 128: Courtesy Marie and
Robert Gauvreau; p. 135: George Grantham Bain Collection, Prints & Photographs Division,
Library of Congress, LC-DIG-ggbain-37319; 172: Courtesy the family of Harry Grogin; pp. 178,
222, 271, 276: Author's collection; p. 180: Courtesy McEvilly/New York Daily News; p. 198:
Courtesy, J. Joseph McGowan, Esq., McCabe & Mack LLP, Poughkeepsie, New York.; pp. 238,
242, 243: Courtesy the family of Harry Grogin; p. 269: Courtesy Levine/New York Daily News;
p. 306: Courtesy P&A Photos/New York Daily News; 78, 81, 104, 142, 298, 304, 310, 319, 322:
courtesy A.P. Images

Cataloging-in-Publication Data is available from the Library of Congress

Book design and type formatting by Bernard Schleifer
Manufactured in the United States of America
ISBN 978-1-59020-046-9
FIRST EDITION
10 9 8 7 6 5 4 3 2 1

To Donna, Corey, and Jeffrey . . .
where the story begins

❖

CONTENTS

FOREWORD

ON JANUARY 6, 1970, the following exchange appeared in the *Ann Landers* column in newspapers across America:

> **DEAR ANN LANDERS:** Although you have never come right out and blasted May-December marriages, you've never endorsed them. Don't you realize age means nothing anymore? It's virtually impossible today to tell if a woman is 20 or 33. The same goes for men, now that hair tinting, toupes and face lifting are so popular. One of the most exciting May-December romances in history was the Peaches and Daddy Browning marriage. Why don't you tell your readers about it? It should give all men hope. —BOCA RATON, FLA.

> **DEAR BO:** Hope for what? A trip to the poor house? Edward Browning was 51 when he met Frances "Peaches" Heenan at a sorority dance. She was 15. They were married on her 16th birthday. The marriage lasted less than a year during which time she spent approximately $1,000 a day in New York department stores. I'd hardly call this a model marriage.

Ann Landers could not have been more succinct. The story of Peaches and Daddy is a study in dysfunction and remarkable excess, yet the lurid details of their brief courtship and marriage captured the imagination of the American public in a way no couple in history had ever done. Their saga appealed to both the prurient and the romantic and propelled them into the headlines and the bylines of the nation's tabloid press for years to come.

In many ways, Edward Browning was the true Gatsby. He was a New York City millionaire, a beneficiary of the Coolidge prosperity, who understood the early 1920s as a time of great personal opportunity. New lifestyles and political forces were reshaping the world, and though Browning clearly profited from those forces, he seemed, for better or worse, to be a man swept up in the excesses of the day.

Frances Heenan was an unremarkable high school girl with unremarkable high school girl dreams and ambitions. Yet she, perhaps more than any other person, would become a symbol of the eccentric 1920s. When she met Edward Browning, she lived alone with her mother in a small apartment at the northern most tip of Manhattan. She worked as an auditing clerk (conspicuously absent from school), earning $15 per week. Peaches and Daddy could not have come from more opposite sides of the economic spectrum or from more divergent social backgrounds. Yet they were drawn together by the same stalwart fanaticism that would ultimately tear them apart.

At another moment in time, Peaches and Daddy might have been a pair of eccentrics whose paths happened to cross. But in 1926, America was ready to let them be much more than entertainment. The recent popularity of commercial journalism left newspaper editors constantly on the hunt for stories that would titillate their readers—and the Brownings loved the public as much as the public loved them. Across the country, big city and small town newspapers alike clamored for every detail of the Brownings and their odd doings. Front-page headlines featuring the couple set readership records and people who had never read newspapers before began buying these photo-filled publications in record numbers.

While some staid and traditional city papers had difficulty making the transition from the informative to the interesting, that newborn brand of journalism—the tabloid, now such a bedrock of the news industry—created itself around the Peaches and Daddy story. The *New York Evening Graphic*, for example, within two years of its inception, had managed a readership of six hundred thousand, while the *Daily News* reached an insurmountable one million readers.

Newspaper circulation is always dependent, however, on the vagaries of human nature and the fickle interest of the public. As with so many stories in today's world, the white-hot saga of Peaches and Daddy would be swallowed up by other momentous events of the day, and the marriage that sponsored so much upheaval in national law, codes, fashion trends, and moral debates vanished almost completely from public memory. The very industry of tabloid journalism that the Browning saga had sponsored abandoned them in the face of fresh and exciting national news. Peaches and Daddy were eclipsed by Charles Lindbergh's famous trans-Atlantic journey, and then, shortly thereafter, by the tragic bombing at a schoolhouse in Bath, Michigan, which resulted in the death of forty-five people, mostly children. In light of these newsworthy items, the Brownings' public was not as faithfully interested in them as either of them might have hoped. Peaches and Daddy were destined to become the forgotten jewel of a bygone era.

Forgotten, perhaps, but by no means irrelevant. This strange and nonconformist romance was no less than a cultural phenomenon, and exploration reveals an impact far greater than the sum of the often absurd events that shaped it. The story of Peaches and Daddy and its vivid press coverage forced 1920s America to confront issues of lasting import—age disparity in marriage, child adoption, contact between men and underage females—and laid the groundwork for what is lawful and acceptable today. The Browning marriage would become the spring- board for many a legislative crusade in the battle for child protection, which survive to this day.

Beyond the obvious legal and moral questions presented by these issues, Peaches and Daddy, like many cultural icons, would effect great social change and contribute to popular notions and fashions of the day. Men and women, young and old and from every walk of American life, relentlessly followed the movements of Peaches and Daddy. They were loved by some, reviled by others, but ignored by none. Their styles were emulated and sometimes castigated, but perhaps no two people had a greater impact on how America looked at itself in the early twentieth century.

As Peaches and Daddy found their way into the courts of New York, so followed many questions of judicial practice and procedure. With modern advances in photography and the advent of mass media, judges across the country were forced to make far-reaching decisions that balanced the public's right to know against the requirement of decorum and privacy in the legal process. The highly controversial judgment to allow press and public access to the proceedings would reverberate for decades to come and would form the basis for the debate that rages to this very day.

The most pervasive impact of Peaches and Daddy was unquestionably felt in the realm of journalism. Intrepid newspaper editors persistently challenged the boundaries of the First Amendment and used Peaches and Daddy as a test case to further their pioneering methods of expression. Though some paid a heavy price, their legacy remains today as a signpost for Freedom of the Press in the face of distasteful content. American mass media as we know it today—its tolerance for truth, decency, obscenity, and imagination—came of age at this unique moment in history.

As I researched this book, the question of the relative motivations of the people involved constantly nagged me. Was Peaches Browning nothing more than an opportunistic seductress? Or was she a star-struck child whose fairytale notions of happiness permitted her less than moderate behavior during the marriage and ensuing separation? Was she even old enough to be held accountable for any of her own actions? Was Edward Browning a true "Cinderella Man" whose greatest ambition was "to preside over a happy home and a family?" He is described in at least one journalistic writing of the day as an "incurable romantic" whose mid-life sentimental frolics replaced an emptiness of heart created by years of financial pursuits.

Yet sinister suspicions of an untoward attraction to young girls permeated the reporting. The Midtown millionaire was no stranger to scandal and his name frequented the columns of the city's tabloids even before Peaches. He said he was fifty-one years old when he met her, but whispers percolated in the press that he might have been a decade older. Because the couple's every action was hashed and rehashed by omnipresent news writers, evidence to support the purest and also the basest motivations of each is readily available. In the end, however, personal motivation is a question of the heart, and it will be upon the reader to decide what to believe.

Whatever it was that motivated the Brownings, the actions of these two extraordinary individuals must be viewed through the prism of the times in which they lived. The story of Peaches and Daddy has as its backdrop the so-called Roaring Twenties, the decade of dance marathons, bathtub gin, the Charleston, jazz, jazz, and more jazz, the Model T, 3-d movies, radio, the peanut butter and jelly sandwich, Rin-Tin-Tin, flappers, women's suffrage, and Calvin Coolidge. It was, as Westbrook Pegler wrote, "The Era of Wonderful Nonsense."

Following the tumult and horror of World War I, the American public sought a sense of personal and social normalcy. Optimism fueled business growth and popular culture flourished. The Eighteenth Amendment was challenged by bootlegging rumrunners, and flappers turned societal taboos of dress, sex, and personal comportment on their ears. The question of morality permeated the day. In Philadelphia, a committee of religious leaders and clergymen endorsed the moral gown, a conservative code of dress designed by a local Dress Reform Committee, but across America nice girls were smoking cigarettes, and hemlines were on the rise. A heroine of F. Scott Fitzgerald's *This Side of Paradise* proudly boasted, "I've kissed dozens of men. I suppose I'll kiss dozens more." Long established Victorian views of right and wrong, proper and improper were constantly challenged and refined in the 1920s, and new ideas of correctness emerged. The courtship of Edward Browning and Frances Heenan confronted the status quo of the day and pushed the envelope of the marital ideal.

The twenties were also, intriguingly, a decade of asceticism and prudence. Though Peaches and Daddy were remembered with a nostalgic eye for years to come, their actions at the time were met with criticism, denunciation, and censorship. In his account of the Browning separation trial, syndicated columnist and noted courtroom commentator Damon Runyon wrote, "I would not think of disclosing some of the allegations in a family newspaper. Your Uncle Samuel would bar it from his mails. They are things that are only put in plays nowadays—the kind of plays that Mayor Jimmy Walker often speaks of censoring. They were pretty raw." "The revel of filth," as the legal proceedings had been described, led one prominent Boston Newspaper to drop coverage of the case altogether.

Nonetheless, Peaches and Daddy were the proverbial automobile accident on the freeway—terrible to see, but impossible to turn away from. Many tabloids happily printed every electrifying morsel. Years later, upon the death of Peaches Browning, columnist and author Robert Ruark wrote, "Reading the papers in those days was an adventure. We innocents didn't know what all the commotion was about, but it titillated us greatly."

The drama and sensationalism of the Peaches and Daddy separation trial would find its place among a pattern of sensational stories that captivated the American public in this Whoopee Era. Some of the stories were of a whimsical nature, some much more serious. They all gained huge notoriety and each were covered in unique ways by the national press.

The first of these sagas took shape in 1922 with the matter of *The People v Frances Stevens Hall*, or the Hall-Mills Case, as it became known. The Reverend Edward Wheeler Hall and one of his female parishioners, Eleanor Mills, were discovered viciously shot to death beneath a crabapple tree. The torn love letters that had passed between the pair had been scattered across the corpses. Reverend Hall's grieving widow was ultimately charged with the crime, and the scandalous details of the case became the subject of debate and conversation at dinner tables across the country.

Though the initial investigation failed to result in arrests, inquisitive tabloid editors refused to let the story die. Under constant pressure to increase circulation, the *New York Daily Mirror* published a speculative reconstruction of the crime on flimsy evidence. In a sensational series of stories, the *Mirror* unabashedly accused Mrs. Hall and several of her relatives of the murders. The coverage caused such a public stir that indictments and a trial soon followed. Upon the acquittal of all defendants, the *Mirror* was sued for libel and the prestige of the paper was irrevocably impacted. More importantly, the frantic press coverage of the case had set a new standard for media treatment of tragedy.

In 1924, another trial of the century enveloped the nation. Richard Loeb and Nathan Leopold, the sons of prominent and wealthy Illinois businessmen, were tried and convicted of the senseless slaying of Bobby Franks, the fourteen-year-old son of a Chicago millionaire. Represented by Clarence Darrow, both defendants were spared the death penalty as a result of Darrow's twelve-hour long summation, which to this day stands as one of the most eloquent and moving arguments against capital punishment ever delivered. "Do I need to argue to your Honor that cruelty only breeds cruelty?" Darrow famously pled. "[T]hat hatred only causes hatred; that if there is any way to soften this human heart which is hard enough at its best, if there is any way to kill evil and hatred and all that goes with it, it is not through evil and hatred and cruelty; it is through charity, and love and understanding?"

One wild headline followed another. Babe Ruth led the New York Yankees to multiple world championships, Richard Byrd flew an airplane over the top of the world, Charlie Chaplin married a sixteen-year-old child-bride, Lita Gray, and Gertrude Ederle swam the English Channel. In Hollywood, film comedian Fatty Arbuckle stood accused of the brutal rape and resulting death of a party guest in his home, while puzzled investigators pondered the still-unsolved murder of famed

Hollywood director William Desmond Taylor. In divorce litigation that lasted for much of the decade, James A. Stillman, the President of Manhattan's National City Bank, sued his wife Anne (Fifi) Urquhart Potter, daughter of the socially prominent actress Cora Brown Potter, asserting that the couple's youngest son, Guy, was in reality fathered by a half-blood Indian guide from Quebec. In Tennessee, the renowned case of *The People v Scopes* pitted creationism against the theory of evolution in the classroom, and enveloped the nation in a debate between science and religion. In describing press coverage of the tumultuous events of 1927, Herbert Asbury recalled it as the Year of the Big Shriek:

> It was a year which produced an amazing crop of big news stories. Scarcely had one stupendous occurrence been emblazoned in journalistic tradition as the greatest story of the age than another appeared in its place, to goad frenzied editors and reporters to new heights of hysteria and hyperbole, while above the din of competition rose the mellow baying of the publicity hound . . .

It is amidst this cultural and social upheaval that the saga of Peaches and Daddy was born.

The romance and ultimate separation of Peaches and Daddy Browning were feverishly covered by many journalists of the day, and their telling of the story is as much a part of the story as the story itself. Both Peaches and Daddy engaged the press not as adversaries but as allies in their cause. They were the ultimate "shameless publicity mutts," as Damon Runyon wrote. For the most part, they willingly provided details of their engagement and courtship to the press, going as far as to stage public photo ops. It was a true symbiotic existence. The tabloid press became involved to the point where two journalists were called to testify in the Browning trial to explain the steps they had taken to obtain honeymoon accounts and explanations of the breakup. (These accounts, it turned out, had been sold to them by Peaches Browning.)

In 1946, syndicated columnist Jack Lait described in a newspaper column an encounter that he had with Edward Browning. At the time, Lait was an editor of the widely circulated *New York Daily Mirror*, and Browning was courting Lait to write a series about his life story. Lait was reluctant. In the rear seat of Browning's chauffeured Blitzen-Benz, a custom built limousine, Browning asked, "Do you like this car, Jack?" "Of course," Lait replied. "Well it's yours—and the chauffer with it."

Incensed by Browning's shameless attempt at bribery, Lait asked to be let out of the car. He wrote, "Browning was the most maniacal publicity hound I have ever met—and I have met plenty." Another description of Browning, penned by Oliver H.P. Garrett for American Mercury Magazine in 1927, aptly concluded, "He was a gentleman who, for all intents and purposes, could not be libeled; who could be ridiculed, buffooned, scorned, or solemnly attacked as a public menace; whose fetid mind could be explored at will; whose sexual practices and honeymoon antics he was only too happy to reveal, and from whom, as rejoinder, might be feared not so much as a single letter to the editor."

The Browning marriage would become a grotesque, if not comical, metaphor for the age in which it took place, and would come to represent a collision between great social and cultural change and the provincial mores of the past. In their time, the Brownings seemed nothing more than a symbol of sensationalism and frivolity. Through the years, however, the true cultural significance of this irrepressible couple would crystallize. Though the details of their story have long ago withered from the fleeting memory of a fickle public, their legacy of social rebellion and cultural nonconformity survives as one of the features of this wayward and unsettled time in the nation's history.

Peaches and Daddy were an emblem of an ever-changing age, where long-settled traditions and customs were challenged and often broken, where Victorian horse and buggy morals were discarded. No longer would the ideal of marriage fit into the tidy traditional mold, and thenceforth, matters that were previously heard only in whispers would be freely discussed and often written about.

Peaches and Daddy would unwittingly lead a revolution against the accepted national order and guide the country into the modern frontier of a new social, religious, and moral conviction. Their story is, on some levels, pure folly. But it is also one that illustrates the human record in a convulsive chapter of the American story.

PEACHES &
DADDY

❖

Hotel McAlpin, where Peaches and Daddy met on March 5, 1926, at a
Phi Lamba Tau sorority high school dance.

PROLOGUE
MARCH 5, 1926

"With the advent of spring I set forth with all the ardor of youth and met Frances Heenan. It was a case of love at first sight and is enthusiastically reciprocated."

—EDWARD WEST BROWNING

In the late evening of March 5, 1926, Edward West Browning waltzed through the doors of the legendary Hotel McAlpin at the corner of 34th Street and Broadway. The peacock blue Rolls Royce that had become the emblem of his opulent lifestyle remained at the front of the building, engine purring, chauffer at the wheel.

On any given day the clatter of wealth echoed through the marble-encased hotel lobby, as out-of-breath butlers carted load upon load of clothing-filled trunks, and impatient nannies hurried flawlessly man-nered children through the walkways of the McAlpin's gender-restricted floors. Fashionable women strolled leisurely among tapestry galleries and dined beneath the arched ceilings of ornate banquet rooms, while their husbands reclined in Russian and Turkish baths amid plumes of cigar smoke and the banter of high finance. Designed with the finest of classic pre-World War I amenities to serve even the slightest caprice of its clientele, the Hotel McAlpin, upon its construction, boasted it was the largest hotel in New York and perhaps the world.

It was roughly 11:00 pm and although the Phi Lambda Tau Sorority high school dance in the hotel's lavish ballroom was already several hours past primetime, the sweet-sounding rhythms of Ernie Golden and his Hotel McAlpin Orchestra could still be heard from the ornate Marine Grill at the basement level of the hotel. Edward Browning, dressed in his blue sack overcoat, snapped his fingers to the familiar ditty as he strolled confidently toward the ballroom. The tops of three rotund cigars stood prominently in the upper outside pocket of his coat, like soldiers at attention during reveille.

"Pretentious" isn't quite the word for Edward Browning. It might have been entitlement that led him to The Hotel McAlpin on that late winter night. Browning was a chief benefactor, some say the founder, of the local Phi Lambda Tau chapter. The newspapers affectionately referred to the sorority as P.L.T., or "Pretty Little Things." Browning himself often presented dance trophies and sorority pins to young ladies at school dances. People had become accustomed to seeing him in the company of young females. They called him "Daddy"—Daddy Browning.

Did his presence raise an eyebrow of suspicion? For some, perhaps, but Daddy was well known to the girls attending the dance, and they adoringly greeted him as he entered the room.

It was, of course, the Golden Age of Hot Jazz, and the sleek sounds of the day flowed from dancehalls across the nation and into the hearts and minds of flappers and gentlemen alike. The Charleston, with its wildly shifting rhythms and heart-stopping tempo, captured the defiant mood of the prohibition era. Enamored with ballroom dancing (and the Charleston in particular), Edward Browning fancied himself a *danseur noble*—and many an underage girl readily agreed. Hardly a weekend passed in which he didn't flutter like a schoolboy from one dance floor to the next, unblushingly strutting his two-step like an aging peacock. Acquaintances aptly described his utter thirst for attention:

> He dearly loves the spotlight and when it is turned in his direction it thrills him to the point where his balance, so evident in business dealings, becomes wholly upset. He loves show. He would rather appear as a person who had been put upon, deceived, outraged and fooled beyond all belief than not to appear at all. He must be seen. When he attends dances he always wants to be the master of ceremonies and offer loving cups to the best dancers. He is absolutely harmless, as free from guile as a new-laid egg and as innocent of evil thinking as an unshucked scallop.

He would joyously skip amongst groups of teenage girls, "chucking chins, pinching cheeks and sometimes a derriere." For their part, the young flapper girls did their level best to appear chic and urbane, brashly donning short shapeless skirts that revealed rolled stockings and bony powdered knees. They wore peek-a-boo hats that fell dangerously over the eye, and they coughed as they puckishly dragged smoke through sleek painted cigarette holders. They gathered in likeminded circles and they slandered their rivals as "Dumb Doras" and "flat tires," but the "sheiks" were the "cat's meow." Their chests were as flat as washboards, and "the intoxication of rouge," as one period publication described the flapper penchant for makeup, became a statement of their reckless rebellion.

Browning himself bore a perpetual red glow which, despite his shamelessness in the public eye, might have been mistaken for a blush of embarrassment. He looked like a young boy holding his breath, or an overtaxed weightlifter. Some even thought his features suggested an imprudent predilection to drink. His bulging eyes glistened within the deep pouches that underscored them. To the delight of many, he spoke in a thick Bowery accent—"bird" was "boid" and "perfect," "poifect." A pocket comb would frequently find its way through the locks of wavy white hair that clung tenuously to his pink and shedding scalp.

Edward Browning's appraising eye was to happen that night upon the round face of a particular young girl. Her name was Frances Belle Heenan and she was fifteen years old. She was not a member of the sorority and she knew only one of the sorority sisters in attendance. She had not been on the list of invited guests and her unexpected arrival aroused some resentment among some of the sisters.

Pitiless newspaper writers would later describe Frances Heenan as a "chubby schoolgirl" and other even less flattering things, but Daddy clearly saw something in her that attracted him. She was sophisticated for her age. Though her face generally bore an expression of haughty distaste and her mouth drooped in an unfortunate frown, when she chose to smile, she was capable of lighting up a room. She spoke in affected tones and she never answered a question with a simple "yes;" it was instead, "pos-i-*tive*-ly." As Allen Churchill wrote, "Though pudgy, pettish and only sweet fifteen, Frances Belle had already proved herself the enviable possessor of the mysterious something called *It*."

Frances Heenan could not help but notice as Daddy Browning flittered into the ballroom, holding court with the coterie of young girls who were eagerly drawn to his side. She turned to a guest and inquired, over the high pitches of trumpet and saxophone notes, "Who is *that*?" It was Daddy Browning, she was told. He had millions, but no one to spend it on. Frances smiled and pronounced, "Well he can pos-i-*tive*-ly spend it on *me*."

What happened next is the subject of some speculation. Peaches would later testify that a mutual acquaintance introduced them and that

Daddy immediately pursued her. "You look like peaches and cream to me," he told her, grinning with foolish delight. "I'm going to call you Peaches." Daddy, however, maintained that the relationship began at Peaches' hot insistence.

Whatever the circumstances of their initial meeting, Edward Browning and Frances Heenan spent the balance of that evening engaged in light-hearted conversation and the wild gyrations of the Charleston. She listened with less than comprehending interest to his boastful soliloquies and he fawned over her skillfully timed blushing giggles—all under the jealous eyes of the sorority sisters and guests.

❖

On March 5, 1926, the temporary rally in American stock prices was abruptly checked as violent swings in the market led to heavy selling. In Paterson, New Jersey, forty thousand textile workers prepared for a walkout among predictions of a nationwide sympathy strike. At the White House, President Coolidge was recalling the Ambassador to Great Britain and the Minister to Switzerland to discuss the approaching disarmament conference of the League of Nations. And beneath the vaulted ceilings of a fashionable Manhattan hotel, Peaches met Daddy.

Thirty-seven days later they would be married, and 296 days after that they would begin the legal battle that would turn their domestic drama into a national scandal.

Edward West Browning, circa 1926. "He had the tender, sweet mind of a child."

CHAPTER I

THREE THOUSAND PURPLE ORCHIDS

"If ever there was an unselfish man, this was he."

—REV. EDWARD H. EMMET

IT WAS A CEREBRAL HEMORRHAGE THAT FINALLY LEFT EDWARD WEST Browning, the man who had built an empire of Manhattan real estate, mentally and physically debilitated, but death had been stalking him for a long time. After surviving the initial critical stage of his illness, Browning was removed to a mansion in Scarsdale, New York, where he suffered from a curious series of delusions. At times he believed himself to be George Washington, leading the Continental Army; at other times he was elected President of the United States and was occupying the White House as the successor to Franklin Roosevelt.

He lived in a vice of extreme paranoia and saw faces peering at him from every window. Kidnappers, he was sure, had marked him as the object of their sinister plots. He often asked his attending nurses to fire rifle shots through the windows to ward off assailants (on more than one occasion these requests were hesitatingly granted). There were hours where he fancied himself commander of world armies and proclaimed the necessity of killing everyone, friends and family included. He became convinced he had lost his fortunes, and moans of anguish from his bedroom could be heard throughout his house.

During the last years of his life, Edward Browning had quietly succumbed to a world of vacuous eccentricity. He nurtured a strict regimen of exercise and cold-water hose baths. He believed that cooked food was not fit for human consumption, and he lived solely on raw vegetables and fruit. He boasted of a 46-inch expanded chest, but it was balanced atop a ghastly 26-inch waistline. In societal whispers he became known as the "grass-eater." He proclaimed, "Do good; help others, keep fit. Get back to nature and you'll get back to health." In the end, however, even this compulsive attention did little to prolong his life.

Though bedridden for much of his time at the Scarsdale estate, Browning occasionally seemed to rally. There was hope of ultimate recovery. But after four months of varying degrees of health and unrelenting battles of the mind, he finally succumbed to pneumonia, with only his sister, Florence, and adopted daughter, Dorothy "Sunshine," at his bedside. It was two days before his 60th birthday.

❖

It was 1934 and the Great Depression enveloped the nation. Hopelessness was a metastasized cancer in the American soul. The careless frivolity of the previous decade had vanished, and nostalgic recollections of years-gone-by preoccupied otherwise unoccupied minds. Edward Browning had come to represent a happier time, a time of carefree gaiety and whimsical idealism. His passing closed the door on that wonderful Whoopee Era. "If there is a gardener in Heaven, I hope he'll keep Edward Browning supplied with orchids," said Reverend Edward Emmett in his eulogy. "He had the tender, sweet mind of a child." Edward Browning passed from this world as he had wished—with his coffin adorned by three thousand purple orchids.

The funeral service was held at Campbell's Chapel in the heart of Browning's beloved Manhattan. Eight years earlier, at the peak of Browning's own flamboyant career, the "pink powder puffed" corpse of Rudolph Valentino lay in the same home while a ghoulish bacchanal of a hundred thousand delirious mourners crowded the streets to pay tribute to the silent screen legend. Edward Browning's send-off, subdued and quiet, would not remotely resemble Valentino's. There were no more than two hundred mourners.

Edward Browning's death stirred up memories of odd and overexposed periods of his life, but also of his philanthropic enterprises. His obituary in the *New York Times* recalled Browning's charitable intentions in liquidating real estate holdings after the market crash of 1929:

A large part of the proceeds of the auction sale of realty was used to establish a Browning Foundation, the purpose of which was to operate and maintain playgrounds for children in various parts of the city, and to provide hospitals with expensive toys and play devises of a permanent character for the benefit of children who were patients.

Rarely, however, were Browning's benevolent endeavors private in nature. They were grandiose affairs, assiduously calculated to attract the maximum amount of attention and press coverage. He became well known for distributing toys to children at annual Christmas parties given at his office. The event had become a yearly spectacle with thousands of children and parents lined up for blocks outside of his building waiting for their turn at the knee of Santa Claus. On one of these yuletide occasions, in 1928, a near riot ensued and police squads were called to quiet the stampeding crowds. Browning was heard to say, "Next year I'll hire Madison Square Garden!" On another occasion, Browning offered the City of New York one million dollars to be used to convert the old reservoir in Central Park into a playground and swimming pool

Children line up to receive Christmas presents from Daddy Browning.

for children. Though the offer was rejected, Browning thrived on the newspaper coverage of the story. Children, many of whom had benefited from Browning's numerous neighborhood philanthropies, solemnly filed past the coffin in the chapel on the Sunday before his burial to pay their last respects to Daddy.

Browning had died largely friendless. It was left to his employees to scour the city and pay for the purple orchids that blanketed his casket. There was no one else to fulfill his funerary wishes. There were, of course, acquaintances, business associates, and lawyers who came to pay their last respects, but it was more likely social obligation or simple morbid curiosity that drew them; affection for the man was hardly the reason for their attendance. Tears flowed from the eyes of some, but the inevitable whispers from the lips of others were inappropriately audible over the droning eulogy. Controversy, it seemed, would follow him into the next world.

And, there was *the* question. Would she come? Could she bear the pain of history? Would she agitate the barely-healed wounds of her past? It had been eight years, but the breathless clamor of their time together had only begun to fade. Those attending the funeral searched for her, men and women alike, necks stretched like giraffes in a fruitless search for some sign of her.

❖

Within days of Edward Browning's death, the personal representatives of his estate began the task of gathering and preserving his property in preparation for the probate process. In the case of Edward Browning, this was no easy charge. With an estate valued between 7 to 10 million dollars (about 300 million twenty-first century dollars), the process would be arduous and time consuming. To properly inventory every asset of the estate, it was critical that all records and financial documents of the business be examined. Ultimately, the estate representatives—Browning's business associates and an appointed board from the Title Guarantee & Trust Company—arrived at his expansive Manhattan offices, which were located on 61st Street and Broadway.

All seemed as expected as the representatives made their way through the records. Books, office equipment, business files—all the typical appurtenances of Browning's ongoing real estate and charitable enterprises. Upon entering his private suites, however, the representatives were drawn to a large vault—a mausoleum that stretched the width and breadth of an entire room. To their astonishment, the vault contained case upon glass-covered case, imbedded horizontally along the walls and vertically from floor to ceiling—and filled to capacity. They were aghast when they viewed the contents.

Letters. Many, *many* letters—all addressed to Edward Browning. Later estimates ranged as high as 2.3 million written items. Edward West Browning had retained what seemed to be every note, letter, correspondence, and writing that had ever been delivered to him.

Many were inscribed simply, "Daddy, New York," "The Millionaire Daddy, U.S.A." and "The Girls' Santa Claus of America." They were written by fans and foes, lawyers and associates, and hopeful young girls. There were marriage proposals and death threats, love notes and financial pleas. There were appeals for adoption and articles of blackmail, business exchanges and charitable requests. They bore worldwide postmarks. Some were little more than a paragraph in length and one was 150 pages long.

And there was more. Newspapers—thousands of them, stacked in huge piles like bricks of a building, and all of them naming, describing, depicting, complimenting, criticizing, or simply referring to Edward Browning. "He played with these printed pieces like a miser with his gold . . . counting, gloating, drooling," wrote Jack Lait in Walter Winchell's *On Broadway* column. Being written to and about was Edward Browning's greatest love, and being forgotten was his greatest fear. He carefully maintained these archives as an open tribute to his own life. They were his insurance policy against obscurity.

The representatives painstakingly examined the contents of the vault, and began to realize the pathetic irony of the man—death had come to him without a flicker of limelight. Edward Browning, who had at one time gazed romantically into the camera lens of virtually every newspaper photographer in New York, was now forgotten.

Edward West Browning's Manhattan

CHAPTER II

EDWARD WEST BROWNING

> "If personality is an unbroken series of successful gestures, then there was something gorgeous about him, some heightened sensitivity to the promises of life, as if he were related to one of those intricate machines that register earthquakes ten thousand miles away."
>
> —F. SCOTT FITZGERALD, *The Great Gatsby*

EDWARD WEST BROWNING WAS BORN ON OCTOBER 16, 1874, IN A RAPIDLY evolving New York City. It was the Gilded Age and the American landscape, previously a collection of provincially isolated communities, began to take on an urban-industrial look. Rural Americans flocked to cities, together with throngs of immigrants searching for new homes and new lives. It was an era marked by great progress and great instability. It was the age of the self-made man.

The Browning family resided in a large house on West 75th Street in New York's Upper West Side and enjoyed a chauffer-driven lifestyle. Edward Franklin Browning, Edward West's father, ensured his family all the privilege and comfort of every modern convenience and a full staff of servants. Young Edward was denied precious little, and he acquired, early in life, a taste for high-society and affluence.

While the entrepreneurial landscape of early twentieth century New York would play an immeasurable role in the man he would become, Edward West Browning was also the product of impressive pedigree. Browning's ancestors can be traced back through eight generations, to a Puritan by the name of Nathaniel Browning who was born in London in 1618. The persecutions of the Anglican Church inspired Nathaniel to cross the sea to Boston and then to Portsmouth, Rhode Island, where he settled in the year 1640. Succeeding generations of Brownings would remain in Rhode Island and flourish as farmers and businessmen. In

Edward West Browning at
the start of a new century.

1833, Edward Browning's grandfather, John Hazard Browning, migrated
to New York and created the family business.

For over a century, the name Browning, King & Co. was nationally
synonymous with clothing and uniforms. From college wear for Ivy League
gentlemen to uniforms for tradesmen and officers, Browning, King & Co.
manufactured and sold clothing to men in every walk of life. Formed by
John Hazard Browning and operated by his sons Edward Franklin and
John Hull, the business adapted to the times and expanded into new are-
nas. In 1849, when reports of western gold reached New York, the company quickly shifted production to workmen's pants and coats, which
were crammed into clipper ships bound for the coast of California. It was
said that Browning "outfitted the gold rush of '49." When the Civil War
erupted, the company wrangled a huge federal contract from the army for
the provision of soldier uniforms. The Spanish-American War brought a
similar contract for the outfitting of the entire United States Navy.

The enormous success of the clothing business eventually provided the members of the Browning family with the means and the caché to branch into other vocations. John Hull Browning found his way into the banking and railroad industries and four times became a presidential elector. Edward Franklin Browning began business life with Browning, King & Co. shortly after graduating from Columbia College in 1859. Though he would spend nearly a quarter century with the company, he would pursue his midlife vocation in, and introduce his son to, the world of New York real estate investment.

In 1863, Edward Franklin Browning was drafted for active service into the Northern Army. As was the common practice of the day for those of means, he appealed for the provision of a substitute to serve in his stead. Edward Franklin candidly described the intriguing arrangement and ensuing story:

> [A]t the same time James Browning, of Manchester, England, came over to this country for the express purpose of going into the Northern Army. Mr. E.F. Browning having applied to an agency for a substitute, was introduced to this Mr. James Browning, and engaged him to take his place, paying him the usual amount paid for such service at that time, namely $300. He entered Company F, 83rd Regiment of New York Volunteers. He served in the army for some time, was in many engagements, and was wounded in a battle in South Carolina, and left for dead on the field. A Southern soldier came along and was about to plunge his bayonet into him, when a Southern officer swore at him and arrested his act. After the soldiers had all gone, James Browning crawled to a Negro cabin, where they nursed and took care of him until he was able to walk. Then they dressed him in Negro clothing and he managed to get to the seacoast, where he hailed a passing vessel, which took him on board and brought him back to New York City. After remaining there a few days he again went into the army and went to the front fighting till the war was over. On June 28, 1865, he was honorably discharged at New York City. He had acquired such a liking for the army, however, that he again enlisted as a member of the Regular Army, and served for several years until his death of fever at Nashville, Tenn.

There appears to have been no blood relation between James Browning and Edward Franklin Browning; the matching of last names was wholly coincidental. Furthermore, there is no indication that Edward Franklin ever met James Browning again after consummating their initial business transaction, yet he clearly followed his exploits with interest and, no doubt, gratitude.

Edward Franklin remained with Browning, King & Co. for twenty-four years. By 1886, however, his eyesight began to fail, and at the age of forty-nine he was forced to retire. Away from the stresses of business life, Edward Franklin was now free to devote more of his time to home and family. He also began investing in New York real estate. Edward West observed his father's business acumen and penchant for prudent investment, and as he came of age, began to develop his own sense of entrepreneurial drive. As he contemplated his future, his father contemplated a business alliance with his son.

As a child, Edward West Browning exhibited a proclivity for athletics and physical culture. He was also infatuated with art, building, and architecture and drew ostentatious plans for mythical homes and estates. Edward Franklin wrote of his son, "He has a natural gift for drawing and designing, and often entertains his friends with his humorous sketches and with legerdemain."

Edward West Browning received his undergraduate education at Columbia University and then attended Columbia Law, though he never became a lawyer. Business was Browning's clear vocational preference. His father identified this preference and invited Edward into a real estate partnership. Regarding his son, Edward Franklin later wrote, "After his father left the firm of Browning, King & Co., his son went into the real estate business in connection with his father, and has devoted himself to the study and management of New York real estate. He has prospered and owns many fine buildings, of which he takes a general oversight." He added, "He is a favorite of the social world."

Through the years, Edward Franklin Browning would bequeath to his son not only tangible wealth but also a sense of unrivalled self-confidence. Edward Franklin's years of experience in the world of New York business would prove to be the fertile groundwork of his son's unfurling industry and unrivaled ambition.

❖

By the turn of the twentieth century, the City of New York, the burgeoning metropolis that was home to Edward West Browning and nearly three million others, convulsed with Victorian prosperity and nascent opportunity. Skyscrapers and the businessmen that occupied them marked New York as the financial center of the nation, if not the world.

Browning bore witness to this and more. He beheld staggering urban growth and the chaotic sprawl of citizenry into every crevasse of the City. He watched as massive waves of immigration placed increasing burdens on new and developing public services. New York and other major cities were expanding at a record pace, and public officials struggled to meet the growing demands of a mushrooming population.

The American obsession with money and status seemed only to mask the destitution of growing numbers of city dwellers. One description of a large American city at the turn of the century could aptly be applied to New York: "In poor neighborhoods garbage mounded in alleys and overflowed giant trash boxes that became banquet halls for rats and bluebottle flies. Billions of flies. The corpses of dogs, cats, and horses often remained where they fell. In January they froze into disheartening poses; in August they ballooned and ruptured." Even the privileged could not avoid the inevitable urban reality of filth, squalor, and disease.

By the year 1900, demographic development, buttressed by wave upon wave of European immigrants, made New York City the most densely populated metropolitan center in the country, exceeding Chicago, its closest competitor, by more than two to one. This huge influx of population not only placed strains on public services but also created a massive need for housing. For those who foresaw this convergence of fortune, mammoth opportunities awaited. Many profited by simply purchasing and holding real estate of every kind—land, tenements, office buildings— while others speculated on capricious property values.

John Jacob Astor, who began business life in the fur trading industry, had set the standard for real estate investment of the day. By the early nineteenth century, Astor had accumulated large tracts of land in New York, and then reinvested his profits in new and larger investments in real estate. Astor benefited not only from rents and appreciating land values, but also from a business policy of securing to himself all tenant improvements made to his properties during the terms of their leases. Astor thus profited in multiple ways. By the time of his death in 1848 he had amassed a fortune estimated at $20 million—over $110 billion today—and was considered the wealthiest man in America. Other industrial giants of the day such as Andrew Carnegie, J. Swift Armour, and John D. Rockefeller would likewise amass enormous fortunes of real estate and reinvent the popular notion of American wealth.

Aristocracy and affluence in the latter part of the nineteenth century became the celebrated byproducts of American industrial innovation and achievement. New York's ruling class filled hours of leisure time at parties, theaters, and opera houses. The palpable reality that anyone could achieve his personal potential and financial dreams permeated the economic landscape of the country. Manhattan real estate was an open door to endless prosperity for anyone with a nose for opportunity or the good fortune to be born into wealth. Edward Browning had been blessed with both. He had a clear understanding of the forces that formed the urban landscape while enjoying the benefit of his father's guiding hand.

The earliest public mention of Edward Browning's individual business dealings occurred in November of 1899. The *New York Times* noted in a tiny block advertisement of its *Real Estate Transfers* section that Browning had been granted two mortgages, for $10,000 and $8,000, respectively, from one Henry B. Stacey on property located on West 31st Street in New York. In April of 1902, the *Times* recorded that he purchased the property located at 452 West 58th Street and sold it the next day to one Anna B. Gilson. In successive months and years, Browning's name appeared more and more frequently in the *Real Estate Transfer* pages, and the purchase prices next to his name gradually escalated.

In 1908, while still residing at the family home on West 75th Street, Browning began his first major real estate endeavor. Straying from the conformity of the typical mid-block loft buildings that were common on the streets of New York at the time, Browning opted to construct a narrow twelve-story apartment building on the parcel located at 11 West 17th Street in Manhattan. Designed by architect Otto Strack, whose architectural innovation had become famous with the reconstruction of the Pabst Theater in Milwaukee in 1895, Browning's odd building was only 27 feet wide but 81 feet in depth.

With the completion of the West 17th Street project, Browning's tendency toward the unconventional began to take shape. At thirty-four years of age, Edward West Browning was about to place his enduring mark on the Manhattan skyline.

❖

Early twentieth century New York was a landscape dotted with "cloud-cathedrals of the religion of success." As Lloyd Morris wrote in his book *Incredible New York*, "For more than two decades New Yorkers were deafened by the chatter of invisible machine guns. In one or another quarter, automatic riveters kept up a ceaseless fusillade. Like human spiders dangling in space, workmen were spinning delicate webs of steel ever higher into the air. The era of super-skyscrapers had opened. Once again, you could watch New York being transformed. Seen from the bay on a sunny morning, Manhattan became an island of glittering pinnacles, a mirage of clustered, slender shafts plumed in the air, the island seemed to float on mist. The reality contrived by engineers resembled an illusion conjured up by poets."

An explosion of capitalistic spirit spurred a cavalcade of entrepreneurial activity. Technological innovations fueled by rapid economic expansion led to massive metropolitan growth, and invention after invention transformed the industrial landscape and revolutionized American urban life. The telephone, demonstrated for the first time in New York by Alexander Graham Bell in 1877, fostered the instantaneous exchange of ideas, and catapulted the City into its role as the communication center of the nation. The harnessing of electricity by Thomas Edison and the formation of the Edison Electric Light Company in 1878 led to the creation of power plants for lighting and motor generation—and to the birth of the electric elevator. Steam-powered elevators were common in the nineteenth century, but were of little use beyond the fifth or sixth floors, thereby making high-rise buildings an impracticality.

Similarly, buildings constructed of masonry were limited by the thickness of the walls necessary to support their structure. The advent of steel frame construction, however, significantly enhanced the architectural integrity of buildings, and erecting larger and taller structures was suddenly possible. With the arrival of these transforming innovations, there was little to stand in the way of massive vertical growth on Manhattan Island—and little to prevent men like Edward West Browning from promoting and profiting from that growth.

On December 19, 1910, Browning strolled into the Manhattan Building Department and filed plans for the construction of the tallest loft structure in the city. At an estimated cost of $250,000, the design called for a 22-story residential building on the north side of 36th Street between 7th Avenue and 6th Avenue. The building was to be equipped with state-of-the-art fireproofing, three elevators, and a façade constructed "of the modern renaissance style of terra cotta." It was considered, according to the *Real Estate Field* section of the *New York Times*, "a notable addition" to the area. The design firm of Buchman & Fox, who played an influential role in the design of many New York landmarks of the day, such as Saks Fifth Avenue and the Times Annex Building, was named chief architect of the project. Browning had cemented an alliance with Buchman & Fox that would endure through the years and add considerably to the Manhattan skyline.

Though Edward Browning's career was just beginning, his name was now spoken in the same breath as Vanderbilt, Astor, and Rockefeller. His holdings, while not yet rivaling those of such names, were nonetheless formidable and steadily growing. In 1913, Browning again gained public prominence with the construction of the imposing 30-story World's Tower office building, on 110 West 40th Street. The slender skyscraper was publicized at the time as the "tallest office building ever built in the world." The tower was constructed on twenty four piers submerged in caissons to bedrock level at a depth of 50 feet. It was faced on all sides with white ornamental terra cotta and set off by more than 1,000 window frames of golden bronze. It was a massive endeavor with many technical challenges that tested Browning's financial and personal resolve. Buchman & Fox drew plans for the tower as well, and achieved an architectural marvel by effectuating the entire resplendent structure on a narrow fifty-foot lot. The project proved to be a resounding success.

No sooner had the last steam-powered crane ambled away from the newly constructed World's Tower than Browning set his sights on a new area of the burgeoning city. Until the turn of the twentieth century, the Upper West Side of Manhattan along West 73rd Street consisted of upper class brick and brownstone single-family row homes. It was known as one of the most attractive places of residence in the city, and was occupied by families of privilege and an "invisible population" of butlers and servants. But as construction swept through the area in the early 1900's, the apartment trend found its way across 73rd Street. In June of 1914, bewildered property owners and residents near 72nd Street observed with more than ordinary interest the demolition of two fine and longstanding residences near Central Park West and Columbus Avenue. The *New York Times* reported that the homes had been purchased by Edward Browning, whose intent was to erect apartment houses on the now empty lots. Within days the plans were finalized. The *Times* declared:

Continuing his policy of erecting tower-like structures, Edward W. Browning will carry out three building projects, this time in a new field. These exceptional operations will mark the first erection of tall buildings in the Seventy-second Street zone and are now under way at 42 . . . [and] 18 West Seventy-second Street, and 126 West Seventy-third Street . . . The plots will be improved with three thirteen story fireproof apartment hotels from design by Buchman & Fox, architects, and will contain all the latest and most approved devises for safety and comfort.

The structures were built at a cost to Browning of $60,000 each and represented the first large apartment house invasion on at least one of the blocks. The buildings were constructed in the so-called Gothic style, with ornamental facades of brick and terra cotta, and were the tallest of their kind on the Upper West Side. Browning had introduced a new kind of residential development into the area, and was the forbearer of the high-rise apartment construction that would accentuate the New York skyline in the 1920s. The three buildings, all still standing today, are identical in appearance, and were constructed within one block of one another. They each stand thirteen stories high and twenty-five feet wide and bear the inscription of Browning's initials, *EWB*, in quatrefoil form in cartouches at the third-floor level.

On May 15, 1912, amidst this backdrop of business growth and financial acuity, Edward Browning's father passed away at the age of 75. The estate, which Edward shared with his sister, was meager in comparison to the fortune he had already amassed through his own efforts. The death of his father, though surely an emotional blow, served only to inspire Browning to further his own business and social legacy.

Throughout the following years, Browning would amass a fortune in income-producing Manhattan real estate, becoming one of New York's wealthiest financiers. His name was by now a familiar sight in the real estate transfer sections of virtually all New York newspapers, and he relished the celebrity he had achieved. He specialized in Midtown and West Side properties and became a pioneer in residential and office development. By 1929, he would own hundreds of buildings, from offices to apartment hotels, from houses to tenements. They ranged from a single story to thirty stories and extended from Houston Street to Washington Heights. They covered a total ground area in excess of 300,000 square feet and contained approximately 30,000,000 cubic feet of rentable space.

In an interview given early in his career, Browning summed up the secret of his success: "I always show a client the sunny rooms first."

❖

The appearance of Edward West Browning in the public record was not confined to matters of real estate. As early as 1906, accounts of a quarrel over the condition of an automobile that he had purchased and a dispute with the Central Union Gas Company regarding the ownership of certain gas ranges crept into the newspapers.

It was, however, a matter of estate planning that first cast Browning's personal life into the public eye. In September of 1912, shortly after the death of his father, Browning drew a will and a testamentary trust that was to create a fund from his real estate income to be distributed in furtherance of the "advancement of learning." The stated purpose of the trust was "to promote the well being and happiness of humanity by stimulating an interest in and a competition to achieve those religious, moral, social, economic and intellectual improvements which seem to me most important." The testament was intended by Browning to be a "monument to his memory." The income from the fund was to be converted to "Browning Prizes" awarded to students and researchers throughout the country through a board of trustees appointed by Browning. The seven board members were leading businessmen, philanthropists, and educators.

A reporter from the *New York Times* learned of Browning's intentions and called on him seeking confirmation of the story. "Good gracious!" Browning was quoted as saying. "I did not want that to become known yet! I have pledged my word as a gentleman to several of the greatest men of the country who want to help me that I would not say anything about the matter yet. I do not know how it could have leaked out. I cannot say a word about it." On September 4, 1912, despite Browning's bitter protestations, the *Times* printed a comprehensive article entitled "*FUND OF MILLIONS TO AID RESEARCH. E.W. Browning, Real Estate Operator, Will Give His Wealth to Advance Learning.*"

Curiously, when the *Times* reporter contacted several of the appointed trustees of Browning's testamentary fund, it was reported that "some of them had not even heard of Mr. Browning before, and at least one declared . . . that he was ignorant of his appointment until informed by a reporter of the *Times*."

Either Browning himself was the cause of the leak that led the *Times* reporter to the story, or his outward display of anger was genuine. Whatever the case, Edward Browning would not remain at odds with the New York press for long.

❖

Though shielded by his prosperity and consumed with his own personal and business matters, Edward Browning was not oblivious to the terrific tensions that had befallen the world during the second decade of the century. The voices of war were rising and America's neutrality was being tested at every turn. The German attack on the *Lusitania* had outraged previously non-aligned countries, and political pressures mounted in the United States to discard isolationist policy.

With America on the brink of war, and amidst rumors of German submarines lurking in New York Harbor, Browning read news headlines with as much trepidation as the rest of the country. At the time of the third registration of the Selective Service Act for men ages eighteen through forty-five, Browning was forty-three years old. He registered as required by law but stated on his draft registration card that he suffered from a "double rupture (hernia) [and] phlebitis (thrombosis) from ankles to hip." Though Browning would not be called to active military service, he would participate in the war effort in another rather unusual way.

It had been just over a decade since the Wright brothers' historic flight at Kitty Hawk, and the strategic use of airpower on the battlefield was in its infancy. In its conflict with Libya in 1911, Italy had become the first country to make military use of the airplane, dropping grenades from a German-built monoplane, and in 1912, dropping bombs from an airship. With the start of World War I, however, the era of active experimentation with aircraft as a military tool had begun. The war years of 1914-1918 saw tremendous growth in the production and development of aircraft and in the understanding of their military implications. Aircraft were becoming faster, more powerful, and more maneuverable, and the world's militaries had begun in earnest to integrate them as a key element of battle plans. The use of aircraft in strategic bombing of targets was becoming a very realistic consideration for both sides during the war.

Edward Browning had developed a concern over the perceived threat posed to American cities by enemy aircraft. He was genuinely distressed by what he viewed as the obvious vulnerability of the country to aerial bombardment, and the complacent manner of a people unprepared to fend off such an attack. Browning spoke passionately on the subject to anyone who would listen and he became known as an "enthusiast for preparedness." Browning's jeremiads were cultivated by his relationship with two tenants of his World's Tower, W.K. Micky, president of General Aeronautic Company, and Leon Mayor, secretary of the United States Air Navigation Company. Both of these executives lent skeptical ear to Browning's paranoia and indulged his spirited enthusiasm for flight. Browning merged his two passions for aircraft and preparedness, and it did not take him long to hatch his next scheme.

On February 17, 1916, Edward Browning announced plans to build a steel aircraft hanger atop his World's Tower, from which he would launch fleets of "aeroplanes" to fly over "the Times Square section of New York . . . dropping dummy bombs [to demonstrate] what is likely to happen to a big city in a country unprepared to defend itself." To Browning's delight, the *New York Times* went with the story the following day, and led with the headline, *"WANTS TO BOMBARD TIMES SQ. FROM AERO—Flying Enthusiast Seeks to Show War Dangers to a City in a Land Unprepared—PLANS HANGER 300 FEET UP."* The story continued:

> Some time next week, before the hanger is built, Mr. Browning said that a number of aeroplanes from Garden City, L.I., would circle the tower and drop imitation bombs with search lights playing on them. Mr. Browning was yesterday preparing an application to the City Bureau of Licenses and to Borough President Marcus M. Marks for permission for these flights and to build the aeroplane cote on top of his building, more than 300 feet above the street. He was sure that no danger was involved in having aeroplanes flitting over streets on which tens of thousands of persons walk daily and alighting on an area of about 50 by 100 feet which will be provided in the hanger.

Remarkably, Browning had persuaded W.K. Micky to work up plans for the proposed hanger on top of the tower, and had also persuaded Leon Mayor to commit the use of several aircraft for the stunt. Though the permits for the act were denied, Browning had clearly achieved his purpose of raising public awareness of this virtually nonexistent threat. Denying any involvement in the project other than the provision of several planes, Leon Mayer was quoted as saying, "If Mr. Browning thinks it is practical to build a hanger on top of his building he is entitled to go ahead. It will be a remarkable thing if he succeeds. I should like to see an aeroplane make a landing in the limited space on top of a building like this."

Undaunted by the failure of his simulated aerial bombardment, Edward Browning modified his aeronautic ambitions only slightly. He decided that his chauffer driven limousine was insufficient for all his transportation needs and proposed to use a hanger atop his office building as a launch point for a private plane for his forty-one-block daily commute. The impracticality of such a proposition did not bother Edward Browning (or any of the newspapers that picked the story up). Browning wallowed in the press coverage like a child in a sandbox. All he cared about were the first words of virtually every article that brought narration to his various antics—"Edward W. Browning . . ."

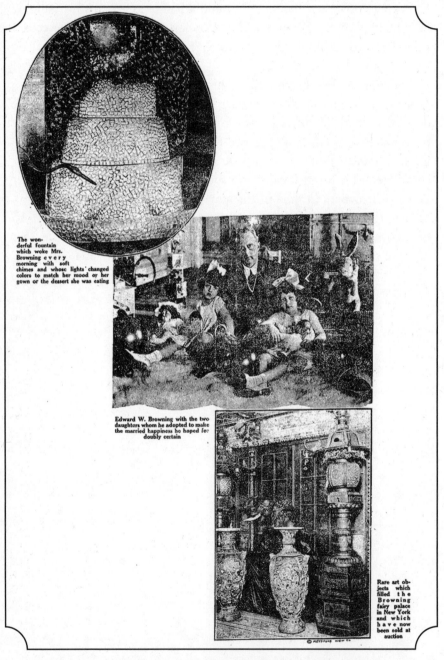

The wonderful fountain which woke Mrs. Browning every morning with soft chimes and whose lights changed colors to match her mood or her gown or the dessert she was eating

Edward W. Browning with the two daughters whom he adopted to make the married happiness he hoped for doubly certain

Rare art objects which filled the Browning fairy palace in New York and which have now been sold at auction

Across America, newspapers celebrated Browning's elaborate home and family life. Here the *Ogden Standard Examiner* reveals life amidst the "Gardens of Babylon."

CHAPTER III

THE GARDENS
OF BABYLON

"But I don't want to go among mad people."
—LEWIS CARROLL, *Alice in Wonderland*

AMERICA'S INEVITABLE ENTRY INTO THE WAR IN EUROPE DREW CLOSER, BUT Edward Browning was not in any way to be deterred from social pursuits. Turning forty years old seemed to mark a change in his focus. At the prime of his life he had already accomplished most of his financial goals and had received public accolades for his many business achievements. By 1915 Edward Browning was, quite simply, New York's most eligible bachelor.

The label would not last long. Browning had taken stock of his life. With the passing of his father, thoughts of creating his own family and perpetuating his own legacy began to weigh heavily on his mind. Edward Browning was quixotic when it came to matters of love. He claimed that he yearned to provide and care for a woman with complete devotion and with his total imagination. His ideal of marriage was not merely one of romance, however, but was born of an age of dominance and chivalry. He would proclaim that "Woman are like mischievous puppies and willful children—teach them how far they can go, and they won't go further. For there is a large percentage of the child in every woman . . . When a woman can look upon the six feet of height of her husband; when she can regard his broad chest and powerful forearm and hands with the crinkling dark hairs, and know that his height and strength and power can be exerted in the primitive way to make her behave—why, there's a marriage where the balance is even and the erratic instincts of the cave-woman, never dying, are disciplined in the modern wife." His actions, however, would betray his inability to maintain a woman's affections in any such dominant manner, and he would even question whether he was ever truly prepared for the ultimate role of *husband*. In the end, Edward Browning's own personal eccentricities would prove to be the decisive element upon which his romantic life would balance.

In 1915, however, doubt was not in Edward Browning's mind. He had conquered downtown Manhattan and amassed a huge fortune. The question as to with whom to share this fortune—and his life—was answered when he walked into a local real estate office in the Bronx and was then and there smitten by the blonde hair and crimson lips of a pretty young file clerk named Nellie Adele Lowen.

Browning was swept away. He wanted more than anything to be the hero of this young woman, to unchain Adele, as she was known, from the mundane efforts of daily life. Whatever misgivings she might have had about Browning and his past peculiarities were easily overlooked in light of the astonishing world of material comfort that he offered her. Edward Browning would introduce her to a life unlike any she had ever known.

They were married on April 15, 1915. "When I married my young wife," Browning said, "I studied to make life different for her and more beautiful than life had ever been for a bride before. I thought I could do this by hedging her in from the pain of ordinary living." He showered his new bride with every material excess, and though he insisted on a prenuptial agreement to protect the "large benefaction for public welfare" instituted by his last will and testament, he created a fully endowed trust fund to provide her with a separate income for her own use during their marriage. Adele happily surrendered to Browning's unquenchable indulgence—the prenuptial arrangement was a mere legal formality.

The marriage announcement appeared in the *New York Times* under the headline "Bridal Pair's Roof Garden," and described in detail the couple's marital home. Browning took the entire top floor of a high-rise apartment building on West 81st Street, overlooking Central Park, and gutted the existing units. He created a twenty-four- room penthouse and adorned it with every possible amenity. He spent $250,000 (nearly five million twenty-first century dollars) on this palatial home for his queen. "I went seeking the beauty and the romance of the past to surround her with outward furnishings that would typify my inward love," he later told a reporter. One commentator declared that Browning had "combined magnificent opulence with inconceivable bad taste."

Adele Browning acclimated to her new lifestyle with obvious ease. She posed for pictures that adorned newspapers across the country. On May 2, 1915, a "Special to the Washington Post" entitled "BRIDE TO HAVE HANGING GARDEN COPIED AFTER THOSE OF BABYLON," described in lusty detail the rooftop garden above the couple's protrusive living quarters. A sunken lake stocked with rare specimens of

Japanese goldfish sat surrounded by an array of exotic and delicate plants, which were kept in a series of glass compartments, with atmospheres regulated according to each individual plant's natural habitat.

A music room and a bird aviary filled the entire home with the sounds of composed as well as zoological song. The dining room—actually three ornate rooms combined into one—bore the Browning coat of arms near the ceiling. The bedroom suite came straight from Versailles. Collections of Chinese and Japanese objects d'art adorned the vast recesses of the Browning home. The "eastern treasures" of the audacious residence were typified by a bronze temple vase, nearly 6 feet in height and 45 inches in breadth, sheathed with entwined dragons bearing offerings of flaming suns, and by bronze bowls and vases in relief depicting elephants and combating lions.

Guests at the Browning residence were greeted in the foyer by an 8-foot antique Japanese temple lantern mounted by a pagoda top bearing spirit bells. Teakwood furniture in the residence, much of it Chinese in style, accented a number of rare Chinese rugs, as well as a Persian palace silk rug and, of course, a white polar bear rug over 10 feet in length, complete with piercing fangs and ferocious eyes. The circular mahogany dining room contained an ornately carved sixteenth century Italian design table with twelve elaborately carved arm and side chairs with Cordova leather seats bearing Italian coats of arms.

Dining in these regal surroundings could not placate Browning's ravenous craving for extravagance. To the center of the dining room, he added an Italian fountain garlanded with turtles and frogs spouting water from their reverently posed reptilian mouths. Even Browning seemed aware of the mindless profligacy of it all:

> In our dining room I placed a fountain because once I heard her say she loved the tinkling of limpid water. And the first night when we dined I admired the crystal ebb and resurgence of the hundreds of slender water jets in our fountain. But she turned away her delicate face in a gesture of dissatisfaction.
>
> 'They are so pale—those waterfalls,' she said. 'I eat my mousse or ice at dessert. It is pink and flushed. Colors mean so much to me. And then I look at the pale waters and they are cold. Color is absent from them. I crave the iridescence of the rainbow.' And when she spoke I understood because I have not crushed poetry from my life. 'Your fountain shall splash in colors for you, my love,' I said. We had in the architect and he asked me what color for her fountain would best please my wife.

'Give her all the colors,' I said. 'Every color to charm her fancy. There is pink—that will go with some of her confections; blue will chime with others. Then don't forget the romance of lavender, the saffron hues of yellow, the coquetries of green. Arrange them with small buttons so that my love shall order them to suit her mood, or the desert she is eating, or the gown she is wearing.'

And so, as the Great War raged in faraway lands, Mr. and Mrs. Browning dined each evening on opposite ends of their Italian dining suite, to the placid tinkling of falling water, in colors dictated by the fickle moods of the lovely Adele Browning.

❖

Over the next several years, victory in Europe became apparent and the shell shock of an injured generation began to pass. America saw a resurgence of optimism. The election of Warren Harding as President marked the end of Wilson's internationalism and heralded an era of national pride and independence. By their votes, Americans made clear their desire to look inward and to live their lives for the betterment of their own country rather than the world at large.

To Edward and Adele Browning, as was the case with many other Americans, the end of the war signaled thoughts of children and of growing families. Browning would later confess, "I thought a marriage could not be perfect with just her and me alone. We needed the patter of small feet running to meet us, the lisp of little voices, the appeal of children to cement our marriage, to fill up our hearts and time." Three years of marriage, however, had failed to produce children for the Brownings. By 1918, their only real prospect of becoming parents lay in the alternative of adoption.

In the early part of the twentieth century, it was publicly assumed that most adopted children were the illegitimate offspring of sexually promiscuous unwed mothers. Statistics, however, prove otherwise. Prior to 1940, the majority of all "surrendering parents" were married. At the time, the dramatic influxes of immigrants to cities throughout America often resulted in unemployed or unemployable parents with little or no means to care for their growing families. Many of these parents were left with the heartbreaking choice of watching their sons and daughters slowly die, giving them up to charitable organizations, or informally leaving them with other families. Despite Theodore Roosevelt's 1909 pronouncement at the first White House Conference on Children that the family was "the highest and finest product of civilization," many American parents were simply left without any viable option except to give a child up for adoption.

In April of 1918, Jacob Herbst and his wife Minnie found themselves in such a dreadful circumstance. Mr. Herbst, though employed as a truck driver, earned an average monthly income of only $125, and was unable to provide in any real way for the wellbeing of his family. There were three children to feed and Herbst feared for the health of their youngest, three-year-old Josephine Gloria. One morning while perusing a New York newspaper, Minnie Herbst noticed a personal ad, placed in the Public Notices section that read as follows:

PROMINENT WEALTHY OLD NEW YORK family of highest standing, with palatial home and no children, would like sweet little girl of about 4 years, who would have every advantage and care, with privilege of adoption. Write full particulars, Knickerbocker, 122 Times.

Such adoption advertisements were fairly common at the time and laws preventing the farming of children were only in the initial stages of development. Orphanages and other childcare institutions were falling out of favor, and the placement of children with families had become the growing trend. Mrs. Herbst hesitatingly brought the ad to the attention of her husband. In their minds, they had little choice but to answer.

The ad had been placed by Edward Browning. He had used the alias to hide his identity and to thwart the inevitable questions of virility. The Brownings initially began their search in several adoption asylums, but were unable to find a child that suited them. The matter was dropped, but shortly thereafter Browning informed his wife that he had placed an ad in various newspapers and had received several promising responses.

Upon meeting the Brownings and viewing the surroundings in which they lived, Mr. and Mrs. Herbst's sense of dread must have been tempered by some degree of relief. They shushed their runny-nosed children and gaped at the Japanese artwork, the flowing tapestries, and the fountains that spouted multicolored water. Could their little daughter Josephine actually become part of this peculiar world of fortune? Edward Browning, in his inimitable style, smoothly convinced them that the answer was yes.

Arrangements were made and legalities handled. A curious footnote to the adoption of Josephine Herbst, however, would have far-reaching implications years after the fact. Browning had a concern that his reputed wealth would be subject to future legal claims that could be brought by Jacob and Minnie Herbst. To avoid this possibility, Browning insisted that the final adoption papers be executed by Adele Browning only. She did what he asked without argument. Though he consented to the adoption, Edward Browning did not legally adopt Josephine and technically she was not his child.

There was no turning back for Jacob Herbst and his wife. As a condition to the adoption, Browning required them to renounce all of their rights as Josephine's parents and to promise never to lay eyes on their daughter again. The demand, though seemingly cruel, was viewed by both families as being in the best interests of Josephine, and for nineteen years the Herbsts would keep their promise.

❖

Edward and Adele Browning attempted to create a quiet and stable family life following the adoption of Josephine. They managed to keep a relatively low profile and, for the most part, stay out of the public eye and away from the New York gossip columns. They did their best to remove all residue of Josephine's prior life with the Herbsts. They even changed the child's name. She was renamed Marjorie.

By 1920, when Marjorie was five years old, the Brownings realized that she needed companionship. The material possessions and arranged playmates provided only so much entertainment, and Marjorie was now a greedily indulged child. She needed a sibling. Edward and Adele were back in the adoption market.

Their search produced a five-year-old girl named Stella Brussel. This time, the legal concerns Edward Browning had had at the time of Marjorie's adoption were nonexistent, as Stella's natural parents were deceased. He adopted the child in his own name to the exclusion of Adele.

Stella's deep brown hair and dark eyes seemed an almost perfect contrast to Marjorie's blonde hair and light features. They were the ideal bookends to Edward Browning's storybook life. As he had done with Marjorie, Browning changed his newly adopted daughter's birth name. She was now Dorothy Browning. For good measure, he added the nickname "Sunshine," which was to follow her for the rest of her life.

Though only five years old at the time of her adoption, Dorothy's road had been a difficult one. She had been adopted once before under the most bizarre of circumstances. Anna Brussel, her first adoptive parent, told of a desperate widow who, on a bitterly cold December day in Newark, New Jersey, thrust a two-and-a-half month old baby into Brussel's arms and hurried away. Brussel somehow maintained contact with the woman, whom she was to know as Doris Lane, and arrangements were made for the child's adoption. Lane later died and Brussel feared that she could not care for the child as she had hoped. Responding to another adoption advertisement placed by the Brownings, Brussel concluded that the Browning family was the appropriate place for Stella, and she agreed to the adoption.

Anna Brussel later claimed that at the conclusion of the adoption hearing, Browning handed her a roll of bills as a present, and when she removed the rubber band, found that all of the bills were in one-dollar denominations with the exception of the top bill, which was a five. Her mind began to swim with uncertainty about the man to whom she had given up her child.

❖

Following the two adoptions, Edward Browning's life seemed complete, his ideal family realized. Little Marjorie and Dorothy Sunshine were tended to by a private nurse, Mollie Callaghan, and were sent to the exclusive Veltin School for Girls, where their playmates included the daughters of some of New York's most privileged and exclusive families (among them, the daughter of Mr. and Mrs. Babe Ruth). Lavish parties and servants that tended to their every need punctuated the fanciful world into which Browning's children were thrown.

The *Annie*-esque irony of it all became a sensation, as word of these two charmed adopted children began to spread. On May 30, 1920 an exposé written by an N.E.A. Staff Correspondent appeared in regional newspapers with the headline, "BROWNING TOTS RIVAL 'ALICE IN WONDERLAND'; ARE IDOLIZED BY ALL LITTLE KIDDIES IN LAND." Photographs of both children and Browning's wife were juxtaposed over the family's rooftop garden and lake, above a mocking caption that read, "The 'Wonderland' garden, the little kiddies who rule there and their mother, Mrs. E.W. Browning. 'Fairy Queen' Dorothy is at the left and her sister 'fairy' Marjorie, in the center. Note the boat in the miniature lake, in the middle of the garden."

The Brownings were the perfect American family.

Nellie Adele Browning

CHAPTER IV

THE SEDUCTION OF NELLIE ADELE

> *"I hate Charles Henry Wilen! He wrecked my life and he'll pay for it if I can bring it about."*
>
> —MISS RENEE SHAPIRO

As the winter of 1921 approached, the nation was nearly two years into the Noble Experiment of Prohibition. Rum-running bootleggers and conspiring city officials thwarted law enforcement at every instance and the decidedly defiant mood of the nation spread through gin mills and speakeasies across the land. Perhaps it was this ubiquitous spirit of rebellion that led her astray—or maybe it was just boredom. But as the cold winds of winter began to cut through the lofty penthouses of Central Park, Adele Browning felt an emptiness that neither her husband nor all his riches could fill.

In retrospect, Edward Browning would wish he had paid more attention to detail. He indulged his family and showered them with treasures, but he was utterly unaware of the discontent that percolated beneath the surface of his fairy-tale marriage. In the end, even multi-colored Italian fountains could not bring gratification to Adele Browning.

What precisely Adele found lacking in her family life is a matter for speculation. Historical memory has not been particularly kind to Nellie Adele Browning, especially regarding her choice to leave Edward Browning. Of course, history is always written by the victor, but even friends and descendents have said that she simply rebelled against the monotony of a too-perfect existence, or that her self-absorbed and ego-tistical nature drove her to seek attention and adventure elsewhere. Browning himself, true to his professed ideas about marriage, would later opine that "It may have been because I could not roar in my family circle . . . Woman love to be browbeaten—even cowed at times." But whether it was boredom or abuse that weakened Adele's commitment to her husband, the opportunity to break free presented itself in a most irresistible manner.

Edward Browning adored his wife's smile, but it was in that smile that the hint of discord took shape. Dentist's bills. Though Adele's teeth seemed healthy and strong and she seldom complained about them, a steady stream of dentist's bills began to arrive at the Browning household. For years, Browning had utilized the services of a kindly old family dentist, but now Adele was frequenting a new dentist whose name Browning had never heard—Dr. Charles H. Wilen.

At first Browning balked. The bills were numerous and quite sizeable. But Adele convinced him that she did indeed require some very intricate dental work and she boasted of Dr. Wilen's kind and gentle manner. She fluttered her eyelashes and coaxed her husband to reconsider. And so the bills came and Edward Browning paid them.

Charles Wilen was twenty-eight years old when he first met Adele. His charming and debonair manner and captivating brown eyes were a temptation to the discontented beauty. Her seduction was as simple as it was inevitable. Wilen's office was located at a trendy Fifth Avenue address, and his reputation for womanizing was well known throughout the bistros and cafes of Greenwich Village. He was frequently sighted amongst a harem of adoring females. In whispers throughout the city, jealously motivated gentlemen and suspicious minded ladies called him the Sheik of Greenwich Village, and mockingly substituted the letters DDS—his professional affiliation—with the pseudonym Devilish Dental Sheik.

Adele Browning's earliest visits to Wilen's office were professional and courteous, but Wilen had heard of the well publicized Adele—and her extravagantly wealthy husband. In very little time, conversations of bridgework and enamel turned to matters of a personal nature. Wilen could sense the dissatisfaction that Adele was feeling in her home life. He steadfastly came across as a sincere listener with an understanding heart, and he quickly became Adele's friend and confidant. Her visits to the office became more and more frequent and soon the gentle compassionate hands of Dr. Wilen found their way from her molars to other parts of Adele.

Irritated patients, many of whom in varying degrees of tooth pain, waited outside Wilen's office for maddeningly long periods of time while Adele and the good doctor made love within. Lovemaking, however, quickly turned into profiteering schemes. Wilen persuaded his new lover to siphon off cash from the ample trust account so lovingly provided by her husband. He accepted gifts of gems and jewelry, including two quite valuable diamond rings, which he quickly converted to cash at the pawnshop nearest his office. He plied cash gifts and lavish dinners from her with sweet words and loving gestures—and all the while, he continued to submit his dental bills to Edward Browning for the painstaking services that he was rendering his wife.

❖

Adele's steaming love affair with Charles Wilen progressed and with each passing day she found herself more infatuated. Unfortunately, however, Adele Browning was not the only beautiful young woman on Dr. Wilen's personal patient list. As he courted Adele and her wealth, he was also busy making promises that he never intended to keep to a petite nineteen-year-old aspiring actress by the name of Renee Shapiro. Hopelessly in love with Wilen and troubled in every way, the auburn-haired, blue-eyed Shapiro described Wilen's grip on her as nothing short of "hypnotic." Under the spellbinding effect of his persuasive gaze and pledges of undying love, Shapiro conspired with her mentor, her adviser, her lover. "I was engaged to marry Wilen."

She was convinced of it.

❖

Shapiro acquiesced to several black-hearted plans that she alleged Wilen hatched to defraud Edward Browning and to tap into his deep pockets. One evening after Wilen made passionate love to her in his office, Shapiro went into a jealous rage about the undeniable relationship he had developed with Adele Browning. Why was her lover spending so much time with this woman? He spoke calmly and gazed at her with sincere eyes, told her not to give a thought to Adele Browning, that he only spent time with her because of money. "You know you're the only girl I love, Renee," he assured her. But perhaps Renee could help him make his affair with Adele worthwhile . . . ?

In one of Wilen's devious plans, Shapiro, as Wilen's fiancée, was to confront Adele Browning and inform her that she had been linked romantically to Dr. Wilen, and that she intended to enlighten the good Mr. Browning of the fact. Then, according to the plan, Mrs.

Browning would become quite fearful and go to Wilen for advice. Wilen would see no way out of the predicament other than to recommend that she pay Shapiro a large sum of money to keep the story to herself.

Wilen's second scheme was to blackmail Edward Browning. Shapiro was to get friendly with the unsuspecting millionaire and then arrange to be "caught" with him by Wilen, Shapiro's "husband," who would then make a demand for money in exchange for keeping the story quiet.

In the end, Wilen did not engage either of his sinister schemes. He had much larger plans for Adele Browning.

❖

When Adele first began her cavorts with Charles Wilen, she was lured by the adventure of it all. She had tired of her perfect world of family stability and affluence, and she yearned for the escape that she had found in his welcoming arms. In time, however, adventure turned to love, and Adele Browning's thinking became more clouded than ever.

Wilen had planted the seeds in Adele's mind and now his talk focused on forever after. They lightheartedly imagined a life together away from it all, and from there Adele Browning followed a very natural course to deciding to leave Edward Browning.

Perhaps she had made many errors in judgment up to that point in time, but Adele made her first *criminal* error in the latter part of 1922, when Wilen convinced her to apply for a passport as the wife of one Harry J. Wolcher, a personal friend—and accomplice of Wilen. Wilen had concluded his plan required complete secrecy and that his own involvement could not be disclosed. The promise of a share in Adele Browning's wealth ensured Wolcher's willing participation in the conspiracy. To Adele, however, it was simply a matter of love and discretion. She deferred to the better judgment of her lover.

❖

The summer of 1923 was sure to be a hot one in New York City. Edward Browning had installed a series of four-blade electric ceiling fans throughout the family home, and the rooftop pond that adorned the penthouse play land would provide hours of cooling fun and entertainment for little Marjorie and Dorothy Sunshine. Browning had seen subtle changes in his wife in recent months, but he, no doubt, attributed those changes to female issues or the vagaries of daily living. He felt new scenery would do them all a world of good.

As much of a city person as Browning was, he loved the outdoors and the tranquility of a country setting. The previous year he had purchased a country home on Long Island away from the bustle of trains and skyscrapers, and as summer approached, he persuaded his now detached Adele to spend the summer there with him and the children. He looked forward to a summer of relaxation and of family activities, of sharing iced tea and rocking chairs with his wife and children.

❖

Eleven years earlier, the *Titanic* had met its doom in the frigid waters of the North Atlantic. A lone and pernicious iceberg had ripped the famous wound in its massive hull and thousands drowned and froze in the ship's wreckage. The R.M.S. *Olympic,* her sister ship, had received the distress signals and she sped north through the moonlit night at full velocity, but *Titanic* was much too far away. Her fate had been sealed.

In the wake of the immortal sea disaster, the most modern of safety measures would be installed in passenger ships across the world. The *Olympic* was sent back to her builders in Belfast and outfitted with a double hull, taller bulkheads, and a sufficient number of lifeboats for all of its passengers. When she returned to service, she was the largest ocean liner in the world—and perhaps the safest.

On June 30, 1923, those boarding Old Reliable, as the *Olympic* had come to be known, had little thought of lifeboats or disasters. The ship was bound for Cherbourg, France, and the *Titanic* was but a bitter memory in a glorious record of seafaring reliability.

The transatlantic run offered by the White Star luxury liner had become a favorite of wealthy and aristocratic families. In the 1920s, New York harbor swelled with the movement of people and property, and stirred with the sounds of exiting bilge and the blasting of steamship horns. Ocean liners overflowing with uppity tourists darted in and out of the bustling port, past Gravesend Bay where ships, crowded with anxious immigrants, lay at anchor awaiting entry into a new land and the promise of a better life.

Olympic's crew completed the final preparations for the North Atlantic journey, with special attention to the needs of its lengthy list of prominent passengers. Among the many notables aboard the liner bound for a summer getaway in France were John W. Davis, the former American ambassador to Great Britain, who traveled with his wife and daughter; Charles S. Wilson, the American Minister to Bulgaria; Marie Tiffany, a performer with the Metropolitan Opera Company; and Mrs. J. P. Morgan.

The elegant vessel steamed away from Pier 59, brimming with over three thousand eager voyagers, and the crew checked the final roll of passengers for the last time. Little notice was given to the names Dr. Charles J. Wilen and Mrs. H.J. Wolcher, which read nearly sequentially in the alphabetic list of travelers onboard the *Olympic*.

❖

Edward Browning left his office early on June 30, 1923. He rolled down the windows of the Rolls Royce and let the New York summer sunshine bathe his face and the warm wind rush through his thinning white hair. It was the day of his anticipated move to the Long Island home and he was of a particularly cheerful disposition.

As the Rolls pulled in front of the high rise, Browning directed the driver to leave the car running. The glum-looking chauffer stopped the oversized limousine and solemnly opened the door and allowed his passenger to exit.

Browning nodded cheerfully as he passed the doorman and made his way through the elaborate lobby. As the elevator rose to his city penthouse, he smiled with the expectation of the happy tumult of movers and laboring footmen busily working under the officious direction of his wife Adele. What he encountered, however, was anything but the commotion he expected. The house was silent.

"Sweetheart?" With growing bewilderment, Browning began searching room after room for his wife and children. The family servants, who were busy with their appointed chores, directed Browning to little Dorothy Sunshine, who quietly played with a doll in her bedroom.

"Where's Mother, Sunshine?"

Dorothy looked innocently up at her father. "Gone—gone away. Mother is gone."

Browning let out an incredulous "humph," as Dorothy returned her attention to the doll in her hands. Could Adele have left for the summer house already? He scanned the apartment and found little sign of baggage or packing—though some of Adele's clothing and jewelry were missing. Recent instances of his wife's odd behavior came flooding into Browning's consciousness. "Come, Sunshine, let's find mother."

He satisfied himself that neither Adele nor Marjorie were anywhere within the confines of the vast residence, and then Browning gathered up his daughter and hurriedly made his way to the Long Island retreat where he hoped upon hope to find his wife and little Marjorie.

It was not to be.

The reality that Adele had taken Marjorie and left him was a staggering blow for Edward Browning. Incredulity, however, gradually gave way to practicality as he slowly came to grips with his unfortunate situation. As wounded as he was, Browning's business sense took over, and he began communicating with his attorneys and a private investigation firm to locate his wife and to learn of the circumstances of her abrupt disappearance.

The Daugherty Detective Bureau leapt into action. Before Adele and Wilen had even disembarked from the *Olympic,* the Daugherty sleuths had learned of their passage to France. They immediately made contact with their Paris representatives who were requested to meet the arriving ship at port and covertly track the movements of the perfidious couple. The French agents were instructed to search for "a very pretty woman, with blonde hair of a Titian tinge, blue eyes, small feet and very red lips, 39 years of age," accompanied by a man "28 years of age and having the appearance of a student."

The resulting discoveries were not good news for Browning. The investigators learned that upon arrival in Paris, the couple checked into the Hotel Chamford in the heart of the romantic city. Later, they took up accommodations at the Hotel Imperial under the name Mr. and Mrs. Wilen. They were together at every instance and they passed their evenings with the gaiety of French cabarets and Parisian dance halls. Adele had left far behind the shackles of her proper and controlled family life in favor of the wild and daring indecency of the likes of Maxim's of Paris and Moulin Rogue. She joined inebriated crowds at the foot of ornamented gantries to watch the untamed undulations of the high-heeled black-stockinged Can-Can. For the first time in years, she felt free.

The liberation was short lived. A photograph of Adele had been sent to the investigators in Paris and the identification was confirmed. Within days, Browning was strategizing with his attorneys and planning his divorce.

In the first agonizing hours after Adele's disappearance, Browning searched frantically for Marjorie. He worried that her cavorting mother had taken her and he was concerned that she might not have been suitably cared for. Browning was soon relieved to learn that his wife had left Marjorie with Adele's parents in New York. Mercifully, the child would not witness her mother's reckless and amoral gallivants.

Relief turned to outrage as the details of his wife's unblushing infidelity were revealed. Edward Browning had given Adele everything in his power, and she had left him with no warning and without a single word of explanation.

By the third week of July, Browning had begun divorce proceedings and his lawyer, Herman Witte, was making provocative statements to the press. "Evidently Mrs. Browning was lured away by a man who doesn't amount to much, for he let her pay her own passage on the Olympic. It is a question whether they are not liable to criminal prosecution if they should return to America." Witte was quick to add, "Mr. Browning assures me he still loves his wife."

Edward Browning's cuckolding was now splashed across newspapers throughout the country. The fairytale marriage was over.

❖

When word reached Paris that their escapades had been revealed, Charles Wilen panicked. His plan had been to assist Adele in procuring a quiet end to her marriage in the decidedly popular divorce mills of Paris, and to spend his days anonymously living off of her private trust fund and eventual hefty settlement. But now the alignment of his name with an international scandal threatened his plans. He had never conceived that Edward Browning would be so willing to publicize the lurid details of his private life, and he naively underestimated the public's fascination with the whole affair. He couldn't have been more unprepared.

Newspapermen from both countries flocked to Paris in an effort to locate and confront the faithless couple. Browning's private operatives, who still tailed Adele, reported that she went out in men's clothing to avoid detection. Contradictory newspaper accounts of their movements and activities surfaced, and Adele Browning began to take on a mysterious and legendary character in the popular eye.

An indigent Wilen made a public statement in Paris denying any romantic involvement with Adele: "My only relations with Mrs. Browning have been to install bridgework. This suit is astonishing from one point of view, but very unfortunate from another. The chief result, so far as I am concerned, is that it ruins one good dentist." He continued, "I am the Browning family dentist, which means about as much to that family as a family plumber. The idea of Mrs. Browning eloping with me is foolish. Only a man anxious to find a ground for divorce would think that. It is true that we came together on the *Olympic,* but that is chiefly a coincidence. I was coming here for personal reasons and she was coming to get a quiet divorce in Paris without publicity."

Edward Browning was unmoved. He named Wilen as a respondent in the legal proceedings, and upon learning that Adele had given him cash and jewelry, he pledged that Wilen was to see not a cent more of his money. He stopped paying bills that Adele had accumulated and he set aside the $100,000 trust fund that he had created in her name, effectively choking off her sole means of income. Adele Browning had denied herself no extravagance, but she now would have to survive on whatever money she had taken with her to Paris. Said Browning, "To me my wife is as though she were dead."

❖

Before long, Edward Browning had an unlikely ally. "When I learned he [Wilen] had eloped with Mrs. Browning I nearly went wild," said Renee Shapiro. "For a few days I thought I would go insane; then slowly the love I felt for him crystallized into hate. And if he bragged of his ability to love, then I now boast of my ability to hate."

Shapiro enlightened Browning about Wilen's erstwhile plans to defraud him. She gleefully told him, "I have seen hundreds of dollars that he said [Adele] gave him, and I saw the two diamond rings she gave him and the money he got when he pawned them." Shapiro informed the press, "I want to help Mr. Browning all I can. I know all about Wilen . . . [He] has made a fool out of me." Shapiro spent the better part of a day with Browning and his attorneys and she happily formalized her vengeful rants into an affidavit to be used against the man who had scorned her so. Hell, indeed, hath no fury.

With the evidence mounting against them, the discreet divorce from Browning and subsequent honeymoon that Adele and Wilen had envisioned as they arrived on the shores of Europe dissolved before their eyes. Adele was suffocating financially and the legal hold placed upon her by her husband stressed her relations with Charles Wilen to the limit. Wilen saw the writing on the wall and he knew his free lunch was over—and so was his relationship with Adele. She had no choice but to return to the United States and fight Browning for her sustenance.

Her troubles, however, had only begun.

NEW YORK TIMES
September 20, 1923

MRS. BROWNING ARRESTED.

———

Divorce Defendant Accused of Fraud in Obtaining Passport

Mrs. Nellie Adele Browning, defendant in a divorce action brought by Edward W. Browning, real estate dealer, was arrested yesterday in her apartment at 137 West 179th Street, the Bronx, and arraigned before Federal Commissioner Hitchcock on a charge of violating the Espionage Act in obtaining a passport fraudulently. She was released on $1,000 bail for a hearing October 3.

On the same charge, Harry J. Wolcher, a salesman, of 955 Prospect Avenue, was released on $2,500 bail.

Leo P. Gastel, a State Department agent, alleged that on Nov. 22, 1922, the defendants told the State Department they were man and wife and obtained passports.

Adele almost couldn't make bail. To Edward Browning the justice was poetic.

"A dentist of all people! How can any sensible woman fall in love with a dentist, particularly with the dentist who has done her own work? The idea is preposterous!" Browning's sentiments were loud and clear, and though he continued to profess his love for Adele, the divorce proceedings rumbled their way through the courts of New York and Paris.

The sordid particulars of Adele's adulterous activities were, of course, the basis of Browning's claims, but she fought back in any way that she could. She publicly and vigorously denied all of the allegations in the suit. She filed a countersuit for divorce against Browning, and levied vague allegations that Browning had taken up with other women during the marriage. Adele employed every weapon available to her, including her child. Newspaper reports surfaced stating that Marjorie never wanted to see her Daddy again. Adele had no choice but to leverage whatever advantage she could. Her financial survival was at stake.

❖

Charles Wilen remained in Europe and reports placed him in the French Riviera. Like Adele, he was indicted by a Federal Grand Jury in New York for his role in inducing her and Wolcher's passport fraud. When he finally got around to addressing the indictment, he pleaded guilty and received a one-year sentence—suspended upon the payment of a $500 fine.

In the coming years, reports began to emerge of Wilen's close association with Suzanne Lenglen, the trend-setting French tennis champion who had reached international acclaim on and off the court. *La Divine,* as the French press hailed her, was the 1920 Olympic tennis champion and had won Wimbledon six times. Her revealing tennis attire and unconventional manner revitalized the sport and won over the hearts of millions. One of those hearts belonged to Charles Wilen. Ever the charmer, he secured himself a place in the attractive star's life. He acted as Lenglen's American adviser in the negotiation of movie contracts, and soon rumors of their pending marriage began to surface.

It was news to a certain Mrs. Belle Wilen of New York. "He's already my husband," she said.

❖

Nearly penniless, Adele was no match for the legal machine assembled by Edward Browning. Despite her desperate initial posturing, she was quickly persuaded to accept an agreement of support and alimony *pendente lite* of $6,000 per year to be secured by a mortgage on one of Browning's many properties. Browning then cajoled his estranged wife into returning to Paris—this time with him, for the express purpose of obtaining a fast and clean divorce in the Parisian courts. The extremely liberal minimum requirement of residency for submission to the jurisdiction of the French courts of the day—a simple registered intention to maintain domicile—ensured that the stay would be a short one. Browning reasoned that the uncertainties of the American court system presented too much of a risk to his fortune, and in his mind there was a certain justice in obtaining his divorce in the land to which his wife had fled.

With very little effort and with minimal expense, the Browning marriage concluded in the Civil Tribunal of the Seine in the Republic of France on the ground of desertion. Adele had little choice but to provide her full cooperation in the summary proceedings.

❖

A Federal Judge imposed the same suspended sentence and fine upon Adele for her violations of the Espionage Act as he did on Wilen. Her legal troubles were over, as was her marriage to Edward Browning. She would raise her daughter and live on the support that Browning provided.

As for Edward Browning, the constant reminders of his disloyal wife and the betrayal that broke up his happy family proved too much for him. His home and its extraordinary contents brought back nothing but bitter and unhappy memories, and in May of 1924, he commissioned a two-day auction of "the entire sumptuous furnishings" of the now gloomy residence. One of the *New York Times* classified ads that publicized the event contained the caption, "The End of a Beautiful Romance!!!!" The auction was considered "the largest and most important apartment sale ever made [in New York]." A newly formed motion picture firm out of Los Angeles by the name of Warner Brothers was the high bidder for Browning's eight-foot pagoda-shaped temple lantern. Moviegoers hadn't a clue of its origin when they saw it on the silver screen.

Browning walked away from his marriage a man disillusioned by the institution. He wrote, "Now I thought enough about love and marriage, in the months since the terrible pain of parting arrived, to realize that there is a fine art of the affections. With love as with business, a man should study his possibilities, and when his limit is found accept it in submission. I know my limit in love, and I accept it. That is why I shall not marry again."

Adele Browning thought otherwise. As the Paris divorce ensued, she was heard to say, "He is interested in other women very much younger than I."

Chosen from over 12,000 applicants, Mary Louise Spas gazes adoringly at the "Cinderella Man." Browning's lawyer, Francis Dale, purportedly said that Spas possessed a "mysterious power, not unlike hypnotic influence."

CHAPTER V

WANTED: PRETTY, REFINED GIRL...

"Feeling is running high among those who have communicated with me and charge it to be an unmoral transaction. And I consider it a highly unmoral transaction myself and the meanest piece of publicity I have ever known."

—BIRD S. COLER, Commissioner of Public Welfare, State of New York

EN ROUTE TO FRANCE FOR THEIR EXPEDITED DIVORCE, EDWARD AND ADELE Browning were understandably estranged. They stayed in separate quarters and shared very little conversation. They did, however, discuss the future of their children. Browning understood that Adele had developed a mother-daughter bond with Marjorie, and he had developed greater bonds with Dorothy. Since the abrupt separation, Marjorie had been residing with Adele and her parents, and Dorothy had stayed with Browning. There was no reason to further upset the situation and subject the children to needless additional adjustment. As each parent had separately adopted one child only, it was agreed that Adele would retain sole and exclusive custody of her daughter Marjorie, while Dorothy Sunshine would remain with her father. The arrangement was formalized through the terms of the divorce decree and the final details were set into motion. When Edward Browning returned to New York, he would be the single parent of an eight-year-old girl.

The city-view penthouse was gone—the memories were too fresh and painful for him to remain there. But Browning found other ways to overindulge his now only child. He took up residence in another Long Island mansion that would soon become Dorothy's fairyland playhouse. Ponies, miniature railways, and carriages were scattered over four hundred fifty acres of landscaped lawns, and proved to be an adequate substitute for the mother and sister who were now absent from her life. A specially designed stretch Rolls Royce was Dorothy Sunshine's choice of transportation to and from her country estate. The limo was equipped with a four-foot-high motion picture screen and a sixteen-tube radio set capable of picking up any station in the country. In ordering it, Browning boasted that he wanted it to be the finest automobile in the world.

Browning was still deeply involved with his business enterprises and his time was precariously balanced between long hours in his Manhattan offices and time in the country with his daughter. The arrangement worked for a while; Browning believed that whatever she lacked in the way of companionship he could make up for with his own personal attentions—and failing that, a fairytale world of exotic possessions. There was nothing that Edward Browning would deny his cherished Sunshine. In the coming months, however, it became clear that his daughter was suffering from loneliness. He sadly recollected Marjorie's unhappiness as an only child and the joy that replaced it when he and Adele had adopted a sister for her. Dorothy Sunshine needed the closeness that only a sibling could bring.

❖

Classified advertisements had proved a rather useful tool for Edward Browning in both his business endeavors and his personal life. He frequently placed ads in New York newspapers seeking workmen, clerical help, and tenants. He advertised parcels of real estate for sale and purchase, and when he couldn't find what he wanted through typical channels, he placed ads to the specifications that he desired. He occasionally bought and sold personal belongings through advertisements and he had twice succeeded in acquiring children through the newspaper.

In the early summer of 1925, however, Edward Browning placed an advertisement in various New York newspapers that would seize a different kind of national attention.

ADOPTION - PRETTY, REFINED GIRL, about 14 years old, wanted by aristocratic family of large wealth and highest standing: will be brought up as own child among beautiful surroundings, with every desirable luxury, opportunity, education, travel, kindness, care, love. Address with full particulars and photograph.

The ad was not particularly different from the ones previously placed by Browning. His display ads had worked in the past, and he was hoping they could work again. His motives would be debated for years, but Browning steadfastly maintained that his intentions in placing the ad were simply to secure a playmate and companion for his daughter. Others weren't so sure. It might have been the wording of the ad, or perhaps the era in which it emerged, but the response was immediate and overwhelming. It appeared that his advertisement "had opened up the gates of fairyland for many a poor child."

❖

Philip Siegel sat quietly on a tied stack of morning newspapers. In his ink-blackened hands he clutched a crossword puzzle booklet, its front cover folded back. The crossword craze had hit the nation only one year earlier and Siegel wasn't the only new devotee. His drowsy brown eyes strained hard behind the Marshwood spectacles that always seemed too large for his thin face. The hum of printing presses droned around him. He was a flyboy for the *New York Times* and the moment of rest between deliveries to the conveyors was a welcome one.

The usually attentive and reliable twenty-one-year-old had much on his mind. Philip Siegel had always been a good boy. He had done well in school and his employers at the paper found him to be hardworking and affable, but today he just didn't seem to be on track. Lately he had begun to daydream. Discontent had overtaken him; he had become obsessed with escaping his banal existence for a life of money and power. Imaginative schemes began to emerge from his otherwise unimaginative heart, and soon Philip Siegel began hatching a plot that no one would have thought he was capable of.

❖

The responses to Browning's ad poured in like a tide. Men, women, and children from all walks of life clamored for the opportunity to become the living heir to the Edward Browning throne. Applications scribed in seven different languages—and two in shorthand—arrived from locations as close as the Bronx and as far as China, Europe, and the Philippines. Photographs of candidates ranging in age from three weeks to eighty-seven years were plastered over the walls of Browning's real estate offices, which quickly became a bustling marketplace of the bizarre. Among the hopefuls was an ex-boxer with only one eye and one

Daddy Browning in his vault of letters.

ear, a middle-aged spinster with dimpled knees, an Indian princess, a Spanish *señorita*, a marathon runner, and a woman who claimed she was double jointed all over. He received nearly one thousand marriage proposals and one plea to adopt a papoose. Before making his final choice, Browning would examine over twelve thousand applications.

At first, Browning's secretaries busily worked the telephones in some semblance of business as usual, making appointments with anxious and uncertain parents who pleaded that their daughters were most deserving of the opportunities promised in the ad. As inquisitive tabloid newsmen caught wind of the curious flurry, however, they followed the trail to Edward Browning's downtown offices. Once the anonymous advertiser's identity had found its way into syndication, the decorum the secretaries had fought so hard to maintain crumbled.

Hundreds of tipi-toed mothers with disoriented children at their sides crowded around the entrance to the office building while pedestrians and drivers alike gawked and caused a maddening traffic tie-up. Rabid for any suggestion of personal access to the millionaire, the throngs were gratified when Browning proclaimed that he would personally interview each and every applicant before arriving at his decision.

Browning was utterly delighted by the public attention and the surge of newspaper coverage. As a ploy for further press exposure, he enlisted the *New York Daily Mirror* to assist him in tabulating the flood of letters and photographs and to submit them for his review. The *Mirror* gleefully printed a copy of Browning's signed letter authorizing the alliance and stated, "[Browning] yesterday appealed to the Daily Mirror for help and authorized this publication to conduct for him a contest among New York orphans for a prize which is a rich man's wealth and a kind man's heart." The *Mirror's* glowing opinion of Browning's intentions would not last long.

He joyously provided the press with less than poignant public statements about his desire for a new child, and he paraded his nervously smiling applicants before salivating news photographers. No sooner had the searing afterimages from the Leica camera flashes dissipated from his eyes than clamoring newsrooms splashed quarter page photographs of tiny New Yorkers at the knee of Daddy Browning in news publications from Akron to Albuquerque.

For most of the parents who found themselves engaged in this unholy charade, the scene was surreal. These parents had become desperate sideshows in Browning's adoption circus. To many of them, this was the deadly serious business of giving up a child, a choice they were forced to make because of their unique instances of distressing hardship. Many earnestly believed that Browning's adoption offer represented the only real possibility for their children to ever leave a world of poverty and want in favor of privilege and advantage.

Perhaps it really was such an opportunity, but the stakes were high and the odds incredibly thin. Each parent, in their own way, made their case to Browning and pleaded that their particular child was the ideal sibling and playmate for his. The often heartbreaking scene was described in the *New York Times*: "The first little girl to come by appointment was fairly good looking and dressed in her Sunday best. She stood shy and reticent in the background while her mother told what a nice child she was and showed her excellent school reports. When the child finally was questioned and asked if she wished to leave her mother and be adopted, she shook her head, while tears streamed from her eyes."

Browning was described as "kind and fatherly" to the children he interviewed and those applicants considered unsuitable were chauffeured home in his automobile with a gift for their trouble. He painstakingly poured over each and every application and he announced that the selection process would take several weeks to complete. He stated that he intended to take the winning applicant into his home for several weeks or even a month on a provisional basis before making the decision final. He used his newfound notoriety to fashion himself an adoption expert and make boldfaced assertions regarding children of the poor as healthier and generally more attractive than children of the rich. He then added that the poor soon learn the ways of wealth, pointing as substantiation to Dorothy Sunshine's choice of an imported car as a present.

Though Browning's adoption ad requested a "pretty, refined *girl*," among the thousands of applications was one sent by a fourteen-year-old boy from Harlem who wrote, "I will amuse you and the little girl by playing the violin for you. When I grow up to be an artist I will pay you back." Browning chuckled and submitted the boy's earnest pleadings to the newspapers.

By mid-July, it appeared that Browning had made his choice. The application of an eleven-year-old child actress by the name of Margaretta Curry had caught Browning's eye and he was sufficiently impressed with her appearance and demeanor to conclude his search and adopt the girl. As the legal documents were about to be signed, however, Margaretta's mother finally began to comprehend the implications of handing over her daughter to this eccentric champion of child rearing. With tears streaming from her eyes, she gathered up her little Margaretta and fled Browning's offices, never to return. Stunned, Browning turned to his associates and quipped, "Perhaps she needs more time to think things over." Perhaps so.

❖

On the morning of July 9, 1925, as Browning's staff began the task of opening the day's torrent of mail, one parcel conspicuously marked "PERSONAL" caught the eye of the secretary. As she slit the envelope and perused the correspondence within, her pulse began to quicken and panic overtook her.

> Mr. Browning: We are in need of some ready money, about fifty thousand dollars ($50,000). We have selected you because you will never miss that much and it is imperative that we have the money. If you refuse we will use other methods. We are quite sure that your little girl's life is worth that much to you, and even your own life depends on whether we get it or not. We will give you ample time to think the matter over and let us know through the Public Notices column of the N.Y. Times of next Tuesday, July 14, if you will grant our request . . . May we add that it will do you no good to notify the police or to hire private detectives. If you are a wise man you will do as we say because we stop at nothing. You or your girl cannot escape us if we go after you. Give us the money and you will never hear of us again, we will annoy you no more. Keep this to yourself, if there is any publicity or if you try any false steps it will mean death.
>
> THE BAND OF FIFTY.

Edward Browning's all-too-public pronouncements had gained him not only the limelight that he so dearly sought but had also awoken the unwelcome and often frightening attentions of a disgruntled underclass bent on snatching away the riches of the man now dubbed the Cinderella Man.

Browning was outraged. The letter could have come from *anywhere*, but how to respond? He contemplated his course of action and in a red-faced fit of disgust stuffed the letter into the inside pocket of his jacket and headed for City Hall.

❖

John Francis Hylan had been the Mayor of New York since 1918 and though he was hardworking and industrious he was considered by most to be of average intelligence. Buttressed by the efforts of William Randolph Hearst, Hylan railed against the infiltration of "interests" throughout government, and rode a wave of disenchantment into the mayoral office. Over the years, and his many real estate endeavors, Edward Browning had developed a course of dealings with "Red Mike," as Hylan had come to be known, and felt that he could rely on him to resolve the problem of the letter.

With an air of urgency and perhaps with a lack of attention to propriety, Browning wheedled his way into Hylan's office and laid the ominous note before him. "I want this handled, John," Browning told him. The mayor did his best to relax his unannounced guest and finally agreed to tend to the matter personally. Browning insisted on no less.

In conjunction with the New York City Police Commissioner and a team of inspectors and detectives, Mayor Hylan began his investigation. He also promptly supplied an officer to tend to the personal protection of his friend. Out of fear for the safety of his daughter, Browning's initial impulse was to respond quickly to the demands presented in the letter. He lobbied hard for inserting a responsive ad in the *Times* as had been requested.

The detectives balked. They wanted to pursue their leads and search for the culprit on their own timeframe and in their own manner. But Browning was not in the mood for chances. He had no idea how serious a threat he was dealing with or the risks involved. He was not going to gamble with his or his daughter's safety. As the letter had demanded, he placed a display ad in the Public Notices section of the *New York Times* that appeared on July 14:

"BAND (Cousin) - Will grant your wishes: Send instructions.
Edward W. B."

Two days later another typewritten letter arrived in Browning's office. This letter acknowledged Browning's acquiescence and ordered him to obtain denominations of tens, twenties, and hundreds, and to take the money to the northwest corner of 86th Street and Central Park, at a designated time and date, where he would be met by a messenger to accept the package. The letter warned Browning against "any false moves, such as marking the bills, or an empty cake package, or having someone with you or in hiding."

It was agreed that Browning would meet the culprit as demanded. Sheets of blank paper were sliced into strips about the size of bank notes and made into packages that were each individually wrapped with five-dollar bills. He was provided with a small leather satchel and the "money" was neatly packed into it. Bag in tow, Browning appeared at the appointed time and location. At several positions in the streets surrounding the drop-off point, detectives peered from darkened doorways and slouched in unidentifiable automobiles, laying in wait. Browning buried the obvious fears that he felt with protective thoughts of Dorothy Sunshine.

A tense young man with an awkward deportment wandered about the area. He paced back and forth and he eyed Edward Browning. The young man glanced about the area and then, as if in a burst of daring nerve, approached Browning, who peered expressionlessly at the curious man. He was a child, barely out of his teens, but Browning was filled with anger and determination to see this rogue brought to the law.

The exchange was quickly made, and the young man made his way up 96th Street. Browning anxiously watched as the posse of undercover detectives quickly went off in pursuit. Later that morning he was to learn that Philip Siegel was arrested on an uptown subway platform.

❖

At first Philip Siegel vigorously denied any involvement in the scheme to extort money from Edward Browning. He insisted that a persuasive talking stranger that he met had requested that Siegel go to Central Park and pick up a package for him. This, Siegel maintained, he innocently agreed to do. His relatives immediately came to his aid and supported his every claim. "Phillie simply could not have done this thing," pleaded his mother. "He trusted everybody. I can understand how he would readily agree to do a small service for a stranger." The police were unconvinced and a vigorous interrogation ensued, but Siegel steadfastly held to his story. He made allegations through his family that the police had beaten him during the questioning and almost immediately these allegations found their way into the papers.

Browning quickly became fed up. He was frustrated by the slow pace of the investigation and he wanted better results fast. He was present during most of the questioning of Siegel and he was absolutely convinced that the police had never beaten the boy. He was also certain beyond a doubt that Siegel's protestations of innocence were completely false. Amid the raw public censure levied against the City, and the mounting pressures placed by Edward Browning, Mayor Hylan felt he had no choice but to personally intervene in the interrogation of Philip Siegel.

Siegel's mother was right—her son basically was a good boy. His crimes were both malicious and imperfectly planned, but Philip Siegel was not stupid. He understood the power of the Mayor's office and when Red Mike ambled into his jail cell at police headquarters Siegel knew the jig was up. Hylan was an imposing figure and his experience as a Kings County judge had given him some expertise at witness examination and fact finding. To Edward Browning's utter delight, Hylan was quickly able to obtain a full confession from Siegel, acknowledging his sole involvement in the scheme.

❖

Browning's frustration with the criminal legal process mounted, even after Siegel's admission of guilt. Shaken to core by the threats levied against him and his daughter, Browning wanted to make an example of Siegel. He urged vigorous prosecution in an effort to discourage others from engaging in similar activities. Browning appeared at every hearing involving Siegel's case, accompanied by an army of lawyers and armed bodyguards. He sought the additional charge of robbery against Siegel, and when that failed he contested any reduction in his bail. At the first bail hearing Siegel's lawyer turned to Browning and declared, "If the Court imposes high bail perhaps Mr. Browning could furnish it. He is charitably inclined." Browning fired back, "Yes—and be murdered for it?" Siegel's family raised the $7,500 bail set by the court and Siegel was temporarily freed.

Several days later, at Browning's urging, the parties were back in court before another judge and the District Attorney was pleading for higher bail. Browning had clearly found the judge he was looking for in John McIntyre, who ruled, to Browning's sheer delight, "If this complainant's story is true, it is the most infamous crime that has been attempted—part of a scheme that has been going on for some time. They were up to murder . . . I must presume the defendant to be guilty rather than innocent on the question of bail." Bail was increased to $25,000 and Philip Siegel was remanded pending trial to the notorious New York prison known as the Tombs.

❖

Meanwhile, a young girl in Astoria, Queens had stumbled across Edward Browning's ad. Little Mary Louise Spas was the antithesis of a modern flapper. She wore her golden hair in long and flowing curls instead of the fashionable cropped bob of the day, and she sported a Mona Lisa smile that transformed her otherwise plain and boorish features. Mary was born in Prague and though her Bohemian parents spoke very little English, she was well versed in the language and customs of America.

When she read Edward Browning's ad, her mind filled with longing and mournful thoughts of what she didn't have and what she wanted so. Writing, music, dance, and education—all of the things that she desired and felt deprived of. Mary sensed that the world was just out of her reach, and that the wealth and power needed to unlock her dreams would be forever inaccessible for a girl like her. She was determined to change her circumstances.

Mary Spas was somewhat older than the fourteen years specified by the advertisement, but she was resolved to appeal to Browning and to present herself as a viable candidate for adoption. She awoke early that late July morning and quietly slipped out of her parents' Astoria apartment. With only five cents in her pocket but with glowing dreams of riches and opportunity swimming through her brain, she boarded a streetcar bound for Manhattan.

She made her way over the Queensborough Bridge and walked the remaining two miles of the trip, across Central Park and finally to Browning's office. The words of a newly published novel written by an upstart young author from St. Paul prompted riders of the *Astoria Line* into Manhattan to peer from the windows of the clattering trains to the sight of the bustling city beyond. "The city seen from the Queensborough Bridge," observed the novel's protagonist, Nick Carraway, "is always the city seen for the first time, in its first wild promise of all the mystery and the beauty in the world." The novel, which had initially been met with mixed reviews, was called *The Great Gatsby*. F. Scott Fitzgerald's stirring dialogue could have come directly from the hopeful mind of Mary Louise Spas.

Mary's wild dreams of wealth immediately gave way to the harsh reality that many, many other girls shared the same dream as her—and were all attempting to bring it to life through the good offices of Edward West Browning. She felt old and big amidst the throngs of babies and little girls that waited for their turn at Daddy's knee. The winding line of mothers and their young daughters that lay ahead of her dashed her hopes of even meeting the mythical benefactor. She collapsed meekly into a far corner of the expansive offices and lamented her return to a dreary life of the mundane.

After enduring what seemed to be an eternity of crying babies and the mindless chatter of little girls, Mary observed a man enter the offices. She stiffened against the wall and watched as he stopped and scanned the bustling throng. She knew who he was instantly. As Browning's gaze crossed hers, Mary instinctively smiled, revealing a modest gold tooth in one corner of her contoured mouth. He fixed his eyes upon her and smiled back, and at that moment Mary's despair withered away. Edward Browning had made his choice—and she knew it.

In the following months and years, much was written about the smile of Mary Louise Spas and its hypnotic like power. A syndicated expose entitled *"The Smile That Upset All Rich Mr. Browning's Plans"* appeared in newspapers across the country. The article suggested that Mary's smile transformed her face, "It becomes a countenance of mystery and compelling power, one that seems easily capable of making slaves of men just as it did for a brief time with Mr. Browning . . . Psychologists believe that there is something actually hypnotic about this smile of Mary Spas—something mysteriously compelling which swayed Mr. Browning from his usually good judgment and made him for a time its obedient slave." Browning's own lawyer, Francis Dale, was actually quoted as saying that Spas possessed a "mysterious power, not unlike hypnotic influence . . ."

Hypnotized or not, Edward Browning was clearly smitten by this young girl and within a few short moments Mary found herself catapulted past the convulsing line of hopeful children and into an oversized

Browning and Mary Louise Spas

chair at the foot of Edward Browning's desk behind the imposing closed doors of his personal office.

Browning was captivated by Mary's tale and was totally blinded by her sweet and disarming manner. Though she came from a loving family, she convinced Browning that they were poor and unable to properly care for her. She hesitatingly admitted to being sixteen years old—two years past eligibility for the Browning daughter position—and pleaded that her maturity would allow her to become not only Dorothy Sunshine's companion but also her big sister. She enthralled Browning with stories of her diverse interests and explained that she had done well in high school, mastered stenography in business college classes, posed for a movie screen test, and danced for a short while at a ballet school used by the Metropolitan Opera House. The question never entered Browning's entranced mind of how this little immigrant girl could have crowded these wide range of experiences into sixteen short years. To him, she was the perfect choice.

At first Mary's parents begged to differ. They were a simple immigrant family who had come to America fifteen years earlier. Mary's father worked hard to provide what he could for his daughter and they were understandably reluctant to give her up to a total stranger. John and Marie Spas had high hopes for Mary and wanted more than

anything to ensure that she received a rich education. Their hopes had
been tempered and the family finances severely drained, however, by
the illness and institutionalization of Mary's older sister, twenty-three-
year-old Mildred Spas. Between Browning's persistence and their
daughter's beseeching, Mr. and Mrs. Spas were persuaded that
Browning could provide Mary with comforts and opportunities far
beyond what they themselves could. Finally, with Browning's pledge
to allow their constant continual contact with Mary, and the promise
that she would ascend as an heiress to his fortunes, John and Marie
Spas capitulated to their daughter's appeals and offered their consent
to the adoption.

As a token of goodwill, Edward Browning then provided to Mary's
parents what was described as a surprise present for the purpose of
defraying the mounting expenses of Mildred's illness. He wrote a check
to each for $500, and he would soon regret ever doing so.

❖

Within days, the Queens County Surrogate's Court approved the
adoption and Browning proudly introduced Mary Louise Browning to
the world. Headlines across America screamed the news—*Gold Tooth
Smile Gives Janitor's Child Rich Home Over 12,000 Rivals; Poor Girl
Is Given Wealth; Browning, Fairy Godfather, Picks Pretty Cinderella.*

Mary Spas' world was transformed in the blink of an eye. When she
wasn't being driven from locale to locale in Browning's glitzy Rolls
Royce, she was dining on the finest cuisines at fancy hotels and passing
time in large country estates with Browning and his circle of friends. She
learned to ring once for a butler and three times for a maid, and she no
longer slurped her soup but carefully positioned the spoon on her lips,
allowing the contents to drop primly into her satisfied mouth. Quickly
acquiring the language of high society and wealth, Mary added a variety of polysyllabic words to her vocabulary. Referring to her janitor
father, she learned to say, "My father is a superintendent."

Mary's every move was photographed and written about by enthusiastic newspapermen; news of the Browning clan was a surefire path
to increased circulation. On one occasion, there was a near riot of
onlookers and flashing camera bulbs that followed Mary and her
Daddy from shop to exclusive shop on New York's Fifth Avenue. To
the delight of the mob, Browning's chauffer and footman loaded into
his Rolls Royce countless bags and boxes that brimmed with pretty

"Cinderella" and her coach.

frocks, expensive hosiery, specially designed shoes, posh jewelry, and dozens of other items of feminine finery. When asked by one of the reporters how much he had spent on the spree, Browning flashed a toothy grin and said, "Oh, I didn't spend all I had." He removed a role of fifty-dollar bills from his trouser pocket, and matter-of-factly added, "This was only a preliminary shopping trip . . . Probably didn't cost me more than $2,500."

The delighted Browning topped off his public displays of affection for his new "daughter" during his first few days with Mary Louise, with promises of a high-powered boat for use on the Hudson River, and an airplane. In true Browning fashion, he intended to bestow upon his new ward every possible luxury and meant to do it in the most flamboyant manner possible. Mary gloated to the clamoring newsmen, "Of course I love my new daddy. He certainly is good to me."

❖

Meanwhile, letters began piling up at Browning's Long Island residence from Dorothy Sunshine, away at camp, and pleading for a summer visit from her father.

Daddy Browning surrounded by Mary Spas and "runner-up" Sylvia Mullen. The placement of Browning's hand (in this particular photo) would cause a stir and prompt the attention of the authorities.

CHAPTER VI

TWO STROKES TO MIDNIGHT

> "... But her godmother, above all things, com-
> manded her not to stay till after midnight,
> telling her, at the same time, that if she stayed
> one moment longer, the coach would be a
> pumpkin again, her horses mice, her coach-
> man a rat, her footmen lizards, and her clothes
> become just as they were before."
>
> —MARCIA BROWN, *Cinderella, or
> the Little Glass Slipper*

WHILE BROWNING WAS BUSY TRAIPSING MARY LOUISE DOWN A ROW OF
exclusive Fifth Avenue boutiques, a hardnosed collection of newspaper
reporters began questioning friends and neighbors of the Spas family in
the normally quiet municipality of Astoria, Queens. Mary's former
address had been purposely withheld from reporters to prevent just such
an annoyance, but the inquisitive mob was without scruples when their
noses told them that a story beneath the story was brewing. The neighbors of John and Marie Spas were all too willing to tell what they knew
about Browning's Cinderella, and what they wouldn't say or simply didn't
know was revealed by a generous public record.

Immediately, headlines decrying Mary's age—and innocence—satu-
rated the streets and began to raise the eyebrow of a cynically fascinated
public. Acquaintances scoffed at the assertion that Mary was sixteen
and even insisted that she was romantically involved with at least one
man and perhaps even engaged to be married. Claims of a plumber's
assistant by the name of Emil Vasalek—that he had been hotly pursued
by Mary and that she had repeatedly proposed an elopement—were
splashed into news columns, and at least one tabloid paper claimed that
Mary was engaged to an Astoria dentist. Missing not a scintilla of the
irony, the article claimed, "The very word 'dentist' sets Browning's teeth

on edge," reminding titillated readers of Nellie Adele's very public antics with Charles Wilen. Whispers that Mary had been a moving picture actress found their way onto reporters' notepads and soon photographs surfaced depicting her in revealing swimsuits and in very adult poses.

Eager newsmen did not stop their probe at the Astoria neighbors and former friends of Mary Spas. As curious eyes scanned county and municipal real estate records, it was quickly revealed that John Spas, far from being a poor janitor, was the owner of the apartment house that he maintained and lived in with his family, and that its worth was in excess of $60,000. Mary's claim of Cinderella innocence and deprivation was crumbling beneath her feet.

At first, Browning appeared undeterred by the damning claims of the newspaper columns. His instinct was to fight fire with fire by publicly denying the allegations and by asserting his own version of the facts. After satisfying himself through Mary's fervent denials, he immediately called a bevy of news reporters to his Manhattan offices to refute the slanderous stories and to openly respond to their mounting questions. Eager reporters armed with note pads and cameramen muscled their way through hundreds of curious men, woman, and children who waited anxiously outside of Browning's Midtown office building, hoping for a glimpse of the celebrated millionaire and his renowned adoptee.

"I have absolute faith in Mary Louise," he began. "I have satisfied myself that my girl is sixteen years old. Such evidence I have is enough to convince me. She was born July 31, 1909. Last week we had a party at her home . . . It was her sixteenth birthday." When asked if he had seen Mary's birth certificate, Browning angrily admitted that he had not. "Talk with her and see for yourself that she is only a child."

Browning then turned his attention to the finances of the Spas family, claiming that John Spas made $30 per week and yielded only a small income from the apartment house that he maintained. He argued that Mary's sister was ill and living in a sanitarium, the cost of which was absorbed by the Spas family. "I call her a poor girl," Browning said of Mary. "She is Cinderella enough for me."

For her part, Mary charmed the news reporters with flashes of her wide smile and straight white teeth. Even the writer for the normally reserved *New York Times* waxed poetic: "Her appearance of youth is accentuated by the long golden brown curls."

With a hot flush in her cheeks, Mary indignantly denied that she was over sixteen, or that she was involved with any man. She appeared hurt that her neighborhood acquaintances would claim that she had been less than forthright, and attributed all of their rants to jealously motivated gossip. "It would appear from the reports that I was pretty busy with the boys in Astoria, but that was not the case. I know they would like to be engaged to me now on account of my good fortune." "I never have had any boyfriends or gentlemen friends. You must have been misinformed," shrugged Mary. On the harping questions of her age, Mary grinned and said, "I don't know anything about this talk. I was a baby when papa and mama came to America from Prague and I know I'm sixteen now." With a sigh of relief, Browning intervened, "You see, it's just idle neighborhood gossip. I believe her and her parents when they say she is sixteen and that is sufficient for me."

As the interview wound down, Mary and her new father made what would prove to be a fatal mistake. In response to a reporter's question about her institutionalized sister, Mary stated that Browning had given her parents money to help in the care of the girl. When the reporter's eyes flashed to Browning's for confirmation, Browning nodded and hesitatingly admitted that he had given the family a trifle to defray the expenses of the Spas' sick child. Browning then put his arm around Mary and abruptly ended the conference. "Please let us go down to Kew Gardens tonight alone. She is tired and we want a little more time to get acquainted."

❖

The various city newspapers, with headlines screaming the details of Edward Browning's latest foray into the world of child adoption, lay sprawled across Bird Coler's desk, amidst hundreds of letters from fellow New Yorkers expressing disapproval of the millionaire's depraved escapades. The telephone was ringing off its hook with calls from people demanding action, and Coler decided *he* was just the man to take that action.

It had been twenty-three years since Coler's unsuccessful bid to become Governor of New York, but the political scars still lingered. He had endured charges of official wrongdoing in the years prior to and after the election, but nothing came of the investigations. Coler's resolve was only stiffened by what he viewed as a political machine that served no one but itself. Fiercely independent and stubbornly defiant, Coler's turbulent career was marked by political battles with Tammany Hall officials who sought to place unqualified government appointees into positions that he alone was charged to fill. By 1925, after serving in a variety of positions in local government, Coler found himself appointed Commissioner of New York's

Department of Public Welfare. His manifest distrust of the City's political machine, however, soon extended to the people whom he served. It came as a surprise to few when Bird Coler began to utilize the political power of his office as a pulpit for a headlong attack on Edward Browning.

Though Coler knew that his department did not have jurisdiction over the matter—Mary was not in the public charge and had been in the custody of her parents at the time of the adoption—he couldn't resist stirring the waters of intrigue. The idea of a divorcee or a bachelor adopting a child was completely repugnant to him, and though the practice was permitted by law, he made it his policy to prevent it whenever he had the opportunity to do so.

Coler immediately denounced Browning's most recent adoption proceedings as a "highly unmoral transaction," and he revealed his intention to conduct an official inquiry that would include the participation of Queens County District Attorney Richard S. Newcombe. He then announced that if in fact Browning had provided a monetary consideration in exchange for the adoption, he expected the District Attorney to act. "It is the most unmoral thing that ever has come to my notice," said Coler. "Somewhere in this country there must be a statute that a parent cannot sell a child. If there is not such a law we will make one!"

Browning's lawyer, Francis Dale, issued a statement to the press characterizing his client's actions as an "entirely praiseworthy and philanthropic act." Browning personally dismissed Coler's claims of wrongdoing as politically motivated nonsense and stated that he too had received numerous letters from the public—virtually all complimentary. "I have a clear conscience," he added.

❖

Anna Brusel—now Anna St. John—had gotten on with her life since she gave up her foster daughter, Dorothy, to Edward Browning. She had remarried and thrust the disquiet of her decision to the recesses of her mind. As she read the news accounts of Browning's current circumstances, however, the lingering scars of that sad episode in her life now festered into an angry open wound.

❖

Like sharks sensing a kill, newspaper reporters left no stone unturned. They quickly learned that school records kept at the New York Board of Education indicated that Mary Spas was brought to the

United States in 1910 at the age of six. That now made her twenty-one years old. Publicly, Browning said he didn't believe the records. Privately, however, his doubts began to grow.

❖

As Mary began to understand the seriousness of the situation, her happy and lighthearted manner began to crack. While questions mounted and talk of investigations ensued, the smile that conquered her millionaire Daddy began to fade into tears. "I would rather be the poorest girl in New York now than go through all this," she said. "Yes, if I had known this was going to happen, I would have starved to death before I would have offered myself for adoption."

❖

On August 6, 1925, Bird Coler received a letter.

Dear Mr. Coler,

Permit me to write you in regard to Dorothy S. Browning, youngest adopted daughter of Mr. E.W. Browning. Your statement in today's papers about Browning's latest adopted daughter proves you are a man of honor. I hope you will listen to my pleas for poor little Dorothy.

I am her first foster mother, the nearest and only known person belonging to or interested in the child. She was deserted by her own kin at the age of four months, at which time I adopted her. About four years later I gave her to Mr. and Mrs. Browning because at the time it seemed the only right thing to do.

Since then I have learned that most of the things they represented to me as true facts were lies. Mrs. Browning deserted the child two years ago, and I cannot believe that Mr. Browning is fit to be her guardian, now that there has developed this disgusting farce of adopting a young woman. My heart is breaking to think of what may be in store for Dorothy.

Don't you think that there is cause to take her away from him? We are plain working people with one little girl, also an adopted child, but will gladly take Dorothy back and give her a decent home. If that cannot be, can't she in some way be placed in the care of responsible people?

I dearly love Dorothy, but have not the money to fight Mr. Browning.

Mr. Coler, if you are interested and will see me personally, please let me know when and where I may call.

ANNA ST. JOHN

❖

Frances Mullen frantically searched through the night for her twelve-year-old daughter, Sylvia. She contacted police and a general alarm was broadcast for the whereabouts of the little blued eyed girl with flaxen bobbed hair. Sylvia had been acting somewhat strangely since learning that she was actually the runner-up in Daddy Browning's adoption race. Her mother had even entered into some preliminary negotiations with Browning regarding the transaction, when, all at once, it was learned that Mary Spas would be Browning's choice. Sylvia seemed distraught by the news.

On the evening of the disappearance, Frances searched well into the night for her daughter. Having all but lost hope, she returned home after midnight only to find little Sylvia snug in her bed beneath her warm blanket. She awoke her young daughter with a flurry of hugs and relieved shakes, and demanded an explanation as to where the child had been. With flushed cheeks and innocent tired eyes, Sylvia murmured, "Why I've been to see 'Daddy' Browning and Mary Louise, momma. I wanted to congratulate her on her good fortune." Sylvia sat up in bed and seemed instantly to awaken with cheerful excitement. "They took me to the country and gave me a wonderful dinner and then drove me back home." With rising incredulity, Frances studied the girl as she continued. "Mr. Browning made me very happy. He said in just two weeks he was going to adopt me. Then I, too, will be a sure-enough Cinderella."

"There was no party last night," protested Browning when the story hit the press. "I retired early and the last time I saw the Mullen girl was in my office yesterday."

Browning's problems seemed to multiple by the hour.

❖

On Friday, August 7, 1925, Browning was summonsed to the Long Island offices of District Attorney Richard Newcombe for questioning. A large and enthusiastic crowd noisily assembled outside of the courthouse where Newcombe's office was located. As Browning ambled into the room, accompanied by his lawyer, the gravity of the situation became unmistakably clear to him. Seated in the office with the District Attorney were not only Commissioner Bird Coler, but also the Director and Secretary of the Bureau of Investigation of the Department of Public Welfare and two Assistant District Attorneys. The assemblage was intimidating even to Edward Browning.

❖

Pummeled by the constant questions of her age and character, Mary Louise was breaking down. While her Daddy was being interrogated by the imposing collection of public officials, crowds that were assembled outside of Browning's apartments at the Kew Gardens Inn heard hysterical shrieks and cries from inside. "I want to go home! I want to go home!"

❖

Browning fully cooperated with Newcombe's tireless investigation. Other than the crusading Bird Coler, it seemed that none of the participants were particularly pleased to be involved in the spectacle. As the facts and legalities of the situation were presented to Browning and his attorney, it became obvious that Newcombe was not looking for a prosecution as much as he was searching for a solution. Clearly the adoption could not stand, and Newcombe's objective was to press for Browning's acquiescence. To do so, he would use every asset available to him. Among the many demons confronted by Browning during the interrogation were statements made by Nellie Adele confirming that her ex-husband had an affinity for young girls. By the end of the day, he would be looking for a way out.

As he hurried out of the courthouse, a drawn and worried Edward Browning was swarmed by a horde of young girls seeking consideration of their name in place of the faltering adoption of Mary Louise. The police drove the crowd back and allowed Browning and his attorney to pass.

❖

Later that evening at the Kew Gardens Inn, as Browning lamented the events of the day with his friend and associate Robert Dunnett, Mary quietly slipped out of the room without notice. A moment later, the men heard a shriek from the bathroom and there they found Mary on the floor with an open bottle of iodine by her side.

She had placed the bottle to her lips and perhaps a tiny amount entered her mouth, but the majority of the poison fell harmlessly to the floor. Browning, of course, had no idea how much she had ingested and he immediately leaped into action. He sought medical assistance in the Inn while Dunnett created an egg solution to induce vomiting. A doctor soon arrived and quickly recognized Mary's attempt as nothing more than a bluff. "I did it because I was hysterical and did not know what I was doing, and because of the nasty things Mr. Coler had been saying about Mr. Browning," sobbed Mary.

Browning sighed with deep relief and realized that Mary must go home.

❖

The next morning, as if nothing had ever happened, Mary awoke and set herself down at the breakfast table with a wide grin and a carefree manner. "It's all past now and I am going on living," she said matter-of-factly. With that, she finished her pancakes and went outside for a game of tennis.

By 2:00 pm, however, when word came that District Attorney Newcombe wanted a word with her, Mary's breezy demeanor had vanished.

❖

Dressed from head to toe in green, Mary arrived with Edward Browning and Francis Dale at Newcombe's office, where her parents waited. John and Marie Spas had been interrogated for several hours already and had quickly admitted Mary's true age of twenty-one. They explained that they had hesitatingly gone along with their daughter's ruse because she was so obsessively intent on its success. They only wanted to make their daughter happy, they pleaded, but now all they wanted was to put this bizarre situation behind them and to take their daughter home.

Though Browning did not yet know it, they had also gone a long way to resolve his potential criminal culpability in the matter. Upon inquiry, Mary's parents informed Newcombe that at no time had Browning offered or given them any money in return for their consent to adopt. The "trifle," as Browning had called it, had been given to them as nothing more than an afterthought and they had been completely surprised by its tender.

❖

Newcombe invited Mary to sit down and he addressed her softly. He began with some harmless questions about her likes and interests and he even complimented her interesting choice of clothing for the day. After gaining her trust, he began probing her thoughts and motivations regarding the Browning adoption. She cooperated fully and she gratefully acquiesced to Newcombe's characterization of her as the victim in the case. Throughout the questioning, however, Mary unwaveringly refused to admit to being a day over sixteen. Despite her mother's tearful pleas to tell the truth, and in the face of clear and incontrovertible evidence to the contrary, she clung tenaciously to the lie. "I am sixteen because I want to be sixteen," she hissed.

❖

Upon leaving the courthouse offices, Francis Dale made the following statement on behalf of Edward Browning to the horde of newspaper reporters waiting outside: "Mr. Browning will present a petition to the Surrogate seeking to be relieved of his present embarrassment. There is no question but that the Court will set it aside. It is probable that Mary will consent. We don't care whether she does or not. Mr. Browning will act so as to wipe out all question of any right to his property. There will be no settlement. None is contemplated and none will be advised. She is now out of the picture. Mr. Browning's attitude is one of resentment that he has been deceived."

Mary was not the only one to be portrayed as a victim.

❖

Perhaps out of pure defiance, Mary refused to return home with her parents. She indignantly stated that she had experienced a new and different world and she never wished to return to the old. At wits end, District Attorney Newcombe recommended and it was agreed that Mary would discretely stay with the family of Browning's friend and associate Robert Dunnett, at least until the Surrogate's Court Judge issued his final ruling to annul the adoption. Mary's secret whereabouts were anything but. By the next afternoon, a large crowd had gathered outside of the Dunnett home seeking a glimpse of the faltering Cinderella, and police were called in to maintain order.

The previous day, Browning had been contacted by an agent of a local tabloid paper seeking the rights to Mary's story. Browning flatly refused, but the communication had made him uneasy. After sleeping on the matter, he traveled to the Dunnett's home to make sure that the venturous agent had not uncovered Mary's location and attempted to make contact with her. He was too late. Making his way past the crowd and into the home, he was dismayed to find a star-crossed Mary sitting across from the agent and negotiating the terms of her story for use in newsprint and on the silver screen.

Browning frantically tried to persuade Mary not to listen to the man; that he would exploit her and ruin her. He clearly understood the power of the press and he knew that any story instigated by New York's tabloid papers would be nothing short of catastrophic for Mary—and himself. Like a woman pressed to a decision in a lover's quandary, Mary rose from her chair, gathered her things and walked toward the door. "He's my best friend," she sobbed, referring to the tabloid agent. "The world has been making me suffer, and now I'm going to get even and make them suffer." She turned to the smiling agent and said, "I haven't any money, but I will fight him."

As Mary defiantly climbed into the agent's waiting taxi, Browning nervously rung his hands and braced himself for the storm that he knew was coming.

NEW YORK DAILY MIRROR
Cinderella Wants Revenge Against Browning
August 10, 1925

"I don't know how much harm he has done me. But I want my revenge. I want to do two things to Edward W. Browning. I want to have him legally punished for trying in every sanctimonious way to work evil against me. And I want to help to get little Dorothy Sunshine away from him before she gets to be the age when she also will come under his baleful influence."

"I know he is not fit to associate with young girls. My story shows why."

"Imagine a man who filled a young girl's ears with nonsense about her 'perfect Venus shape' and 'kissing love letters all night' and things like that. I think he is a very evil man and I hate him . . ."

"I am 21 and I never told Mr. Browning anything else . . . I asked him right away: 'What about my age? I'm too old for Dorothy Sunshine . . .' Right then he suggested for the first time the lie that he made me tell afterward...He petted me and said: 'Don't worry about your age. Forget your age. You look 14 or 15. To make it safe we could say you are 16 . . .'"

"Then he said: 'In a little while you will learn to call me "Darling" and "Honeybunch" and I shall always call you "Paddy"' because he used to like to sort of spank me—paddle me."

"I had to laugh when he got awfully serious and said: 'And then we will get married and go to Europe and live in castles, won't we, Mary Louise? Just think, Mary Louise, I have never had anyone love me enough to really make me happy and call me loving names.'"

"I got very scared."

For a fee of $500, Mary had strolled into the offices of the *Daily Mirror,* and dictated the first installment of her spellbinding adventures with Edward Browning. Excerpts of the "gripping human narrative" were reprinted across the country and readers absorbed every word with ebullient approval.

❖

Prior to the highly anticipated annulment hearing, the typically reserved Richard Newcombe publicly lambasted both Mary and Browning to awaiting reporters. He lectured that Mary had accomplished nothing but to bring "shame and disgrace" upon herself, her family, and "all young American womanhood," and he scolded her for attempting to capitalize on her notoriety. As for Browning, Newcombe condemned his actions as the "reprehensible and disgraceful ostentation of wealth." He continued, "You can't flaunt common decency and truth, which are the bulwarks of the American home, and get away with it."

Reprimand complete, Newcombe delivered his accumulated evidence to the Surrogate judge and gratefully closed his file on the matter.

❖

On August 11, 1925, a massive throng of curious onlookers waited outside of the Queens County Surrogate's Court, hoping for the slightest glimpse of Mary Louise and the Cinderella Man. Even the rooftops of adjoining buildings were awash with spectators straining for a better view of the unfolding drama. Inside, a trembling and disheartened Mary hastily skimmed the document that annulled her adoption and forever discharged any and all claim that she may have had to Browning's massive fortune. Her parents looked on with nervous anticipation. With one sweep of the pen, the hands of the clock had struck twelve and Cinderella was once again Mary Spas of Astoria, Queens.

As she frolicked in play at her girls' camp in Barton, Vermont, Dorothy Sunshine was blissfully unaware of her father's current predicaments, or the unsettling intentions of her first foster mother. Counselors and administrators at the camp nervously watched the child's every move in apprehension, fearful of overlooking any person or intruder intent on doing her harm. "I love Daddy Browning," Dorothy was heard to say. "He's the best father in the world. I'd love him just the same if he were poor."

After investigating Anna St. John's requests to remove Dorothy from her father, Bird Coler concluded that the 1920 adoption of the child was valid and, more importantly, out of his jurisdiction. He informed Anna that he wouldn't be taking action on her complaint.

A disappointed Anna St. John would watch Edward Browning's future doings like a hawk.

❖

In an effort to avoid the bustling cordon of reporters and delirious spectators outside the courthouse, Browning and the Spas family attempted to exit through a door at the side of the building. By that time, the scene outside had become more wild and ruckus than earlier, and the furtive group was easily detected by the roving mob. Through the efforts of a burly police officer with a foreboding nightstick, Browning made his way to the waiting Rolls Royce limousine. As it rolled away, the officer swung his club at foolhardy reprobates clinging to the running board of the vehicle while others brazenly stood in its path and tussled for a look at its occupants.

With another segment of the crowd streaming toward them, the Spas family dove into a waiting taxi. With a fleet of twenty-five cars and taxis in wild pursuit, the bizarre cavalcade surged its way through the towns of Long Island and finally across the bridge to Manhattan. Throughout the odd incident, Mary was seen in the rear of the cab in a state of hysteria.

The winding procession found its way to the Belleclair Hotel where Browning, by prior arrangement with John and Marie Spas, had agreed to meet with Mary after the court hearing. Patrons at the exclusive hotel restaurant gasped as the screaming and frantic Mary Spas was led firmly by the arm to the elevators and the room waiting for them upstairs. All who witnessed the scene heard Mary frantically shouting, "I won't be forced into it! I won't sign that paper!"

❖

Later that night as a windswept rain overtook the area, a loud pounding at the door of the St. John the Baptist Convent in Newark, New Jersey, awoke all inside. A weary Mother Superior nervously opened the door, and a wet and sobbing young girl fell immediately at her feet. "Oh I'm so tired of everything," she cried. "Please take me sister, everything is ashes. I want to be a nun." After drying herself and calming her nerves, the father of the order explained to the girl that she was in no state of mind to make such a momentous decision. He explained the many sacrifices that came with a life of devotion to God, and the girl soon realized that perhaps her decision did require some further reflection.

As the father sent her on her way, he whispered, "Go in peace, Mary Spas."

❖

Philip Siegel pleaded guilty to the misdemeanor charge of "sending an annoying letter" and was ultimately freed on a suspended sentence. Edward Browning, however, received a sentence of extortion attempts and death threats that would follow him for the rest of his life. Though he had received the worship and adoration of millions, he had also been the object of utter hatred and ridicule. He would never again feel truly secure in the city he loved.

❖

A day after the court issued its order of annulment, Browning once again called reporters into his office. He offered for their review two unsigned letters, ostensibly prepared by Mary on the night of her suicide attempt, which emphatically declared her love and devotion to "Daddy" Browning, and characterized him as the most "honorable man on earth." He also produced a statement that he alleged Mary had voluntarily signed after the court hearing, categorically retracting the allegations made by her against Browning in the *Daily Mirror* series. "Mary double-crossed me," he said. "I have been a damn fool but I have not done anything I need to be ashamed of." He added, "Will I adopt again? Absolutely never. I am through trying to do good for people."

Frances Belle Heenan in 1926. "Studying her problem dispassionately," wrote Allen Churchill, "it is possible to see that her best chance in life was to marry a millionaire."

CHAPTER VII

THE LIFE AND TIMES OF FRANCES BELLE HEENAN

> *"If one judges by appearances, I suppose I am a flapper. I am within the age limit. I wear bobbed hair, the badge of flapperhood (and, oh, what a comfort it is). I powder my nose. I wear fringed skirts and bright-colored sweaters, and scarfs, and waists with Peter Pan collars, and low-heeled 'finale hopper' shoes. I adore to dance. I spend a large amount of time in automobiles. I attend hops, and proms, and ball-games, and crew races, and other affairs at men's colleges."*
>
> —ELLEN WELLES PAGE,
> *A Flapper's Appeal to Parents*

A REVOLUTION WAS AFOOT—OF CULTURE AND MORALS; OF FASHION AND entertainment; of language and expression. It was, quite simply, a revolution against the accepted code of American order. Though a general wave of prosperity had encompassed the nation, by the start of the 1920s, a kind of post-war cynicism had gripped America's youth. "The older generation had certainly pretty well ruined this world before passing it on to us," wrote one disillusioned young man. An entire generation had been altered by the horrors of World War I, and the effect was a cultural backlash that would change the country forever.

The Victorian code of conduct that had been the implied (and often written) law of American morality was founded on the conservative values of pre-war traditions. Respectable girls sported their chaste innocence like a badge and avoided the burning temptations of youth, while young men strove to impress with lofty pursuits and impeccable manners. The guarded and chaperoned attitudes of American society remained as the foundation of stability. But this system benefited certain groups more than others, and among a disgruntled underclass of youth, whispers of defiance had planted the seeds of rebellion.

Soon, bewildered parents watched helplessly as their children—now members of that frightful cultural movement known as the Younger Generation—transformed before their very eyes. Their petulant teenage daughters donned ever-shortening skirts and rolled skin-toned stockings below their knocked knees. They smoked cigarettes and wore hip flasks filled with giggle water. The era of Prohibition seemed only to embolden their attitude of defiance.

Mass media energized this air of social change. Motion pictures that promised romance and sex in every flicker across the screen kept patrons glued to seats, while publishers such as Bernarr MacFadden launched true confession magazines that offered salacious thrills on every page. Rosalind, F. Scott Fitzgerald's heroine in *This Side of Paradise*, embodied this new self-indulgent air of carefree impertinence. "Well Rosalind has still to meet the man she can't outdistance," Fitzgerald wrote. "Honestly . . . she treats men terribly. She abuses them and cuts them and breaks dates with them and then yawns in their faces—and they come back for more . . . She's a sort of vampire, I think—and she can make girls do what she wants usually—only she hates girls . . . Does Rosalind behave herself? Not particularly well. Oh, she's average—smokes sometimes, drinks punch, frequently kissed—oh, yes—common knowledge—one of the effects of the war, you know."

Petting parties, impulsive overnight drives in the family car, and the excited gyrations of new forms of music and dance highlighted this era of restless social upheaval. The American flapper became a caricature of herself. She discarded the restrictions of the corset in favor of the freedom and boyish appeal of straight sleeveless tubes with elevated hemlines, and she embraced every conceivable fad and trend. She had an obsessive yearning to acquire the intangible and inexpressible "It" as her pervading statement of lifestyle. "The 'It' Girl," from the term coined by Elinor Glyn, possessed a sort of "personal magnetism" that every teen and prepubescent craved. "Either you had It or you didn't, but, look, you simply *had* to or all life went punk."

❖

By 1926 Frances Belle Heenan had attained "It." Though only fifteen years old, she displayed an air of haughty maturity that rivaled Fitzgerald's Rosalind. When she stared into her own pleading blue eyes in the mirror, she fancied herself the animated and slender Flapper Jane or the sultry star of the silent movies Clara Bow—despite the fact that the woman in the reflection was a robust and curvaceous strawberry blonde.

She was five foot six and physically developed beyond her years; she could easily have passed for twenty. The columnist Damon Runyon described her as "large and blonde." His oft-quoted description continued, "She has stout legs. I hesitate to expatiate on so delicate a matter, but they are what the boys call 'piano legs.'" The morose look of sad resignation in her eyes and the perpetual frown that formed the natural shape of her moist lips seemed often to veil her otherwise attractive features. But when she smiled, her expression remade her—her countenance changed and she was considered by most to be sweet and beautiful. One commentator described her as "the cat's meow," while in the same breath declaring her to be a "buxom child." Another baptized her as a "chubby fifteen year old with an overdeveloped body."

In his 1974 autobiography, Milton Berle recounted a chance meeting that he had with Frances Heenan after his appearance in 1925 at the Regent Theater in New York. He was approached by four or five girls after the show seeking autographs. "One girl interested me in particular," he wrote. "It wasn't that she was so much prettier than the others. She wasn't. She was cute and a little on the plump side, and inside her middy blouse there was a lot of woman developing. She seemed quite sure of herself. I was sort of interested until I asked her age and she told me she was fourteen. I decided not be interested." It would not be the last time that Frances Heenan and Milton Berle would meet.

Virtually nothing concrete is known about the formative years of the girl who was destined to become an iconic legend of the Roaring Twenties. Frances Belle Heenan appears in the public record quite suddenly upon first meeting Daddy Browning; most details before that day in 1926 are hazy.

She was born on June 23, 1910 in Columbus, Ohio. By the age of two, her parents, William and Carolyn Heenan, had decided to forgo the industrial mills of the Midwest in favor of the big-city opportunities of New York. Labor strikes against Columbus's city rails had caused general public unrest and prospects for secure employment seemed bleak for William Heenan.

The move from Ohio to New York proved difficult, however, and dreams of a better life did not go entirely as planned. Before long,

William and Carolyn Heenan divorced. Frances Belle, now eight years old, seemed unaffected by it all. Her world centered upon school, friends and gossip. By the dawn of the Twenties, however, Frances was all Carolyn Heenan had in the world, and the child was endlessly indulged.

Frances Belle came of age early. She began to shed the graceless bonds of childhood in favor of a robust and womanly charm. She looked older than she was, even as she first entered adolescence. She was, however, still several years away from being baptized with the name that would follow her all the rest of her days. "Peaches" was an unwitting child entering a Mad Decade on which she was destined to make an indelible mark.

For years to come, Frances Belle Heenan would be the subject of both mocking and venerable written portraits and descriptions in press accounts all across the nation, but in the early part of 1926 she was simply a young girl, bound by the mind of the modern day flapper. Frances's early penchant for social exploits gave her a reputation as a party girl or, even worse, a courtesan in the Washington Heights section of Manhattan where she and her mother settled. This middle-class residential area at the uppermost tip of Manhattan Island was, until the completion of the subway extension into the neighborhood, a mostly undeveloped rural enclave dotted with country homes of the wealthy. By the 1920s, a boom of residential construction had brought apartment buildings and tenements to the area as well as a culturally mixed influx of population. Washington Heights became the home of the Polo Grounds and the New York (baseball) Giants, as well as the city's first American League team—the Highlanders, who would later become the New York Yankees. In a period of less than twenty years, the area would become a bustling neighborhood brimming with commercial and residential activity.

As a young child, Frances splashed away hot summer afternoons with neighborhood friends at the Audubon Pool down the sloping incline of 158th Street to the Hudson River and was often sent on food errands to Fleischer's delicatessen on Broadway. She was a fun loving child, a very typical child of New York in the 1920s.

As she grew into her teens, however, her tastes for fun matured, and though she sprung from the most common of middleclass roots, she gained a fondness for the trappings of wealth and a passion for the wild side of life. She was seen often in the presence of men much older than she, drinking bootleg hooch and dancing the Charleston in hot spots throughout New York.

In a real sense, Frances was nothing more than a product of the times in which she lived. No longer were composed gatherings of tranquil companions quietly soothed by the symphonic tones of orchestral pieces. Instead they gyrated to the stirring cadence of the saxophone in a "syncopated embrace . . . as if glued together." One news organization decried the scandalous nightly scene: "The music is sensuous, the embracing of partners—the female only half dressed—is absolutely indecent; and the motions—they are such as may not be described, with any respect for propriety, in a family newspaper. Suffice it to say that there are certain houses appropriate for such dances; but those houses have been closed by law."

After a lively evening of such unchaperoned careening of bodies on crowded dance floors, it was not uncommon for Frances to be spotted in a parked Tin Lizzie engaged in a passionate stint of necking. Far from an awkward adolescent, she had become adept at the ways of the world—a Sheba of the night. An acquaintance described Frances Heenan simply as "a nice girl who petted."

Frances apparently delighted in her experiences with members of the opposite sex. Both of her parents confirmed that she had many boyfriends and her father admitted that she didn't like being with boys of her own age. Like notches in a bedpost, Frances meticulously documented her love relations and petting episodes with entries into a personal diary that she kept through the months and years of her adventurous adolescence. Without any trepidation that the writings in this private journal could ever become public fodder, Frances imprudently included the names of the gentlemen with whom she had courted and with intriguing detail transcribed her petting parties like an author of an article in a true confessions magazine. Observant neighbors living in the tenements of Washington Heights could have corroborated every scintillating word.

When her name began appearing in national publications, Frances Heenan's alleged promiscuity became a topic of much discussion. Certainly the change in sexual morals that the country was undergoing in the 1920s contributed to her sense of freedom and her willingness to socially engage in ways that women in prior decades had not. It is, perhaps, difficult to assess broad psychological reasons for individual behavior, but in the case of Frances Heenan, an overriding desire for male affection and adoration is readily apparent. Whether the divorce of her parents at an early age contributed to this need for affirmation or an open and indulgent lifestyle after the divorce promoted it, we may never know. What we do know is that Frances Heenan had a strong emotional need to be taken care of. Her party girl reputation and active social schedule might have been nothing more than the fulfillment of an essential need to feel secure.

Frances's mother, Carolyn, worked evenings as a nurse in a local New York hospital and offered little in the way of responsible parenting. Her divorce from William Heenan had left the two alone with meager finances, and Carolyn spent most of her time working to provide what she could for her daughter. Frances learned at an early age that the real pleasures in life would come from the wallets of the gentlemen who courted her.

In the fall of 1925, Frances had been a student at Textile High School on West 18th Street in New York City. The school was established in the early 1920s as a vocational institution to aid in the City's flourishing textile industry, and was considered the first technical high school devoted to a single industry. Frances was not particularly enamored of schooling or the rigors of the educational process. The hours were long and her demanding social pursuits made it difficult for her to awaken early enough to be in class before the morning bell. She felt a distinct superiority over the school and the girls who attended it, and she grew to loath the entire prosaic learning environment.

Rather than insisting that her daughter act responsibly and attend class with all of her peers, Carolyn indulged the girl's idle and lazy disposition and wrote a train of notes to school officials begging their pardon for her daughter's truancy and fabricating plausible reasons for it. As the tardy mornings and spotty attendance accumulated, however, the notes trickled to a stop and she informally withdrew from school. By November of 1925, Frances Heenan had become a de facto high school dropout.

Apparently feeling some degree of ambition—or, more likely, pressure from her peers and her mother—Frances took up employment as a shop girl in one of New York's many department stores. At the time, women in cities across America were straying away from the home and striving for the financial independence that careers could provide. At the start of the decade, department store work was considered rather tawdry, but as time went on girls stood in line for such opportunities. It was idleness, as opposed to occupation, that now had to be defended by the unmarried woman. To Frances Heenan, however, the bourgeois nature of counter work soon proved to be beneath her aristocratic inclinations (if not, perhaps, below her middle class blood), and she quit in favor of the fulltime pursuit of dating, dancing, and petting. By age fifteen she had become a lady of leisure. In his expose on the "Era of Wonderful Nonsense," Allen Churchill wrote of Frances, "Studying her problem dispassionately, it is possible to see that her best chance in life was to marry a millionaire."

Peaches dances the Charleston upon a table while Daddy Browning looks on in delight.

CHAPTER VIII

PEACHES AND DADDY

> *"When a man finds such a true soul mate he must claim her for his own, no matter what. Age, wealth, poverty, public opinion—all melt before the searing flame of love."*
>
> —EDWARD WEST BROWNING

IT WAS PERHAPS INEVITABLE THAT THE PATHS OF FRANCES HEENAN AND Edward Browning would cross. In the months following the Mary Spas affair, Browning filled his recreational time organizing and participating in various dancing clubs, and awarding prizes and loving cups to a variety of youth-oriented societies and organizations. With little apparent concern over the blistering news reports of his penchant for young girls, Browning engaged himself whenever possible with underage females and attended youthful social functions. Rather than attempt to rehabilitate his faltering reputation, he wholeheartedly embraced the moniker of "Daddy" with every attendant image that the word conjured in the minds of suspecting and cynical adults. Framed upon the walls of his Manhattan offices were photographs of teenage girls dressed in middies and bloomers, innocently receiving class pins and prize-winning awards from the shameless Cinderella Man.

Browning publicly founded and supported various high school sororities. He announced his willingness to sponsor their dances, pay their expenses, and provide their membership pins. He viewed the enterprise as wholly philanthropic in nature and never paid a moment's notice to the rising eyebrows of the sentinels of social propriety. "I belong to at least twenty dancing clubs, and by supporting the Sorority I give these picked girls an opportunity for healthy entertainment," he claimed. Having footed the bill, however, Browning informed each of the society heads that he expected invitations to all of their Midtown hotel dances—a request that was nervously granted.

Daddy Browning found his way to many if not all of these high school functions. He fluttered about ballrooms, entertaining crowds of young girls with naughty jokes and lecherous antics. He would stuff literally hundreds of multicolored handkerchiefs into his pockets and, like a circus clown, award them to young ladies as they passed or gathered around him. His loud and gaudy sense of humor was designed simply to delight the room and to garner to himself as much attention as could be had. To many, Browning himself was the joke—a harmless and rich old fool whose money had gained him access to a world where he didn't belong. On the evening of March 5, 1926, however, as Daddy Browning first laid eyes upon Frances Heenan at the Hotel McAlpin, the joke was about to turn from the comically harmless to the patently absurd.

❖

"Peaches is the Cinderella of my heart!" crowed Browning to tabloid reporters who gathered at his downtown offices when news of the courtship finally broke. "I knew the first time I saw her that she was the girl of my dreams. I loved her. I saw the blazing reflection of my own love in her eyes. Here was my perfect mate! I could not trust myself alone with her. I was too overwhelmed with love. My heart was in a tumult. Was I too old? Could I make her happy? I could. I must." Despite the scandalous experiences of his past and the searing public scrutiny into his character, Browning unabashedly cast himself back into the flames of controversy, and without so much as an iota of self-consciousness, bound himself in the arms of a girl nearly four decades his junior.

In the days and weeks following their meeting, Browning's blue Rolls Royce was seen constantly at the door of the Washington Heights apartment building that was home to Frances Heenan. He showered her with expensive gifts of candy and jewelry and madly courted her with roses and poetic words. They went for long chauffer-driven rides through the country in Browning's limousine and they were frequent patrons of Manhattan's finest restaurants and theatres. They danced the Charleston in Midtown jazz clubs and upscale locales such as the Majestic, the Plaza, and the Waldorf, and of course, they paid multiple visits to the exclusive Fifth Avenue shops and boutiques where Frances enjoyed Daddy Browning's now renowned shopping sprees. They saw each other every evening, and when the girl's mother objected to the late hours, he responded by taking

Daddy Browning with the "Cinderella" of his heart on a Bronxville dance floor.

her out every afternoon. One way or another, Browning was determined to spend as much time with his new sweetheart as possible.

To Frances—well, her ship had come in. In an instant, she was propelled from shop girl to princess. Browning had found himself another Cinderella, and Frances Heenan was only too happy to assume the role. "My other boy friends were forgotten," she proclaimed. "I had glances for none save Mr. Browning, my silver-haired knight, his gentle caresses, his quiet dignity, his savoir faire." She eagerly accepted Browning's lavish indulgences and, without the bat of an eyelash, she discarded her given name. Forevermore she would be known by Browning's doting sobriquet of "Peaches."

❖

It would be debated for decades exactly what it was that Peaches felt for Daddy Browning upon the whirlwind of their first days together. The inevitable reports circulated that she was nothing more than a gold-digging adventuress whose interest in the millionaire derived solely from a selfish desire for wealth and social position. Friends and acquaintances quoted statements allegedly made by Peaches that would indicate a manipulative and scheming quality to her actions, and Browning himself would later state that it was Peaches who, in fact, was the aggressor in the birth of the relationship.

There is no doubt that Browning's extensive wealth had much to do with Peaches' glowing interest in the man. Through her early years, she had developed an undeniable taste for the fineries of life, and her personal circumstances in the early part of 1926 did not indicate any ability to satisfy those tastes on her own. Daddy Browning represented her only real opportunity to attain the aristocratic life that she so ardently desired. Conversely, it is also clear that any female of fifteen years in Peaches' position in the 1920s would have been completely overwhelmed by the open and lavish displays of fervent love and affection that Browning demonstrated for the girl. It would be natural and completely understandable for her to have fallen in love with the man, or at the very least, to have confused the emotions that she felt in response to his amorous declarations as love. She would make inconsistent statements on the subject for years to come, but in 1926 Peaches declared her undying love for Daddy Browning.

As Browning openly wooed his Peaches, he similarly brought to bear all of his charisma and wealth upon her mother, Carolyn. He plainly understood that his affections for Peaches would be for naught without the assent of the girl's mother, and as Daddy bestowed Peaches with arrays of flowers and extravagant gifts, Carolyn found herself equally showered with exotic candies and sweet tokens of her own—and all the while blushing at Browning's flattering compliments. "Such a lovely girl could only have come from an even lovelier mother," he crooned.

At first, Carolyn expressed understandable misgivings about Browning's amorous intentions toward her daughter, and she openly worried about the dramatic disparity in their ages. In time, however, Browning placated Carolyn with gifts of comic books and candy bars, and before long she was blinded to the reality that her teenage daughter was being courted by a man old enough to be the girl's grandfather. Browning utilized every tool in his arsenal to charm and captivate Carolyn Heenan, going even so far as to display a sampling of the still growing collection of letters that he received on a daily basis from girls proposing marriage to the fabled Cinderella Man. Ultimately disarmed by Browning's persuasive and overpowering nature, Carolyn Heenan was won over. "Mr. Browning is a very fine man," she declared. "He is a kind and honorable gentleman. I have no doubt but that he could provide for her."

❖

One lesson that Browning had learned from the Mary Spas episode was to confirm age when relevant. In later statements, Browning insisted that Peaches had initially represented herself to be twenty-three years old, and when pressed, she admitted to being twenty-one. He was skeptical from the start and he sent his secretary, John Aldrich, to investigate. He quickly learned, with very little surprise, Peaches' real age of fifteen.

Completely undeterred, Browning's protective and fatherly instincts immediately took over and he began formulating plans with Carolyn to send Peaches to a private school in New York to finish her high school education. He provided the family with money for clothing and food and expressed his strong preference that Peaches not work anymore as an extra at Earl Carroll's Theatre, as she had recently done. He took Peaches and Carolyn to meet Dorothy Sunshine and he did his best to assimilate them as part of his own family.

Nearly from the moment they met, Browning unhesitatingly expressed to Peaches his desire to marry her, and though rather coy in her initial response, Peaches had every intention of becoming his wife. He promised every extravagance and pleasure to the girl, going even so far as to pledge that the 135-acre estate that he was now restoring in Bellmore on Long Island would be hers. While each would later contend that it was the other who ultimately proposed, there is no dispute that the matter of marriage between Peaches and Daddy was seriously broached not two weeks after the couple had first met.

Both Carolyn Heenan and her ex-husband William hesitatingly offered their blessings to the union. William, now a car salesman on Long Island, professed his intention to investigate Browning and to ascertain that the millionaire's intentions toward his daughter were pure and true. But whatever concerns he and his former wife had about their daughter's suitor, whether feigned or real, were easily rationalized away with thoughts of his prolific wealth. In the end, the promise of Browning's financial empire and the opportunities that it offered their daughter—and perhaps to themselves—would prove too much of a temptation for them to resist.

It was informally agreed that Peaches and Daddy would be married shortly after the bride's sixteenth birthday on June 23. Peaches' lofty dreams of fortune and wealth seemed to be at hand, though a nagging and insecure part of her mind doubted Browning's true willingness to take her as his wife. Could a well-established man of such astonishing means truly be interested in marrying her? Could he ignore their disparity in age and social status? Would reality finally take hold of his senses? She anguished at these thoughts.

❖

From the moment of their engagement, the couple's world would take on a surreal and star-crossed quality. Even before their wedding, their relationship had begun to spin wildly out of control.

❖

On the evening of March 19, 1926, the ecstatically happy Daddy Browning and his soon-to-be bride attended a birthday party in honor of the Metropolitan Opera tenor Beniamino Gigli at the Hotel Majestic in Manhattan. It was not unusual for the well-connected Browning to attend such events and to be seen in the company of New York's elite. Springtime had come early to Manhattan this year. The evening was warm and the atmosphere festive. Joining the couple was Peaches' seventeen-year-old friend Stella Lubin, who had been invited to join the celebration in honor of the couple's still unpublicized engagement. The three had spent the day together having lunch and then at a matinee performance of the ever popular *No No Nanette!* (The plot of which ironically involves the exploits of an aging millionaire and his young female wards).

At the party, Stella happened to strike up a conversation with Martin Ansorge, a well-known New York attorney and former United States Congressman from the 21st Congressional District. The two clearly engaged one another, and soon both couples left the party in favor of dancing and cavorting at another local hotel. By the end of the evening, Ansorge had made plans with Stella to spend the following afternoon with her. Stella spent the night with Peaches at the Heenan residence and the following day, as planned, Ansorge arrived in his open roadster to pick her up. They remained together through the early evening and upon her return home, Stella became violently ill. She attempted to fight the illness and even went to work the next morning, but soon was back at home, too sick to do much of anything. A week later Stella was dead.

❖

In the late morning the following Saturday the shrill ring of the telephone awoke Peaches. It took all she had to simply reach over to the nightstand and answer. The late hours about the city with her aging suitor were catching up to the girl and it seemed that Browning rose earlier in the day than she.

"Why aren't you up yet, Peaches?" chided Browning on the other end of the line.

"Very sleepy . . ." she moaned. The couple had plans for an early movie matinee and Browning's patience for her tardiness was thin.

"I'll be there by 12:30 and I expect you to be up and dressed, child."

"I will, Daddy." She hung up the phone, pulled the blanket tightly around her shoulders and promptly fell back into a deep sleep.

That morning, Carolyn Heenan was tending to a patient in a home three blocks away. The patient suffered from a nervous ailment that required constant attention, and it appeared that Carolyn's nursing services would be required for the entire day. Peaches was alone at home, but Carolyn had left a number where she could be reached if needed.

At about 11:00 AM, the telephone rang at the patient's home and Peaches' frantic voice on the other end screamed for Carolyn's help.

"Momma, are you coming home? Please come home! I've been burned! I think someone has burned me!" In less than five minutes her anguished and alarmed mother was tending to the child at her bedside.

Through flowing tears and agonizing groans of pain, Peaches reported that about forty-five minutes after speaking with Daddy Browning she had been suddenly and without forewarning awakened from her deep sleep by a stinging and burning sensation about her face and neck. She claimed that she had been viciously attacked with a vial of acid, but offered no explanation for what had occurred or who could have been responsible for the attack. She insisted that she heard no one, saw no one, and had no idea why anyone might wish to harm her. Nonetheless, she now lay in her bed afflicted and in pain, inexplicably suffering from acid burns to her chin, neck, and arm.

Carolyn immediately tended to Peaches' injuries, cleaning and dressing her wounds and gently reassuring the girl that she was fine. She repeatedly attempted to contact the family physician. She also called Browning, informed him of the incident, and pleaded with him to come.

When Browning arrived on the scene, he rushed to Peaches' bedside, and to her outstretched arms. "Oh *Daddy!*" she pleaded. He gently examined Peaches' wounds and tenderly assured her that he was there and that he would take care of her always. He instructed his assistant, John Aldrich, to secure a physician for Peaches, and he then rushed to the corner drug store for some absorbent cotton, bandages and sweet oil to dress the wounds.

By the time Browning returned, Peaches was being treated by a local doctor. Browning pledged to Carolyn that he would arrange for the care of the finest skin specialists in New York and that Peaches would have nothing but the best of medical treatment available to her. He professed his deep love for the girl, despite what permanent damage the acid burn might have effected, and he repeated his enthusiastic intention to marry her. Whatever doubts Carolyn might have had about Daddy Browning then and there disappeared and she openly warmed to the prospect of his marriage to her daughter.

In the coming weeks, Peaches remained confined to her home and bed, recovering from the injuries that she had suffered and receiving treatments from doctors and specialists employed and paid for by Daddy Browning. That the attack aroused in Daddy Browning his caring and loving instincts cannot be denied. William Heenan was quoted as saying, "I met [Browning] last night at my daughter's bedside. When he had left I asked Frances if she was really engaged to him. She cried, then laughed through her tears and whispered: 'Yes, it's true. He told me he would get me the finest engagement ring in the world.'"

Miraculously, the romance of Peaches and Daddy remained out of the newspapers for nearly a month after their meeting, but as the public investigations into the acid attack on Peaches began to unfold, inquisitive newspaper reporters began to pick up the scent. By the end of March 1926, Browning was once again delightedly courting a mob of clamoring reporters and revealing the details of his latest romantic saga.

He could add nothing in the way of answers regarding the acid incident because there simply were none to the give. He told the group in frank and honest tones what he knew, but his words seemed only to deepen the mystery, as investigators remained tight-lipped about their inquiry. When asked to describe the latest object of his affections, Browning smiled broadly and squinted his eyes. "She is a lovely girl, 5 feet 7½ inches tall, weighing 145 pounds, with light brown hair, curly but cut short, you know." Browning held back. He wanted to avoid the same wild public spectacle generated by the Spas episode, and so he conveyed his thoughts in a cautious and deliberative manner. By the time of the interview with reporters, marriage rumors had already begun to spread and of course Browning was asked to confirm what was circulating. "It would not be right to talk about marriage when that beautiful little girl is suffering," he responded. "That is why I cannot say definitely whether or not we will marry."

Another group of reporters circled about John Aldrich, Browning's secretary. Aldrich clearly hadn't gotten word of the confidentiality of the affair. "Yes, of course the reports are true," he admitted.

By the next morning, the Associated Press had wired accounts of Browning's news conference to newspapers across the nation, and front-page stories began to appear on newsstands from New York to California. "BROWNING, ERSTWHILE FAIRY GODFATHER, HAS CINDERELLA;" "ASSERT 15 YEAR OLD HIGH SCHOOL GIRL TO MARRY MILLIONAIRE IN JUNE;" "REALTOR IS IN THE ROLE OF GODFATHER TO CINDERELLA." The measured *New York Times*, in an effort to maintain its air of refinement, buried the story on page 26—"BROWNING MAY WED NEW CINDERELLA, 15." Taking note of Browning's sanitized description of Peaches during his news interview, the *Daily Mirror* sardonically reported that "Many a girl wouldn't mind being described in weights and measures if she could marry a man like Browning." As word circulated, however, of the tragic death of Stella Lubin and of the surreal acid attack upon Peaches, at least one newspaper was prompted to pose the question: "BROWNING JINX?" atop a story of the prodigious millionaire's latest affairs.

CHAPTER IX

CRUELTY TO
CHILDREN

*"We have on principle been opposed to a man
of his years carrying on an affair with a girl of
fifteen. Furthermore, regardless of the disparity in their ages, Browning ought to be kept
away from young girls."*

—VINCENT T. PISARRA,
Superintendent of the New York Society for
the Prevention of Cruelty to Children

VINCENT PISARRA NERVOUSLY TWISTED THE FINELY COMBED WHITE HAIRS OF
his Teddy Roosevelt mustache as he regarded the morning newspapers
of April 1, 1926. He narrowed his blue eyes at the announcement of the
Peaches and Daddy marriage plans and thought to himself, *I just may
have the bastard now.*

Pisarra had become well acquainted with the doings of the so-called
Cinderella Man through Browning's well-publicized botched attempt to
adopt Mary Louise Spas. Now, Pisarra, as the reigning superintendent
of the New York Society for the Prevention of Cruelty to Children, felt
that his time had come.

Vincent Pisarra was an Italian-born naturalized American citizen,
and in 1899 he had learned that the Children's Society was in need of
an Italian-speaking investigator. He was interviewed and hired by the
founder of the New York chapter, Elbridge Gerry, and for the next forty
years he would dedicate his life to the Society's cause.

Pisarra's illustrious career featured a number of very high profile
cases. In 1907 the Children's Society received a letter from a Chinese
merchant stating that a six-year-old girl was being held in bondage by
Mock Duck, the notorious leader of Hip Sing Tong, the famous New
York Chinese-American crime organization. Vincent Pisarra, accompanied by a bevy of police officers, hurried to the scene and found the child

asleep at the foot of a bunk on which Mock Duck lay with an opium pipe. Needing little more evidence than that the child was in fact Caucasian and had been disguised to appear Asian, the court had no trouble in removing her from Mock Duck's home. Vincent Pisarra was widely credited with the recovery.

Later in his career, Pisarra would take an active role in what the *New York Times* would call "the greatest police effort in the history of the city"—the search for the kidnapped baby of Colonel Charles Lindbergh. Upon word of the "vicious outrage," Police Commissioner Ed Mulrooney mobilized every detective and patrolman at his disposal in an attempt to locate the child. The resources of the Children's Society were tapped and Vincent Pisarra led a meticulous search of hospitals, hotels, baby farms, and other homes in the urgent pursuit of clues. He and his team of agents explored both registered and unregistered institutions and urged the administrators to carefully scrutinize their new arrivals. Despite the painstaking inspection of every egress and exit to the city and the eventual payment of a demanded ransom, the badly decomposed body of the Lindbergh Baby was found several months later on the side of a road not five miles from the famed aviator's home.

Though today a seal of confidentiality justifiably shrouds the cases and investigations of the Society, in the early part of the twentieth century its work was often part of the public record. Vincent Pisarra enjoyed his stature and never shied away from the flash of the news camera or the probing inquiries of reporters. In 1922, when asked by a newspaperman what causes young girls to go astray, he responded, "Rides, reels and rum." He was well acquainted with the vices of the day and the dangers that those vices presented to the nation's youth.

Child protection in America found its origins among a wave of reform movements in the mid 1800s. Rampant crime and child neglect and exploitation became a fixture of the rapidly crowding cities as immigration and industrialization changed the landscape of the country and taxed the already floundering public service system. Ironically, the first anti-cruelty laws were passed for the protection of animals; the American Society for the Prevention of Cruelty to Animals was organized in 1866. Recognizing the clear applicability of the association to the plight of children, the very founders of the ASPCA soon became the enlightened champions for the cause against child neglect and maltreatment. In 1874, through the marriage of progressive thought, religious faith, and government-supported private initiative; the Society for the

Prevention of Cruelty to Children was organized. One of its founders, Elbridge Gerry, proclaimed the Society's laudable purpose:

> To rescue little children from the cruelty and demoralization which neglect, abandonment and improper treatment engender; to aid by all lawful means in the enforcement of the laws intended for their protection and benefit; to secure by like means the prompt conviction and punishment of all persons violating such laws and especially such persons as cruelly ill treat and shamefully neglect such little children of whom they claim the care, custody or control.

The New York Society for the Prevention of Cruelty to Children was incorporated on April 27, 1875, and became the first child protection agency in the world. By the turn of the twentieth century, new laws had been enacted recognizing society's undeniable responsibility for the welfare of its children. The notion of organized agency-based child protective services had been accepted and was finding its way across the nation and around the world. By 1900, in New York City alone, the NYSPCC had investigated 130,000 complaints, brought assistance to 370,000 children, and prosecuted 50,000 cases with a conviction rate of 94%.

❖

Vincent Pisarra's position at the NYSPCC, though quasi-political, was not an elected office. He conducted the affairs of the Society mindful of the political considerations that affected the organization but with the independence required by its private charter. Confident in his longstanding work with the chapter and driven by his own moral compass, Pisarra was nonetheless aware that many of New York's citizens and public officials would look to him for a response to Edward Browning's provocative courtship of the fifteen-year-old Peaches. Pisarra needed no further motivation than his own personal outrage over Browning's actions—as well as those of the girl's mother.

Pisarra considered Bird Coler's earlier faltering attempt at the prosecution of Browning to be inadequate at best and, more likely, a stunt designed to ingratiate the well-connected politician with his public. Since Mary Louise was over the age of maturity and beyond the reach of the Society's jurisdiction, a frustrated Pisarra had been powerless to act during the Spas affair, but now, in light of what he was learning of Edward Browning's most recent scurrilous behavior, he felt duty-bound to take action.

"Yes indeed, we are going to be married," chirped Peaches to reporters at her bedside. "Daddy Browning has promised me a ring from a Fifth Avenue jewelry store just as soon as I get well." Despite Peaches' upbeat demeanor, the visible burns about her head, face, and arms were a silent reminder of the vicious acid incident that had confined her to home and bed. Wax casts had been removed from the burns the previous day, revealing fierce scars and blisters, and now led the newsmen to the obvious questions about how, why, and by whom her injuries were inflicted.

Browning had previously informed the papers that he had volunteered himself for a skin-grafting procedure to aid in Peaches' recovery, but was told that such a measure would not be necessary. Wild speculations regarding the attack hummed through the press, suggesting a jealous girl or even Browning himself as the culprit. "I think it was a girl who had been treated kindly by Mr. Browning and who misinterpreted his kindness," declared Peaches as she squirmed under the bed sheets. She stated that she was, in fact, sure of the person's identity.

The real purpose for Peaches' availability to the newspapers, however, was not to discuss the acid attack, but to set the record straight. She had read various accusations in the press that her interest in Daddy Browning was entirely mercenary and that a girl of her age could never have genuinely fallen for the gray-haired eccentric. Concerned about her reputation and gently goaded by Browning, Peaches agreed to a conference, and now skillfully guided the reporters to the topic at hand. She wanted to "correct the impression that I am an adventuress," she told them. "Mr. Browning is serious in his affections for me. I am not marrying him for his money. Neither am I marrying him for a career. I don't want a career, but only want a home and a man with whom I can discuss serious things for hours."

With that, Peaches told the newsmen that she was tiring and wished to sleep. Her mother, who had listened intently to every word of the interview, smiled approvingly and escorted the men out of the room.

The NYSPCC investigation lurched into gear. Pisarra knew that the marriage was planned for June and he was determined to take all steps necessary to prevent or at the very least delay it. The Peaches and Daddy investigation was Pisarra's first priority and he had every intention to conduct it quickly—and personally. Pisarra was deeply offended by Browning's actions and clearly believed that adult men had no place courting or enticing teenage girls. The Spas affair had convinced Pisarra that Browning had an unnatural predilection toward young girls and he considered it his duty to protect Peaches from the likes of such an individual.

Pisarra's twofold plan was first to test the competence and fitness of Carolyn Heenan as the parent and guardian of Peaches, and second to engage the trio in enough of a legal quagmire to make a continuation of this shameful relationship difficult, if not impossible. His objective was to bring Peaches under *his* jurisdiction, so that Carolyn could no longer continue with the profusion of irresponsible decision-making on her daughter's behalf.

He immediately met with and interrogated various witnesses, including personnel from the Textile High School, a former landlord of the Heenans, and Daddy Browning himself. With intimidating vigor, he questioned Peaches and Carolyn Heenan at their Washington Heights apartment. Of particular interest to Pisarra was Peaches' unexplained absence from public school, her activities with Daddy Browning during this period, and the mysterious details of the acid-throwing incident. He interviewed many of Peaches' friends and acquaintances and he inquired into the circumstances surrounding the death of her friend Stella Lubin. His investigation also addressed the odd circumstances of the couple's meeting and he followed up on Browning's involvement with the Phi Lambda Tau girls' sorority, interviewing its members and administrators. "What object can a middle-aged business man have in founding a girls' sorority?" he asked rhetorically to a gathering of reporters outside his offices. Pisarra was particularly infuriated by the physical description of Peaches that Browning had provided to the newspapers. "What is it that induces a man of his age to describe a little girl's hair, her eyes, and her figure? It is obvious to any one that he is at least rather indiscreet." "We will hale Mr. Browning into the courts if this proves necessary," he continued. "If a gray-haired man more than fifty years old takes a little school girl out for night rides in a Rolls-Royce and takes her to dances, all this without a proper guardian, it is time that something should be done about it."

Pisarra's inflammatory public comments had the desired affect on Carolyn Heenan. She was unnerved at the accusation that she had been an improper guardian and was terrified at the prospect of losing Peaches, or worse, having her institutionalized. The accusatory nature of the news accounts and Pisarra's powers of intimidation were alarming to her and to Peaches, but Browning assured them that he would capably handle the matter and implored them not to panic. He continued his romantic courtship of Peaches and on Easter Sunday, he presented her with a huge pink Easter egg, which thenceforth earned him the nickname Bunny Browning in at least one of New York's tabloids.

Publicly, Browning remained silent and wisely avoided any comment on his marriage intentions. His primary remarks in the initial days of Pisarra's rigorous investigation astonishingly focused on his annoyed indignation over tabloid reports that he was fifty-eight or fifty-nine years old. As he angrily made his way out to the streets of New York to buy up every edition of the libelous rag that he could find, he protested his true age of fifty-one to every newspaperman that would listen.

❖

As word spread of Peaches and Daddy's romantic entanglements and of Pisarra's crusade against them, the attention of other state and municipal departments was awoken. The Bureau of Attendance of the Board of Education began investigating Peaches' long period of truancy from the Textile High School and sent an investigator to the Heenan home to question Peaches and her mother.

Panicked by the onslaught, Carolyn untruthfully informed the investigator that her daughter had been sent away from the area to recuperate from pneumonia and was therefore unable to attend school. The skeptical investigator raised a doubtful eyebrow as he reviewed the notes written by Carolyn during her daughter's absences from class, noting no reference to illness or recuperative journeys. In follow-up interviews, Daddy Browning, in fact, disclosed that he had accompanied Peaches to many parties and shopping sprees throughout New York at the same time as this supposed period of sickness. Stagehands at the Earl Carroll Theatre also eagerly informed the investigators that Peaches had performed on stage as a dancer on one evening during the period in question, but that her performance did not warrant her retention as a regular in the show. Daddy Browning would later maintain that he was adamantly opposed to any stage performances by Peaches, but the public investigations concluded that on the evening in question Browning had occupied a front-row seat and proudly took a bow when introduced as the Cinderella Man. The Bureau of Attendance had all the answers they needed.

Amidst this mounting pressure, the New York City Police Department began an investigation of its own into the sudden death of Stella Lubin. They questioned virtually every guest in attendance at Beniamino Gigli's party at the Majestic Hotel, as well as Peaches Heenan, Daddy Browning, and Martin Ansorage. Though Browning cooperated fully with the authorities in their investigation, he expended considerable effort in the days following Stella's death to distance himself from the tragedy. He knew what Peaches would soon learn: that regardless of outcome, the death of this young girl would forever be linked to their romance.

Information provided by Stella's mother together with a full examination of the medical evidence in the case prompted the authorities to conclude that the girl had a history of heart disease, making her untimely death an inevitability. Though no evidence was ever revealed to indicate any responsibility of Peaches and Daddy, or any other party, for that matter, the New York tabloids could not resist the temptation to intimate that there *had* to be some connection between Daddy's activities with the girl and her unfortunate passing. They published innuendos and rumors and misquoted public officials in an effort to suggest the inevitable nexus that simply did not exist.

To their credit, the authorities refused to bite at the same apple, despite some political pressure. In light of the lack of culpable evidence, the Bronx District Attorney declined to pursue the matter and promptly closed his file. Martin Ansorage, the last person with whom Stella Lubin was seen in good health, issued a statement to the press claiming that he knew nothing of Edward Browning's affairs and that he did not "crave any of his publicity."

❖

The New York City Police likewise conducted an exhaustive investigation into the matter of the acid attack upon Peaches. They interviewed scores of friends and associates, seeking evidence of malevolence or ill motive that would lead to such a violent premeditated assault. They hunted for any proof whatsoever of an assailant or of any forced intrusion into the Heenan home on the morning in question. Browning himself voluntarily submitted to a grueling two-hour interrogation with lieutenants and detectives at the Wadsworth Avenue Police Station and offered whatever assistance to the case he could.

The investigations revealed nothing but an unexplained mystery. Peaches had seen no assailant and could not imagine why anyone might want to harm her in such a way. Rumors of jealous friends or scorned lovers circulated through the city, but no arrests would ever be made and no proof of any such schemes would be offered. The inquiries revealed no evidence of an intruder or any forced entry into the Heenan home, and they discovered that no acid was ever found upon Peaches' clothing or bedding. "If the acid was thrown . . . by another person, it was done with remarkable accuracy."

No one was ever formerly charged with the crime of marring Peaches Heenan on that late March morning, but whispers that Peaches herself had committed the act in a desperate attempt to secure Daddy Browning's loving and protective attentions have echoed through the decades since. Prior to the conclusion of his investigation, Superintendent Pisarra publicly stated his opinion on the matter, to the consternation of the police detectives working the case. After questioning the police, school officials, and Peaches herself, Pisarra averred that the attack was, in fact, a fake and designed to keep the girl from having to attend school for the continuing future. "Either that," he said in his report, "or she inflicted the injury herself."

If Peaches was, in fact, her own assailant, she dramatically underestimated the strength of her acidic confection. It would later be written, ". . . to her dying day seared, puffy flesh was unpleasantly visible on her chin, throat, and left arm. To some the scars completely spoiled her hefty good looks."

❖

Prior to October of 1924, Carolyn Heenan and her daughter had rented a first-floor room in a rooming house owned by a Mary Conlin on West 96th Street. It was a modest home and the rooms were somewhat close-quartered and cramped, but Mrs. Conlin prided herself in running a clean and orderly building for her guests.

At first, the Heenans went about their business quietly and for the most part kept to themselves. As Frances emerged into her early teens, however, things began to change and Mrs. Conlin took notice. Loud and ruckus parties conducted in the Heenans' room often disturbed fellow tenants in the otherwise tranquil building. Bootleg liquor and its inevitable consequences were readily present while the Heenans entertained their varied guests. The other residents began complaining to

Mrs. Conlin, and after several unheeded warnings and a spell of uncomfortable acrimony, she was forced to evict Carolyn and her young daughter from the building.

Nearly two years later, when Mary Conlin read in the daily papers about the girl they now called Peaches and the investigations of the Children's Society, she could hardly wait to tell her story to Vincent Pisarra.

❖

"This marriage will never take place!" Benjamin Antin pounded his fist on the oak panels of the speaker's rostrum. His rising voice echoed through the halls of the New York State Senate chamber as he implored his fellow senators to take action before it was too late. As Chairman of the State Child Welfare Commission, Antin, who found himself personally offended by the Peaches and Daddy fiasco, introduced a new Child Marriage Bill into the state legislature that would forbid the marriage of girls under the age of sixteen without the consent of a justice of the State Supreme Court. "This national scandal is a disgrace and I hope the legal proceedings in the matter are not ended before the Governor signs the bill," barked Antin.

Vincent Pisarra smiled as he listened to Senator Antin's tirade. He knew he had a staunch ally in Antin—a dedicated soldier on a now very personal vendetta to stop Edward W. Browning.

❖

To Vincent Pisarra, Mary Conlin's sworn affidavit was the mortal blow that he had been hoping to land upon Daddy Browning's matrimonial intentions. On April 6, 1926, armed with a slew of damning formal statements, Pisarra appeared before Judge Franklin Chase Hoyt in the Children's Court.

Hoyt, a mild-mannered but stern jurist with golden-red hair, was the product of a distinguished bloodline: he was the grandson of Salmon P. Chase, Secretary of the Treasury under Abraham Lincoln, and later Chief Justice of the United States Supreme Court. It was the austere countenance of Salmon P. Chase that appeared on the ten thousand dollar note of U.S. currency. Franklin Hoyt was instrumental in the creation of the court in which he sat. In 1908, at the age of thirty-three, he became the youngest judge ever appointed to New York's Court of Special Sessions. He led the fight in 1915 for a state constitutional amendment creating a separate Children's Court. The criminal courts, posited Hoyt, were no place for New York's children. Through his career, he would wear the label "The Bad Boy's Friend" like a badge of merit.

Well aware that he could not launch a direct legal attack on a marriage that had not yet taken place, Pisarra instead focused his argument upon Carolyn Heenan. In a lengthy conference in Judge Hoyt's chambers, Pisarra set forth, in condemning detail, his case that Mrs. Heenan was unable to properly care for her minor daughter, as a result of her demanding work schedule as a practical nurse and of her demonstrated past neglect. He pointed to Carolyn's complicity in Peaches' extended absence from school, and supplied affidavits, including but by no means limited to Mary Conlin's, indicating that the girl had been maintaining ungodly hours in some of Manhattan's most renowned nighteries. He attacked Peaches' one-night appearance as a dancer in Earl Carroll's *Vanities* and pointed out that Daddy Browning himself was seated front and center in the audience. Finally, Pisarra offered his very strong opinion on Carolyn's enthusiastic approval of her daughter's courtship by a man thirty-six years her senior. Pisarra lay down sworn statements and police reports supporting his position. In short, Pisarra argued that Frances Heenan was a neglected child requiring the installation of a surrogate decision maker to act on her behalf. He demanded the issuance of a summons to compel Peaches and her mother to appear in court and answer to the charges.

Judge Hoyt regarded the evidence before him and would not have been able to help but think of the broken and beleaguered class of wayward young who daily crowded into his courtroom. He had dealt with many cases of severe neglect—the kind that resulted in injury, abuse, or even death—and he attempted to reconcile the matter now before him with the dreadful circumstances of other cases on his docket. The disconcerting activities of Peaches Heenan and her aging suitor, while disturbing for a variety of reasons, were not necessarily at the level of delinquency required for judicial intervention. However, Hoyt certainly found Browning's actions suspect, and considered Pisarra's allegations to be of adequate severity to warrant, at the very least, a closer look.

Later that day, a detective of the New York Police Department served a summons executed by Judge Hoyt upon Carolyn Heenan and her daughter.

❖

Heeding the advice of his lawyers, Edward Browning remained conspicuously absent from the proceedings involving Peaches and her mother. Callers to his downtown offices were curtly informed by an exasperated male secretary that Browning had sailed for Europe. Vincent Pisarra only wished that it were so.

❖

On April 8, 1926, a pale and sullen Carolyn Heenan appeared, without her daughter, before Judge Hoyt in the New York Children's Court, accompanied by an attorney named Ralph Newman. Upon Hoyt's inquiry into the girl's absence, Newman produced a certificate signed by Dr. Howard Fox, who had been tending to Peaches' injuries, stating that the lingering affects of the acid burns continued to restrict her to home and bed, and prevented her appearance in court. Newman then requested Hoyt to adjourn the proceedings for two weeks pending Peaches' recovery and ability to appear.

Until then, Vincent Pisarra had quietly watched the proceedings from a wooden bench at the side of the gated bar. Though he was not surprised by Newman's appeal for an adjournment, he was nonetheless incensed at the request. He was worried that time was one luxury he lacked. If Hoyt did not act immediately to bring the child under the protective eye of the Children's Society, Pisarra believed that her misguided parents would cave to the appalling intentions of Edward Browning. Unable to fight down his anger and desperation, Pisarra leapt to his feet, both hands firmly clasping the oak grained rail before him, and interrupted the proceedings.

"Your Honor, Mr. Browning has publicly declared his intentions to exchange vows with this girl and I feel that you must act to prevent it. I respectfully request, for the wellbeing of this child, that you enjoin any attempt on the part of Mr. Browning to marry her, pending final inquiry and decision of this court!"

To Pisarra's dismay, Judge Hoyt, shook his head and reminded the gathering that he was powerless to prevent any marriage that would otherwise comply with law. While Browning's actions and intentions might have been repugnant, he continued, the current evidence did not provide a legal basis to prospectively act against him.

Pisarra then argued that Browning's actions constituted a violation of the New York Penal Code by endangering the morals of a juvenile, and that judicial action should be taken against him directly. Hoyt refused, concluding that if the child's parents consented to the relationship, there was nothing that he, as a judge, was able to do. The current state of New York law was clear. A marriage license could be granted to a child under the age of sixteen, regardless of age discrepancy of the spouse, if the child's parents consented to the union. Hoyt even brought up Senator Antin's pending Marriage Bill. "There is a law we are trying to put through the Legislature which requires the consent of a Supreme Court Justice when a child under age wishes to marry. As that law is not in effect at this time I can do nothing." Hoyt must have been moved to some degree by Pisarra's impassioned speech, however, because he then granted a shortened extension of one week and promptly adjourned the proceedings.

Senator Antin, who had made a special trip from Albany to witness the Heenan proceedings, bristled with anger as he exited the courtroom. Antin let his anger erupt to the barrage of newspaper reporters waiting outside the building. "Everything will be done to block a marriage between that child and a man old enough to be her grandfather!"

On April 10, 1926, newspapers across America printed an announcement by Browning's secretary that the Heenan affair was a closed chapter. As prattling readers lamented the end of the libidinous romance, an unconvinced Benjamin Antin now surmised what Vincent Pisarra already knew; Edward Browning was biding his time.

Emile Gauvreau, Managing Editor of the *New York Evening Graphic*. He was a "box within a box within a box, or perhaps a fox within a fox," as Lester Cohen wrote in *The New York Graphic: The World's Zaniest Newspaper*.

CHAPTER X

NOTHING SO POWERFUL AS TRUTH

"Some of my tricks may be vulgar but there are vulgar puns and vulgar stage devices even in Shakespeare's plays. No one can dispense with vulgarity who wants to attract a crowd."
—EMILE GAUVREAU, *Hot News*

ON A HOT SUMMER MORNING IN 1924, EMILE GAUVREAU HOBBLED INTO the *Graphic* city room on the fourth floor of the old *Evening Mail* building. The impish grin that almost always adorned his thin lips was missing on this, his first day on the job as Managing Editor of the city's newest crusading daily tabloid. He wondered whether he was at all prepared for the task that lay ahead.

Gauvreau was small in stature—not 5'3"—and a confessed but celebrating sufferer of a serious Napoleon complex. He had been injured in a childhood Fourth of July accident that had resulted in a perpetual limp, the familiar sound of which announced his frenetic comings and goings. The disability, however, served only to remind him of the like frailty of Napoleon, and he gained a full measure of inspiration from the cast iron bust of the fearless emperor that he kept on his office desk at all times. His various offices were littered with books about Napoleon and there were paintings of the conqueror upon the walls. On any given occasion, Gauvreau could be observed pacing the floors like a nervous general, striking poses with his hand in vest, and plotting elaborate circulation flow charts as if they were strategic wartime maps. One of Gauvreau's editors later wrote he "was a box within a box within a box, or perhaps a fox within a fox."

Gauvreau's concerns about the vagaries of his new position may have been well founded, but his nagging self-doubt was not. He had been well groomed in his profession, and he understood the mechanics and the business of a large city newspaper. His instinct for sensationalism—what he called "Hearst journalism"—was hatched early on. One afternoon as a boy he was perusing the *New York Journal* and came across a terrifying story under the headline of "The Kissing Bug." The story highlighted a full-page close-up drawing of an insect and explained that one sting from it on the lips would prove fatal to its victim. Unable to resist the temptation, the young Gauvreau showed the story to his even younger sister. A moment later a fly settled upon her face, and she ran into the house in hysterical tears as her older brother snickered in delight. He could not have had better empirical evidence for the power of print.

Gauvreau's informal entrance into the world of journalism began in grammar school, where he developed ample talent for sketching. A train wreck that had occurred close to his home one afternoon provided a stirring subject for the young artist and, as one of the first on the scene, he proceeded to place pencil to paper in an effort to create a rendering of the event. Satisfied with his depiction, he rushed to the offices of the *New Haven Union* and handed it to several men who seemed to be swallowed up in a tumult of journalistic activity. To the boy's utter astonishment, his drawing, with attribution, appeared on the front page of the next morning's paper.

At the age of eighteen, Gauvreau landed his first paying job as a journalist with the *Journal-Courier* in New Haven, Connecticut, where he worked as an obituary editor and a cub reporter. He quickly gained a reputation for tenacity and a nose for sensationalism, exposing the graft of public officials and cracking the case of a long unsolved murder. After the start of the war in Europe, he gained a foothold at the *Hartford Courant* and within three years, he had become the youngest managing editor of one of the most important daily newspapers in the country. Though Gauvreau was considered a rising star in the newspaper industry, his tenure at the *Courant* was riddled with controversy. The *Courant* historian would later write of Gauvreau that he "attracted off-beat news as a magnet attracts iron filings."

Gauvreau was a young man editing one of the oldest papers in the country and he was frustrated by its conservative and longstanding traditions. The major stockholders and editorial staff of the organization refused to engage in competitive ploys to up circulation and looked upon Gauvreau's attempts to do so with mild amusement. They were content to have the paper read by the intelligent few. Gauvreau, however, maintained that change was inevitable and that clinging to the sober methods of the past would mean the ultimate demise of the paper. He believed that the role of a major newspaper was to engage in causes for the greater good rather than to simply report the news as it happened. He was roundly criticized, however, when he reported on the legislative appeal of a young mother petitioning Congress for the right to vote. The heretical woman spoke to the bemused lawmakers while her little daughter stood bravely by. That little daughter, Katharine Hepburn, would grow up to become one of America's most celebrated actresses.

Finally, in early 1924, Gauvreau's brash methods of newsgathering came to a head. He had learned of a diploma mill in the State of Connecticut whereby medical degrees were being dolled out to fraudulent recipients throughout the State. He knew that printing the story would bring embarrassment to the political leaders in the State—as well as serious repercussions for his own career. He also knew that if he didn't go with the story, at least one of his competitors certainly would. Gauvreau, in his own words, "slammed the story under three eight-column headlines on [the] front page, and shocked the state." Immediately upon publication, Gauvreau found himself embroiled in a bitter backlash that would ultimately result in his dismissal from the paper. Bernarr MacFadden, the founder of the *Graphic,* was no friend to the medical profession or arrogant mainstream publishers. MacFadden viewed Gauvreau as a martyr for freedom of expression and offered him the position at the new tabloid on their first meeting.

❖

In the summer of 1924, advertisements had begun appearing in the New York papers announcing the arrival of "the most unique daily that would ever be seen since Johannes Gutenberg did his first printing." A skeptical public, already satiated by an abundance of two-penny papers, paid little attention, unaware that never was advanced a more truthful claim. Through its short and turbulent life, the *New York Evening Graphic,* under the militaristic talents of Emile Gauvreau, would challenge the longstanding dogma of the newspaper industry and stir the very foundations of American journalism. This self-anointed king of Tabloidia would stretch the definition of news like the slingshot that slew Goliath.

"The World's Zaniest Newspaper," as it was dubbed by one of its editors, operated in a vacuous world where sensational news wasn't just reported—it was created. From the moment of its inception, the *Graphic* was a chaotic venture of entertainment, art, and science that would result in the most infamous journalistic exploits in history. Perhaps a reflection of the clamorous era of the 1920s, or more likely the audacious personalities of its management, the *Graphic* attracted the censure and attention of anti-vice leagues across New York, and found itself banished from the more discriminating newsstands. The "Porno-Graphic," as it came to be known, was widely regarded "as the worst form of debauchery to which a daily newspaper has ever been subject."

The *Graphic* found its place among a dramatically changing journalistic landscape in the City of New York. At the end of the nineteenth century, aging editors of such prestigious newspapers as the *New York Times,* the *Herald-Tribune,* and the *World* complacently went about their business of reporting the fine details of important news. A focus on political matters, economic concerns, and international issues reinforced the dignity and prestige worthy of their established place in the world and appealed to their sober target audience. It was widely felt by industry moguls that stories of interest, while proving to be a frivolous distraction for the masses, added little to the high status of these established papers and took a backseat to the imperative of reporting the real news.

Into this fat and contented world of journalistic conceit burst a new form of daily newspaper. With the appearance in the overcrowded streets of Manhattan of the *Illustrated Daily News* and its hideous prodigy, the reigning dogmatists of the ancient order were quickly turned on their heads. The tabloid was already a beloved institution in England. This new American version was nearly half the size of the traditional newspaper, and encapsulated the events of the day with bold headlines and sensational photographs designed to hook readers at the first glance. Unlike their traditional counterparts, tabloids focused completely on the needs and values of the unpretentious wage-earning common man, "Sweeny," as he was affectionately called in the industry, and sought to communicate the day's news on his level without ego or arrogance.

"At first," wrote Oliver H.P. Garrett in a 1927 issue of the *American Mercury Magazine,* "there was an inclination to regard the new fungus with gentle compassion, as a novel experiment little likely to succeed. There were news stories and even kindly editorials, wishing the newcomers well." As it soon became clear, however, that the tabloids were attracting and creating huge numbers of new readers, the established papers changed their tune. Convivial greetings soon turned to disregard, and disregard became outright contempt. Anti-tabloid crusaders appeared on the scene and by the mid-1920s the tabloid had become, to them, "a genuine and full-fledged Menace, certain, in the opinion of right-thinking people, to disrupt the home, ruin the morals of the youth and precipitate a devastating wave of crime and perversion."

When the *Graphic* came upon the scene in 1924, the intention was to draw market share from the two other major tabloids in the City—the *Mirror*, William Randolph Hearst's foray into the world of tabloid journalism, and the *Daily News*, New York's inaugural tabloid, whose readership was now fast approaching the one million mark. Initially, few took the *Graphic* seriously, but the antics of this and New York's other tabloids forced an undeniable shift in journalistic focus. Sex and crime were the hallmarks of theses scandal sheets, which together, in a mad rush for increased circulation, would usher in a new era of eavesdropping, theft, and outright fakery under the guise of First Amendment freedom. Suddenly, reporters were burgling the offices of public officials and surreptitiously photographing executions of condemned criminals. Firsthand accounts of gossip and romance among the famous and privileged were sold to the highest bidder, and stories with attendant graphic photos were stolen from competitors like penny-candy in a country store.

The new methods of newsgathering prompted a predictable backlash. One commentator described the tabloids as "an unholy blot on the fourth estate—they carry all the news that isn't fit to print," while another simply branded them as "a perversion of journalism." The publicist Aben Kandel wrote tabloids "reduce the highest ideals of the newspaper to the process of fastening a camera lens to every boudoir keyhole." There was an undeniable element of truth to these condemnations, but it is also undeniable that the introduction of the tabloid newspaper to the bustling New York newsstands in the 1920s changed the face of American journalism forever.

❖

Prior to his plunge into the newspaper business, *Graphic* founder Bernarr MacFadden built a multi-million dollar physical culture industry premised on a maniacal dedication to diet and exercise, and the *Graphic* unmistakably reflected his idiosyncratic personal beliefs. He would ultimately become a maverick in the magazine publishing industry, promoting his bizarre health penchants and the liberation of sexual thought.

He was born to a poor farming family in the Missouri Ozarks as Bernard Adolphus McFadden. As a child, he was small, sickly, and often malnourished. He received little formal education and survived, in the early years, on the charity of friends, neighbors, and relatives. As he began to work and travel outside of his hometown, his individuality germinated. He changed his name to Bernarr, thinking his birth name too weak and commonplace, and replaced the "Mc" of McFadden with "Mac"—for more powerful and descriptive connotations, he believed. The middle name, Adolphus, never had a chance.

Influenced early on by trips to Barnum's Circus in St. Louis, and Chicago's World's Fair, MacFadden developed a keen interest in exercise and bodybuilding and attempted to replicate the look and the feats of the trapeze artists that he had carefully watched. He honed his skills as a weightlifter and wrestler and toured the Missouri countryside under the self-appointed name of The Professor, challenging any willing foes and participating in wrestling exhibitions and promotions. At these events, MacFadden also satisfied a growing zeal to convey his knowledge of physical culture to others. At the end of each exposition, he would gather the crowd around him and deliver a passionate sermon on the benefits of good health and physical fitness.

In 1894, MacFadden migrated to New York, where he opened a gymnasium, training and counseling out-of-shape businessmen in the art of bodybuilding. He created an exercise machine—one that attached to the wall and featured dangling springs and gadgets to create tension—and he began writing articles on the subject of physical culture for the purpose of promoting his invention. He toured England, lecturing and promoting his ideas on fitness and bodybuilding. In time he abandoned his machine concept and focused his writing exclusively on diet and exercise.

MacFadden was unable to interest any magazine editors in his writings, but was only emboldened by the constant rejections. He hatched the idea of creating his own publication. From a four-page promotional leaflet originally designed to arouse interest in an exercise product, he launched *Physical Culture* magazine in 1899. Through it, MacFadden was given a broad platform from which to espouse his personal philosophies, beliefs, and goals. The cover of the first issue was adorned with photographs of a muscular zealot—himself—cast in classic bodybuilding poses alongside the magazine's slogan, "Weakness is a crime; don't be a criminal."

Bernard Adolphus McFadden—Bernarr MacFadden—Founder of the *New York Evening Graphic*. "Weakness is a crime; don't be a criminal."

As MacFadden's eccentric beliefs evolved, his magazine began advocating bizarre and alternative health methods. In the pages of *Physical Culture* he waged a battle against conventional medicine and drugs. MacFadden advocated fasting to cure diseased kidneys and gallstones, and hot and cold compresses, vegetables, and cold water as a treatment for heart disease. He believed that natural remedies were superior to medically prescribed solutions and he paraded a bevy of untested therapies through his magazine. Offbeat natural cures for maladies from cancer to hair-loss enraged the medical community and ultimately prompted the American Medical Association to call for a ban on the publication. MacFadden engaged in a life-long wrangle with the medical profession over the evils of compulsory vaccinations—"the rotted bacteria of a vile disease" as he called them—and, perhaps prophetically, he accused individual physicians of being the puppets of a villainous commercial network made up of organized drug producers.

Through *Physical Culture,* MacFadden also waged a continuous battle against the "censor" who, in his words, became the "quintessence of prudery" and who represented the "mystery, secrecy, ignorance, superstition, and for the most depraved conception of all that should be divine and holy." In 1905, Anthony Comstock, the chief agent of the New York Society for the Suppression of Vice, conducted a raid of MacFadden's offices and confiscated various promotional materials for a physical culture exposition scheduled for Madison Square Garden. Comstock viewed the materials as lewd and pornographic, even going so far as to confiscate pictures of mythical gods in their classical nude poses such as Apollo, Bacchus, and Aries, all of which he considered to be "dirty." The First Amendment principals which drove MacFadden in his fights against Comstock permeated every venture that the offbeat publisher would thenceforth engage in.

Physical Culture magazine spawned a slush pile of mail and manuscripts to the publisher each claiming a particular exercise technique or natural remedy. Others provided inspiring testimonials of muscle growth and resulting stories of girl meets boy. It became apparent to MacFadden that this reservoir of public revelations could itself be a revolutionary basis for a new self-help magazine, and the idea of *True Stories,* was born.

True Stories was just what its name suggested, a publication devoted to first person accounts of human experiences written by those who lived them. The narratives had their share of sexual content, but there was also a wide range of social consciousness including family relations, prejudice, and love. The magazine offered a monthly prize for the most compelling narratives and in a short time was receiving thousands of entries each week. The sincerity and passion of the personal vignettes was essential to the success of *True Stories.* The magazine's editors were not permitted to edit the accounts in fear of losing their primal and realistic quality. It was said that MacFadden hired "average people" such as taxi drivers and store clerks to evaluate the articles, and when he learned that two of his staffers had honed their skills with a college creative writing class, he fired them.

True Stories became an instant success, earning $10,000 a day at its peak and serving as the primary source of MacFadden's huge and growing fortune. It would also provide MacFadden with the resources to further his exploits in the publication industry and became the natural springboard into the zany venture that would become the *Evening Graphic.*

Emile Gauvreau was unprepared for the scene that would greet him in the city room at the *Graphic* upon his arrival on that summer morning in 1924. ". . . A tanned, athletic creature attired in sandals and a leopard skin sprang from somewhere and in one leap landed on a desk and commanded everybody to rise. A large number of the workers, male and female, climbed up on their own desks with surprising agility. Others stood up in the aisles. The entire department was set off into violent calisthenics, swimming in the air, inhaling, exhaling and legs kicking back while the leopard man, his voice reflecting a lust for life, exerted the limb swingers into a furious temp."

On any given day, the pressrooms and corridors swam with MacFadden protégées. Muscle-laden eccentrics of health—all avid readers of *Physical Culture*—found a home at the *Graphic*, spending time tearing telephone books and doing chin-ups from creaking doorframes. Gauvreau described a man hanging by his long black hair from a ceiling water pipe, claiming that he had the strongest hair in the world. The journey through the corridors to the *Graphic* city room almost always entailed the sampling and measuring of flexed arms and expanded chests, while Gauvreau's astute secretary trailed behind, notebook in hand, pacifying these Titans by jotting down their vital statistics as they passed. On one occasion, a member of the International Weight Lifters Association picked up Gauvreau by the chair and placed him atop his desk. Searching for the editor's diminutive bicep, he asked "How did Barney happen to pick you out for editor?" and left in disgust. Gauvreau sheepishly slipped out of the office and found refuge on a fire escape at the rear of the building, where other kindred souls gathered to covertly puff their cigarettes and eat their ham sandwiches.

It was up to the talents of MacFadden's new managing editor to staff and build the venture from the ground up. Gauvreau's charge was to create something new—something never before witnessed. "I want to tell the truth in my newspaper in a way in which it has never been told before," he later wrote of MacFadden's edict. "I want to give the nation a paper which is stripped of hypocrisy. I want to conduct it in such a way that everybody will talk about it. Give them the news, but make it *hot news!* Give it to them sizzling from the griddle . . . Talk to them in pictures, flaring, glaring pictures. Sit down on the curbstone and chat with them! Catch their eyes so that I can pour my message into their brains!"The *Graphic* was to be, quite simply, a newspaper created in the image of its most eccentric founder, and like the evils of Pandora, the journalistic talents of Emile Gauvreau were unleashed to bring his employer's diabolical creation to life.

❖

On September 15, 1924, in an aging building on a gloomy side street near City Hall, the *New York Evening Graphic* opened its doors. One writer called it the "blackest day in the history of American journalism."

MacFadden was not interested in being a mere newspaper publisher. As with his prior endeavors, he intended the *Graphic* to be a platform from which he could proliferate his personal beliefs. He was a crusader, and the *Graphic* was to be a crusading newspaper. He applied the same principles that made *True Stories* the success that it was—he introduced the revolutionary first person treatment of stories to the newspaper industry. The *Graphic's* abandonment of the typical third person narratives in favor of first person confessions written by the actual participants was, at the time, a new and radical way of conveying the news. Now, of course, it is commonplace.

I KNOW THE MAN WHO KILLED MY BROTHER!

FOR 36 HOURS I LIVED ANOTHER WOMAN'S LOVE LIFE!

WE FACED DEATH TOGETHER IN THE FLAMES!

HE BEAT ME—I LOVE HIM!

The *Graphic* was to be written *by* and *for* its readers. It claimed to be staffed by ordinary plain folk and displayed open hostility for the sobriety and arrogance of the established papers that had become the mainstay of New York journalism. On the top of the *Graphic's* inaugural issue editorial page appeared Daniel Webster's oft-quoted axiom: "*There Is Nothing So Powerful as Truth—and Often Nothing So Strange.*" Directly below, the paper promised, "We intend to interest you mightily. We intend to dramatize and sensationalize the news and some stories that are not new. But we do not want a single dull line to appear in this newspaper."

As managing editor of the *Graphic,* Emile Gauvreau was given wide latitude in the running of the paper and was permitted to exercise his journalistic judgment within the purview of MacFadden's vision. Gauvreau's staff hirings were sometimes controversial and always interesting. A gossip column that would come to be known simply as "Your Broadway and Mine" would launch the career of a pink-skinned vaudeville dancer by the name of Walter Winchell. For two generations, the indomitable Winchell, who got his start in the business with the *Graphic,* would be considered a leading gossip columnist and wordsmith, aptly credited with creating the art of keyhole journalism. The stormy relationship between Gauvreau and Winchell is well documented, but there is no denying that Walter Winchell had an avid fan base, which resulted in a massive increase in the paper's readership. Winchell was but one of the many colorful and dedicated staff—many of them incurable workaholics—who graced the City Hall Place offices.

One junior member of Gauvreau's sports department immediately caught the attention of the editorial staff not by his steadfast and dedicated work ethic but rather his lack thereof. While his comrades moved about the building in a flurry of activity, this young staffer seemed content to lounge around, firmly attached to his chair, congenially talking to people. Those who mistook the man's friendly, easy-going demeanor as an indication of indolence, however, were soon proven wrong. His work was always completed—and on time. He simply had a wonderful knack for accomplishment with minimal effort. He worked quickly and efficiently and was the beneficiary of a wonderful mind and uncanny memory.

As word spread of this affable writer with unique work habits, contacts throughout New York began to emerge and he soon developed skills as a well-known organizer and avid promoter of events around the City. "He'll go places, that boy of mine," said a hometown acquaintance of the young man. The boy *did* go places. In the coming years, this young sports editor whose career emerged in the narrow spaces of the *Graphic* sports department would revolutionize the entertainment industry, introducing names such as Elvis Presley and the Beatles to American households. He was, of course, Ed Sullivan.

The *Graphic* editorial staff was encouraged to experiment and innovate. Contests, created for the sole purpose of stimulating circulation, were a mainstay. From searches for the most courteous man in town (in which a woman plant from the *Graphic* ventured into the city subway system to see if gentlemen riders would offer up their seats) to an offer of $10,000 for the marriage between the perfect Diana and Apollo couple, there were few contest ideas the paper did not pursue. When a relatively unknown word game that offered $1,000 to winners first appeared in the paper in December of 1924, circulation jumped by 30,000. This new crossword puzzle was soon adopted by newspapers across the nation.

In all that Emile Gauvreau did as managing editor of the *Graphic*, the overriding objective was readership. Increased circulation meant increased advertising revenues, and increased revenues meant the over-all perpetuation of the paper and the proliferation of MacFadden's own philosophies on life. By the mid-1920s, Bernarr MacFadden had developed a fiery, albeit delusional, longing for the Presidency of the United States, and he viewed the *Graphic* as the cornerstone of his candidacy. Fierce competition amongst New York's various tabloids placed enormous pressures on Emile Gauvreau. At *all* costs, the mass readership of the paper was to be augmented and maintained.

By 1926, the *Graphic* had become ensconced in a bitter three-way struggle for circulation with the well-established *Daily News* and the Hearst upstart, the *Mirror*. Each desperately searched for that one story or that one angle that would put its particular paper over the edge in overall readership. The readership must increase—must *always* increase. But how? What new sensation, what new approach would grab the public and hold its interest?

Emile Gauvreau worked over the situation daily in his mind. What could he add to the already overpopulated landscape of sensationalist journalism? How could he further exploit the exploited? And then a delicious devilish idea began to churn through his brain. At first he disregarded the notion—it was too . . . evil to be taken seriously. But the more he tried to bury the thought, the more it became *inspiration*. Random stories, he posited, were not sufficient to hold the fickle minds of his readers. Could he not *create* a character or several characters that could be manipulated through a series of exciting experiences, like Punch and Judy, for the benefit of circulation? Why merely report the news? Why not *make* the news? Years later Gauvreau proudly remembered, "I would give the post-War generation that couldn't take a drink except for the kick that was in it, that couldn't read a story except for the thrill, the stimulation its polluted palate craved!"

When word came that the eccentric millionaire Edward "Daddy" Browning intended to take the impetuous child Peaches Heenan as his bride, Emile Gauvreau licked his lips with lusty delight like a young boy before digging into a double scoop of chocolate fudge ice cream. "I began to scent rich copy in this middle-aged gentleman," Gauvreau later wrote.

"Bill, don't worry, she's the best girl I've ever known," Browning assured
William Heenan.

CHAPTER XI

'TIL DEATH DO US PART

> *"To The Most Wonderful Prince Charming in all this World, You really are my Prince Charming, for you are a true Prince. I love you more than any thing else in all the world. I love you for so many reasons. First, because you are just yourself. Next, because you are so good to me, you try to give me everything I want. I know my Daddy dear has so many business troubles and I will always try to make you forget your troubles and be happy. I'll always love my Daddy."*
>
> —PEACHES

> *"I wish them happiness but I know very well it can't last long. This is just another toy but then he needs something to keep him interested. I thought he might have chosen one 16 at least. I hope Frances will get all she can get."*
>
> —NELLIE ADELE BROWNING

AS VINCENT PISARRA WAS MAKING HIS IMPASSIONED PLEA BEFORE JUDGE Hoyt, Edward Browning was plotting to thwart the charges levied against him and Carolyn Heenan. Francis Dale, Browning's attorney and long-standing confidant, spent hour upon hour and day upon day counseling and advising his beleaguered client of every potential risk and liability and the most appropriate manner of avoiding them.

The strategy obvious to everybody, and the one that Pisarra feared most, was to quickly make Peaches and Daddy husband and wife, before the courts or the state legislature could take any action to prevent it. This was the solution that the couple earnestly desired and the one that Dale, as a lawyer, could readily advocate as the most complete and effective remedy to their existing legal problems. With the consent of the minor bride's parents, the accelerated marriage could take place and Pisarra would be powerless to act. Carolyn Heenan continued to be terrified of Pisarra's mischievous doings and would cooperate with just about any plan to prevent the removal of her daughter from her custody, and Browning had already won over William Heenan. The final legal hurdle—the requirement of parental consent—would be easily satisfied, clearing the way for Browning's brazenly provocative marriage to his eager and avaricious child-bride.

❖

Francis Dale, though renowned as an urbane Manhattan lawyer, was, in fact, a longtime resident of the quaint Hudson Highlands village of Cold Spring. Far removed from the clamor of metropolitan New York, the pleasant Victorian township provided a tranquil respite from the rigors of urban life and the acrimony of the New York legal world that Dale found himself a part of. Not quite Atticus Finch, but nonetheless a friendly and philanthropic gentleman, Francis Dale had many friends and acquaintances in Cold Spring and was well known among most of its nearly fifteen hundred inhabitants.

Browning and his lawyer surmised that the tiny hamlet would be the ideal location for the clandestine wedding; it offered the privacy and seclusion that would be required to keep the affair away from the watchful eyes of Vincent Pisarra. Quietly but diligently, Browning and Dale worked together devising wedding plans that Carolyn Heenan would, in later moments, admit to herself were vastly different from what she had at times envisioned for her only daughter's wedding.

On April 9, 1926, a day after Pisarra's hearing in the Children's Court, Browning's machinations with Francis Dale were nearly complete. On that morning Carolyn received an urgent call from Browning asking her to attend a meeting with himself, Francis Dale, and John Aldrich at Dale's offices on 42nd Street. She tended to a few matters at home and quickly made her way downtown. Upon entering the offices she was ushered into Dale's private smoke-filled suite, where she found the men chewing on cigars and gathered about newspapers blaring Daddy Browning's name.

After a short and cordial greeting, Dale leaned forward in his chair and told Carolyn of his concern over the current legal proceedings involving Browning and her daughter. He insisted that the only sure way to hinder the actions of the Children's Society was to quietly hasten the marriage plans. The wedding, she was told, would legalize Browning's relationship with Peaches and clear Carolyn of the parental responsibility she was being criticized for neglecting, but they must act quickly before any official action could be taken against them.

The primary emotion that Carolyn Heenan felt at that moment was one of jubilant relief that the actions levied against her by Vincent Pisarra would, as Browning and Dale now promised, be frustrated. Browning peered earnestly at Carolyn and asked if she was all right. Brushing away whatever lingering doubts her common sense imposed upon her, she replied that she was and she listened intently to the men who now held her daughter's fate in their hands.

It was agreed that Carolyn would accompany Dale to Cold Spring later that afternoon to finalize a lease on a house and to set up telephone service and a mailbox. Dale had, of course, handled the rental details ahead of time, locating an unused fifteen-room cottage set on a secluded two-acre lot, and obtaining through the absentee owners an agreement for its occupancy. Upon a promise that he would be awarded the contract to upgrade the plumbing in the home, Gilbert Forman, the Cold Spring Town Clerk and local plumbing contractor, amiably yielded to Dale's promptings to overlook the six-month legal residency requirement, and agreed to issue a marriage license to the blissful couple. Roy Christian, the proprietor of the town's only taxicab service and resident justice of the peace, promised his availability on the following day, Saturday, April 10th, for an event, he was informed, that might require his official services.

Prior to boarding the train for Cold Spring to finalize plans for her daughter's wedding, Carolyn telephoned Peaches and quietly informed her of what was afoot. Peaches knew that her marriage to Browning was inevitable but she screamed with delight upon learning that it was now perhaps only hours away. Whatever lingering pain she may have been experiencing as a result of the acid burns now vanished.

In Cold Spring, Francis Dale and Carolyn finalized details of the wedding and made arrangements with Grant Wright, another of Dale's acquaintances in nearby Garrison, for the use of a quaint farmhouse where the actual ceremony could be conducted. It was then up to Carolyn to confirm and settle the issue of the marital home. The property chosen by Dale for Peaches and Daddy's Bower of Bliss had been empty for over a year and was in dire need of paint and general repair. Not at all what would be expected for the honeymoon suite of this most flamboyant of real estate moguls, the unpretentious property betrayed the shotgun decision-making that was required for the situation. Dale explained to Carolyn that there simply wasn't ample opportunity to secure something more befitting of the fashionable couple on such short notice. After a cursory inspection of the house, however, a short hand-written lease for a one-year period was presented to Carolyn, which she signed and bound with a $100 deposit taken from a roll of bills that had been placed in her hand by Daddy Browning as she left for the train trip to Cold Spring.

By the time Dale and Carolyn returned to Manhattan it was nearly midnight, but the day's work was only beginning. They stopped at Dale's office, where he contacted Browning's paid bodyguard, Lee Swint, and ordered him to clear any plans for the next day or two and to go to the Heenan apartment as soon as possible. In Cold Spring, arrangements had also been made with Roy Christian, who as well as being the local taxi driver and Justice of the Peace was also a rather capable bruiser and very willing to be added to the security detail for the wedding. He was like-wise directed to meet Dale at the Heenan residence.

The entourage arrived at the apartment, where a dizzily joyful Peaches was now joined by her school-friend Pearl Bear and a longtime friend of her mother's, Catherine Mayer. Daddy Browning had arrived earlier in the evening and was entertaining the three with hackneyed jokes and amusing stories from his youth. Despite the late hour, the con-fused excitement of the occasion kept the group sharp and inevitably anxious. Curiously, Browning saw no reason to interrupt his daughter Dorothy Sunshine's semester at boarding school and had conspicuously excluded the ten-year-old from any involvement in her father's upcom-ing wedding. He would travel with his new bride to meet the child, he reasoned, as soon as circumstances permitted.

That evening, it was agreed that Browning would remain in the city while the rest of the group traveled to Cold Spring through the dead of night. Browning would make an effort to be seen about his offices on the next morning and would then depart for Cold Spring, leaving one of his cars outside his office building as a decoy.

While Vincent Pisarra and the rest of New York slept, the peculiar group disappeared from the apartment building and quietly stole away into the night.

❖

On the following morning, in addition to tending to the personal preparations of his wedding day, Edward Browning handled a lingering matter of business. He executed deeds of conveyance to place various mid-class apartment buildings, then held in his own name, into the name of a corporation—EDBRO Realty Company, a separate business entity over which he maintained exclusive ownership and control. As Browning made his way to Cold Spring to meet with his new bride, a secretary from his realty office filed the deeds in the New York City Hall of Records. Upon later inquiry, Browning would maintain that it was his rule to transfer property into the corporation upon the expiration of leases.

A skeptical press would suspect otherwise.

❖

The village of Cold Spring awoke on the morning of April 10, 1926 to a chilling frost that spread across the rolling hills and still brown lawns. By mid-morning however, the crystal-like rime had given way to the warmth of a sunlit sky and the algidity of the earlier freeze dissipated. The air was clear and full of the cheery fragrances of the coming spring. It was the perfect day for a wedding.

Like a master of ceremonies, Francis Dale rustled the occupants of the hastily assembled Browning residence out of their beds. Peaches and her mother fought back the yawns, products of their very recent long car ride, and leapt into frantic action. With unpacked suitcases and boxes haphazardly strewn about the house, they anxiously searched for stockings and undergarments. They hurriedly applied each other's lipstick and rouge in a flurry of joyous activity. The bride's elegant appearance was only slightly marred by the bandages that still shrouded her chin and neck. A spring suit of blue with a matching hat was the chosen wedding gown for Peaches, and Carolyn was likewise smartly dressed in a new suit paid for by the groom.

As noon approached, Daddy Browning joined the gathering, as did Peaches' father, William Heenan. Within the hour, the group was making its way to Gilbert Forman's plumbing shop to obtain the marriage license. Tripping about the sawed pipe and porcelain toilets that littered the floor and shelving of the garage, Daddy Browning managed to avoid soiling the light colored trousers, vest, and suit coat that he had specially chosen for the occasion. As always, a gaudy multi-colored ascot tie was carefully woven into a slipknot beneath the rounded attached shirt collar, and a matching handkerchief was meticulously folded into his front coat pocket. He thought it best to extinguish the well-chewed cigar that had smoldered in his mouth for much of that morning. Boater hat in hand, he eyed the Town Clerk suspiciously. The circumstances were unorthodox, but it seemed that Francis Dale had come through.

In preparing the statutory affidavit for issuance of the marriage license, Gilbert asked several questions of the bride and groom to which they solemnly responded. Browning openly attested to his age and Peaches attested to hers. When asked of her place of residence, Peaches answered "Cold Spring," as she was told to by Francis Dale. The temper of the group was upbeat and the atmosphere was undeniably joyous. Each of the participants nervously looked about the garage, gauging and appraising the other members of the strange assembly. The timbre was good-natured; there was audible chuckling at the farcical surroundings.

As required by the law at that time, both William and Carolyn Heenan signed the marriage license application before Gilbert Forman, attesting to their consent to the marriage of their minor daughter. Upon signing, William Heenan turned to Daddy Browning and said, "She's a might good kid, Mr. Browning. You take good care of her." Browning winked and replied, "Bill, don't you worry, she's the best girl I've ever known."

❖

Fifteen-year-old Lucy Lee from Dubuque, Iowa had tired of the mundane midwestern existence. She yearned for more. Having read about Daddy Browning's adopted daughter and the promise of a charmed lifestyle that Browning still represented to so many, she resolved to seek adoption as the millionaire's next Cinderella Girl. She carefully crafted a letter to Dorothy Sunshine telling her what a wonderful addition to the family she would make and asked if Dorothy could help her to realize her dream.

To Lucy's happy astonishment a response from Dorothy arrived soon after. Lucy's ambitions *could* be realized, she wrote, but time was running out. She must hurry to New York.

❖

Marriage license in hand, the procession of three motorcars, led by Browning's blue Rolls Royce, wound its way to Grant Wright's small country farmhouse in nearby Garrison, where the marriage party was ushered into the parlor of the home by Mr. Wright. Wright, an unassuming veteran of the Seventh Cavalry in the Spanish-American War and the Indian Wars of the 1890s, had known Francis Dale for years. Over the strenuous objections of the extremely curious Mrs. Wright, Mr. Wright rounded up his protesting wife and, with a tip of the hat, graciously left his home for the remainder of the day.

Once inside, the group located as many chairs as they could throughout the home and arranged them in several rows across the parlor. Roy Christian leafed through the pages of the Methodist Hymn Book as several of the guests arranged a makeshift altar—a reading table and two candelabras. Peaches, clutching a bouquet of red roses, approached the table and joined hands with Daddy Browning before the Justice of the Peace. Several times, Lee Swint nervously drew the lace curtains aside and peered through the window, expecting at any moment a barrage of camera-toting newsmen or officers of the law bearing cease and desist orders from some New York City court. To his relief, the only visible sign of intrusion was a hound burrowing into a gopher's hole in the front yard.

In a short yet surprisingly poignant ceremony, fifty-one-year-old Edward West Browning and fifteen-year-old Frances Belle Heenan promised to have and to hold, for better or for worse, for richer, for poorer, in sickness and in health, to love and to cherish, from that day forward, until death did them part. From that moment on, they would be known to the world as Peaches and Daddy Browning.

Crowds on Fifth Avenue clamor for a closer look at Peaches during one of her many shopping tours through the city.

CHAPTER XII

AMERICA'S MOST TALKED ABOUT NEWLYWEDS

"Why I have scarcely begun my shopping yet. I have ever so many things to get."

—PEACHES

BY THE TIME THE PROBING NEWS REPORTERS HAD SNIFFED OUT BROWNING'S well-concealed marriage plans, it was too late. The ceremony had occurred and the couple had left town. Carolyn Heenan remained at the Cold Spring property with her friend, Mrs. Mayer, to oversee some tidying up, and though under strict orders not to provide any details of the matrimonial events, a jubilant Carolyn chose not to contain her elation. She directed Browning's security force—several Pinkerton detectives and a local constable—to allow the reporters onto the property. With an air of invulnerability she confirmed her daughter's marriage to Browning and, in remarks surely directed to Vincent Pisarra, declared what she perceived as her complete victory: "No power on earth is going to take my little girl away from me now," she bragged.

With the full expectation of encountering a gilded country estate in the Village of Cold Spring, the reporters were surprised at the homely nature of the sprawling cottage and the wretched state of its repair. When asked if Peaches and Daddy intended to make the property their permanent home, Carolyn responded, "Why, you don't know my Frances if you think she would live in such a house."

❖

After the wedding service at Grant Wright's farmhouse, Peaches and Daddy bade goodbye to their guests and left for the Hotel Gramatan in Bronxville, where Francis Dale had reserved a third floor suite for the couple's wedding night. In the commotion of the hastily planned ceremony, Browning had completely forgotten to purchase a wedding ring for his bride. Along the road in the Town of Peekskill, Browning found a jewelry store where he and Peaches picked out a gold ring that he told her would bond their love forever.

❖

Rumors of a European honeymoon circulated throughout the newspapers, but the days following the Peaches and Daddy wedding were actually a whirlwind of mob scene shopping escapades on the streets of Manhattan and tiring commutes between the Gramatan and their Cold Spring residence.

Irate over what he viewed as Browning's flagrant contempt of morality and the rule of law, but nonetheless aware that the custody of Peaches Browning was all but a dead issue, Vincent Pisarra publicly chastised Judge Hoyt's refusal to intervene and announced his steadfast refusal to drop the currently pending Children's Court proceedings until he could further investigate the matter. As he openly pronounced the Browning marriage to be doomed to failure, Pisarra proclaimed his intention to confer with the appropriate authorities and to further examine any remaining legal options available to him.

Well aware that his bride was under summons to appear before the Children's Court, but equally aware that he had successfully removed Pisarra's primary legal weapon, Browning irreverently announced that the order of the court would be respected and that he would do everything in his power to see that Peaches appeared as required.

No sooner had it appeared that the Browning's legal troubles were drawing to a close than word emerged from the Putnam County seat of Carmel, jurisdiction over which the Village of Cold Spring fell, that acting District Attorney Clayton Ryder was looking into irregularities of the Browning's marriage license. The law required that the license must be applied for in the county in which the bride or groom had resided for at least six months. It followed, according to the inquiry, that if Peaches' statement to Town Clerk Gilbert Forman that she resided in Cold Spring was false, then the license could be invalidated and the marriage potentially voided. More importantly, however, the issue raised the possibility of a perjury charge against Peaches for misrepresenting her residency under oath.

From the start, Ryder expressed distaste for the matter and indicated that though he would follow up with the Town Clerk, he would not be questioning Mrs. Browning, nor was he expecting that any charges would be brought. Vincent Pisarra's agents for the Children's Society had made their way to Cold Spring and were throwing around their weight, threatening Roy Christian with subpoenas to testify and aggressively questioning citizens of the sleepy township. Brawny Christian politely informed the agent of what he could do with his subpoena, and as word spread to the County seat of the big city tactics being exerted by the Society, pressure to quash the investigation began to mount.

As well intentioned as his efforts might have been throughout, it now appeared that Vincent Pisarra's attempts to prevent or nullify the marriage of Peaches and Daddy Browning had failed. On April 16, 1926, Judge Hoyt was presented with a certified copy of the unchallenged Browning marriage certificate and promptly dismissed all proceedings related to the matter. With one eyebrow raised, Hoyt could not resist stating from the bench that he was *convinced* that both the Attorney representing Carolyn and the physician tending to her daughter had acted in the utmost good faith in submitting affidavits attesting that the girl had been too ill to appear at the initial court hearing.

The summary nature of the judicial hearing on April 16th obviated the requirement of Peaches and Daddy's appearance in court. As the judge's gavel fell and the proceedings adjourned, Peaches was cheerfully groping her way through mobs of onlookers on Fifth Avenue, while a nervous and agitated Daddy Browning ominously entered the New York License Bureau to renew his permit authorizing him to carry a firearm.

❖

Since the Philip Siegel affair, Browning had maintained a high level of personal vigilance and a low tolerance for threat. He fully recognized that his high profile lifestyle would engender a certain degree of negative attention and he frequently retained security personnel. As newspaper accounts of his wedding to Peaches circulated throughout New York, however, it was inevitable that the threats would increase—and increase they did. Though the marriage produced a large number of congratulatory notes and admiring calls from well wishers, a stream of menacing and hostile messages also began pouring into Browning's office.

Several days after news of the wedding broke, a long rope ominously tied into a makeshift noose was found slung over the doorknob of Browning's office; at the threshold lay an old pair of men's shoes. The message was unmistakable and Browning refused to take chances with his or his new bride's personal safety. Immediately, Peaches and Daddy were surrounded with a privately engaged six-person security entourage. Wherever Browning and his young wife traveled, they were seen amidst a cordon of strapping men—two in front, two behind, and one at each side. As an added measure of security, Daddy Browning often had his right hand buried in the side pocket of his overcoat, nervously clutching a Derringer pistol.

In the first tumultuous days of their marriage, security for Peaches and Daddy was anything but mere precaution. Wherever the couple traveled around the city, throngs of curious onlookers flooded the streets and sidewalks and snarled area traffic. Sometimes accompanied by her mother and other times by her beaming husband, Peaches, who only a few short weeks earlier had been a fifteen-dollar-a-week shop girl, now joyously skipped among the most exclusive stores and boutiques of New York, waving to the ravenous crowds and posing for pictures. She showed little inclination toward humility or discretion. On one such occasion, as her nervous security entourage anxiously cleared a narrow path through the pulsing crowd of over three thousand, an undaunted Peaches flashed a smile and brazenly boasting of her nouveau aristocratic lifestyle. "We have been married for a week and I've spent $7,000. Isn't it wonderful?" she cried. "I've spent a great deal of money," she continued. "Some days it has been $1,000. I usually keep $500 on hand, and when I need more I send for it. Daddy wants me to spend all I wish and to have a good time."

Dour-faced police reserves, patently unimpressed, vainly attempted to clear the sidewalk, battling the crowds with their Billy clubs while shielding the girl with their bodies as she made her way to the waiting limousine. Frenzied young women and smartly dressed shoppers surged about the car, shamelessly plucking at the crystal embroidery that adorned her satin coat, while curious pedestrians shouted out well wishes in an effort to gain the favor of her attention. Despite the danger and inconvenience she was causing, she paused in an evocative pose when a stealthily positioned news-photographer shouted "Peaches, a smile for your fans?"

❖

Despite Daddy Browning's justifiable concerns over security, he insisted that his child-bride continue her education and he made arrangements for her enrolment at the Haldane High School in Cold Spring, not far from their new residence. Though she would have to interrupt her day of shopping, Peaches was only too happy to comply with Daddy's request, as it meant a trip to her old Textile High School to retrieve her school records for transfer to Haldane.

Clearly Textile High could easily have parceled the transcripts to the new school, but Peaches insisted that she personally tend to the issue. In truth, she relished the thought. As Daddy Browning's well-known chauffeur-driven blue Rolls Royce pulled to the front of the school building, former schoolmates of the former Frances Heenan were awestruck by the triumphant return of the Cinderella legend. As she strutted through the halls of the school, large groups of girls clustered about her and stared at the ostentatious jewelry and clothing she flaunted. After an unimpressed glance at the girlish spectacle, the boys focused their attentions on Peaches' posh automobile and the liveried footman, whom they peppered with questions about the inner workings of the machine.

Almost forgetting why she had come to the school, Peaches retrieved her records, made her way back to the limousine, and left the yard shooing away the group of curious onlookers. A perfect homecoming.

Later in the day, Peaches met her mother and new husband for a luncheon at the Biltmore. As they dined, the new bride held up her hand to a bevy of reporters that had gathered around their table, to show three rings that Daddy had purchased for her. The first, a four and one-half carat diamond engagement ring; the second, a platinum wedding band encircled with diamonds; and lastly, a platinum ring with two diamonds to celebrate Peaches' upcoming sixteenth birthday. She leaned over to a reporter and whispered (as if it were just between them) that Daddy intended to build her a castle with miniature lakes and animals on a 135-acre tract that he owned in Bellmore, Long Island. Browning patted her on the hand and smiled. "She can have anything now she wants, and it's worth it. It's Peaches for life for me now."

❖

In between chaotic shopping sprees and fancifully posed photograph sessions, Daddy Browning brought his new bride to meet Dorothy Sunshine, who was finishing the spring semester away at boarding school. Sadly already aware of her father's current exploits, even Dorothy was uneasy having a new mother so close to her own age. As the trio spent time together it took little time for that unease to grow. Dorothy was becoming a refined young girl and she saw none of that refinement in Peaches. She began to dread the end of the school year and the thought of spending time with family.

The relationship between Daddy Browning and MacFadden's *New York Evening Graphic* had taken off during the Mary Spas episode. The *Graphic*, and nearly every other city tabloid, carried a series of stories on the affair, most of which portrayed Browning as a lecherous debauchee with an aberrant interest in young girls. As circulation of the paper leapt at the expense of the eccentric millionaire's already tarnished reputation, Emile Gauvreau received a call from Browning.

Expecting a "frightful exhibition of rage," Gauvreau was surprised by Browning's friendly and affable manner. Far from the expected demand for retraction and threats of lawsuits, Browning was complimentary to Gauvreau and eager to collaborate in the *Graphic's* journalistic efforts. He provided the paper with exclusive angles and scoops and happily posed for photographs while he worked with the editors to ensure maximum exposure of the story. Browning's near pathological desire for fame proved to be the *Graphic's* greatest driver of readership. Gauvreau later wrote of Browning, "A moral exhibitionist, he relished his notoriety. It gave him a thrill to see himself lampooned in the press. Publicity went to his head like synthetic gin."

After the wedding, both Gauvreau and Browning were thinking the same thoughts. Each knew that there were salacious aspects of the marriage that would be of great interest to the public, but they also knew that they required each other to bring the story to life and to keep it alive in the papers. Though Browning refused to limit his public exposure by dealing exclusively with the *Graphic*, Gauvreau could not protest. He had the man's ear and had created a relationship that he was sure would give the *Graphic* the lead on nearly every angle of the story. "I became his adviser, playing the Mephistopheles to his Faust," wrote Gauvreau. Through Daddy Browning's insatiable lust for publicity and Emile Gauvreau's dedicated nose for sensation, the persona of *Peaches and Daddy* was created.

❖

Though Daddy Browning was one of the most prolific owners of real estate in the City of New York, through the spring and summer of 1926, Peaches and Daddy lived a nomadic existence, traveling among Manhattan hotel suites and commuting back and forth on occasion to the rented home at Cold Spring. For much of the time, Carolyn Heenan lived with the Brownings, taking rooms separate, but often adjoining that of the newlywed couple. Much was made of Daddy's plans to gentrify the existing cottage on the Bellmore property, but in the meantime the couple flittered about the city, free from the constraints of housekeeping. "A home is nice," mused Peaches, "but servants are a great problem."

The rumored European honeymoon never came. Daddy insisted to reporters that Peaches was still recovering from her burns and that travel was out of the question. Burns notwithstanding, the newlywed couple, dressed in the finest of evening attire, danced most nights nearly to dawn on the dance floors of New York while Gauvreau's writers and photographers memorialized every step.

At the Hotel Gramatan, the pair's pseudo-residence, reporters from the *Graphic* set up shop, hiring several rooms, behind the doors of which the incessant tapping of typewriters could be heard through all hours of the night. "Day and night I watched over their lives, weaving the web of their destiny," wrote Gauvreau in *Hot News,* his memoir (thinly veiled as a novel). They were "my most magnificent inspirations. They were the raw material out of which I evolved a new journalistic technique."

Browning insisted that every printable aspect of their married life be dispensed like gin at a speakeasy. "He wanted the newspaper men to know everything about us—what I wore, the color of my nighties, the size of our bed," Peaches later said. He conspired with Gauvreau for the production of "Peaches' Honeymoon Diary," a fully illustrated four thousand word multi-installment exposé that revealed the intimate thoughts and experiences of the millionaire wonder-bride.

Overnight, Peaches Browning had become *the* authority on love and fashion, espousing her beliefs on the attributes of a dutiful wife and the secrets of the bridal chamber. Daddy insisted that Peaches continue to cause as much of a public stir on the city streets as she possibly could. The shopping sprees were incessant and, to the consternation of Peaches' chauffeur, Daddy required that each purchased item be packed in its own separate box to make the event appear as glutinous as possible. The story "was eaten up like a strawberry sundae every day by every little flapper who hoped to marry a millionaire," and daily circulation of the *Graphic* was driven to nearly 600,000. In every vaudeville act from Boston to San Francisco, a song, a joke, or a skit was devoted to the joyous child-bride and her aging benefactor, while conservative newspapers reluctantly carried details of the marriage of Mr. and Mrs. Browning.

Other city tabloids, anxious not to lose readership to the *Graphic,* abandoned any attempt to cover important news and filled column after scintillating column with the captivating doings of the Manhattan millionaire and his child-bride. Daddy flaunted the two-penny rags like a proud father, buying hundreds of copies and distributing them to friends and associates and retaining the rest for his personal collection.

❖

Not all was right with the world. On May 15, 1926, in the dead of night, a fire engulfed the buildings located on a huge tract of land in Bellmore, Long Island. It had been widely reported and well known to the residents of Bellmore that Daddy Browning owned the property and intended to convert it into a country estate for his bride, Peaches. Local police found evidence of accelerants on the scene—it was arson.

Several days after the Bellmore fire, in what appears to have been a totally unrelated incident, a short, shabbily dressed man with a dark complexion checked into a San Francisco hotel and signed the register "N.O. Body." The following morning, the man was found by hotel maids lying in bed with a self-inflicted bullet wound to the temple. A blood splattered handwritten will was found beside the body which bequeathed the man's remains to medical science, and gave all of his earthly possessions—the $25 in his trouser pockets—to Peaches Browning, the Cinderella Girl. A bewildered Daddy Browning could only state that had no idea who the unfortunate man was.

❖

On June 23, 1926, Peaches turned sixteen. Daddy hired the popular Victory Club where an eclectic mixture of giggling teenagers and gray-haired cigar-smoking tycoons gathered in celebration of the event. Like the radiant guest of honor that she was, Peaches made her entrance, gliding into the room to the cheers and well wishes of the assembled crowd. Overheated spotlights reflected their colors off the silver bandeau in her hair and the matching spangles splayed across her red gown. She whirled across the dance floor on the arm of a buoyant Daddy Browning, dancing to a full jazz ensemble.

Later in the evening, Peaches was led to a three-story birthday cake that resembled one of Browning's skyscraping towers. Daddy impatiently called for quiet, and when the festive crowd finally settled, he fished into his pocket and presented his bride with a carefully wrapped package containing a diamond bracelet that had been valued at $2,500 (roughly equivalent today to $30,000). As the gasping Peaches tore at

Peaches at her sixteenth birthday party.

the wrapping, Browning nodded to a waiter and a cloth sheath fell away from a previously unnoticed frame revealing a life size painting of Peaches reclining in an antique chair like a renaissance queen, with two delicate love birds gently perched in her elevated hand.

❖

By the end of June, Lucy Lee, whose pleading letter to Dorothy Sunshine had been so hopefully answered, had saved $55 as a waitress and had made her way from Dubuque to New York and to Daddy Browning's office. Upon learning that Browning had been married and was no longer looking to adopt a child, the exhausted and dejected girl fell to the floor and burst into tears. As agents from the Children's Society were called to return the girl to her home, she pleaded, "But I want to be Daddy's Cinderella Girl!" Dorothy Sunshine's attempt to wrestle her marauding father's attention from his determined young bride had failed.

Every day of the Browning marriage was a flurry of activity. Peaches was awash with invitations for social engagements and public appearances, and, between the requisite Fifth Avenue shopping escapades, she could be seen attending breakfasts, luncheons, teas, and dances throughout the city. Prominent patrons of New York's finest dance halls and enthusiasts of the Charleston, the Brownings were frequently requested to judge dance contests and award prizes. A charitable event at the Polo Grounds attended by 20,000 people in the summer of 1926 culminated in a Charleston contest judged by the buxom and rosy-cheeked Peaches who, with the help of Al Jolson, presented a huge silver loving cup—donated by the Brownings—to the winner. The cup was inscribed with the words, "With love from Peaches."

Peaches and Daddy were seen that summer on Coney Island and on the beaches of the Jersey Shore, where police were forced to break up crowds who had gathered to catch a glimpse of the vivacious Peaches, who posed for pictures in a daringly provocative swimsuit. A lugubrious Daddy stood nearby, still impeccably dressed in a sweat-saturated business suit. A day later, amidst a whirlwind of news reporters and camera flashes, the oddly out of place Brownings greeted prominent members of the community at a Greenwich Village dinner hosted by Richard Byrd to honor the men who helped him complete the historic journey to the North Pole. In the summer of 1926, wherever the limelight was focused, Peaches and Daddy would come into view.

❖

By the 4th of July, the Brownings had taken up residence at the exclusive Fairfield Inn near Central Park. Emile Gauvreau, searching for the next chapter in his continuing saga, calculated that a family pet might add a unique dimension to the household dynamic. Gauvreau, having a natural tendency for the bizarre, was pleased when Daddy Browning took interest in a gentleman on Staten Island who maintained a family of African Honking Ganders on his property.

On a day trip (with a bevy of news photographers in tow, of course), the Brownings made their way to the "Forgotten Borough" and

Peaches and Daddy stroll the beaches of Atlantic City.

Daddy arranged to purchase one of the more frolicsome birds of the lot. Some unopened boxes from one of Peaches' shopping trips were removed from the trunk case at the rear of Browning's limousine and the gander was placed within. As the entourage made its way to Long Beach, those inside the limo struggled to be heard over the relentless honks and squawks of Browning's new pet. Peaches was coaxed into tying a red ribbon with a large bow to the bird's neck, and before long the couple was happily walking the foul-tempered gander along the boardwalk, to the delight of curious onlookers and snickering news photographers.

After a gleeful day of aimless gallivants and posed photographs with their noisy fowl, the couple made their way back to Manhattan. By nightfall, the flailing wings and nervous squeals of the gander could be heard throughout the luxurious confines of the Fairfield Inn. In the safety of their posh suite, Peaches shrieked in dismay as the untrained bird clumsily bobbed about the room, soiling floors and furniture alike. Daddy, his face purple with laughter, ordered his scurrying chauffer to get the beast under control.

Gauvreau would immortalize Browning's African Honking Gander. It revitalized Peaches' "Honeymoon Diary" and circulation of the *Graphic* once again catapulted. Gauvreau would later write, "I smiled cynically to myself when I considered how, with a few clownish pranks, a few pictures and headlines, I had succeeded in compelling the entire nation to take notice of an elderly vulgarian and his bride."

❖

President Calvin Coolidge thought that the first lady, Grace, had selected the ideal retreat for the 1926 summer White House. The secluded mountain camp buried deep within the heart of the Adirondack woods provided an idyllic setting for the recreation and quiet that the weary leader so craved. Coolidge was not so naïve as to believe that he could avoid the usual throng of news reporters and photographers even in such a secluded setting, and his belief turned out to be well founded. The small lakeshore village of Paul Smiths was flooded with city slicking reporters, dressed in their finest summer suits and lugging heavy camera equipment through the woods in the summer heat, to the delighted entertainment of the local citizenry.

Several days into the President's summer getaway, however, things had become eerily quiet. The previously clamoring newsmen had all but disappeared and a bewildered Coolidge, not sure whether to celebrate or lament, inquired of his aids where everyone had gone.

"Peaches and *who*?"

It seems that the elusive Browning honeymoon had finally come and had landed the provocative couple right into the lap of the President of the United States. As the oversized Browning limousine, stuffed with two chauffeurs and four trunks, rattled down the dirt mountain roads toward the peaceful backdrop of Lake George, word spread that the Brownings were on their way. Soon every available newspaperman was

Peaches and Daddy pose for photographers while honeymooning on Lake George. Newsmen deserted President Coolidge for a peek at the vacationing couple.

heading for the *real* story. For the next several days, a bemused President Coolidge quietly moved checkers across the board and engaged in unmolested walks in the woods while hoards of photographers watched Peaches, in dresses embroidered with little sailing ships, and Daddy, in his gaudy colored finest suits, take boat rides on the lake. For photographic verve, they attached dead trout to their fishing poles when the fish just wouldn't bite.

In newspapers across America that summer weekend, photographs of Daddy Browning and his first mate Peaches blissfully reclining in a small lake-faring boat appeared beneath the caption "Steal Calvin's Thunder." Grace Coolidge discretely removed the page from the President's Sunday paper.

On the way back from their honeymoon retreat through the Adirondacks, Peaches and Daddy stopped at the Equinox House in Manchester, Vermont. In earlier years, Robert Todd Lincoln, a nearby resident and the son of Abraham Lincoln, dined nightly at the elegant summer resort.

The Brownings arrived with four trunks and twenty-six pieces of luggage. A young college student working that summer at the Equinox as a bellhop spent much of the afternoon lugging the baggage to the Browning suite, hanging the clothing, and icing the champagne, all the while patting sweat from his furrowed brow. Daddy Browning had given his wife a one hundred-dollar bill as a tip for the hardworking bellhop and had promptly retired for an afternoon nap.

When the work was finally complete, Peaches, dressed only in a slinky robe, walked the young man to the door. As the unsuspecting bellhop would later recount, she handed him a ten-dollar bill and with a mischievous smile let the robe fall open, revealing her curvaceous nude body. Undaunted, and cautious not to remove his eyes from those of Peaches Browning, the bellhop reached into her other hand and took the hundred-dollar-bill. The shrewd young man, who was never to forget his chance encounter with the youthful newlywed, was Adam Clayton Powell, Jr. and he would, in the coming years, become the legendary United States Congressman from New York.

When Peaches and Daddy returned from their honeymoon road trip, it was apparent to Carolyn Heenan that her daughter was not herself. Peaches had developed a slight tremor of the hands and was looking rundown and unhappy. To the rest of the world, the Cinderella bride had been given the most wonderful fairytale life that any young girl had ever dreamed of, but Carolyn Heenan knew what Daddy was about to find out. All was not well with Peaches Browning.

CHAPTER XIII

A BIRD IN A GILDED CAGE

"She's only a bird in a gilded cage,
A beautiful sight to see.
You may think she's happy and free from care,
She's not, though she seems to be.
'Tis sad when you think of her wasted life
For youth cannot mate with age;
And her beauty was sold
for an old man's gold,
She's a bird in a gilded cage."

—ARTHUR J. LAMB,
A Bird in a Gilded Cage, 1900

IN THE WANING DAYS OF AUGUST 1926, RUDOLPH VALENTINO LAY DYING in a New York hospital bed, though he didn't seem to know it. He pleaded to be released to his hotel room and he begged his doctors so tenaciously for a cigarette that on at least one occasion they relented despite the severity of his condition. At times, Valentino appeared to improve, but in spite of valiant medical efforts, nothing could be done to slow the infection. As the stricken sheik of the silent screen slipped away, a very public grief rose steadily through the streets of New York and throughout the country as a whole. Women the world over would mourn Rodolfo Alfonso Raffaello Piero Filiberto Guglielmi like no man had ever been mourned before.

Prior to his death, when the pain of his illness did not overwhelm him, the iconic legend Valentino was brightened by the deluge of calls, letters, and telegrams wishing him well. Lovers, friends, and admirers sent so many gifts and flowers that they were banked outside his door and down the hallway as a grim tribute to the dying luminary. Many tried to gain admittance to the hospital for a parting glimpse of their idol, and many more simply called to inquire as to his condition. Of course, few messages were relayed and even fewer admirers permitted access.

Several of the messages that *were* conveyed to Valentino belonged to Peaches Browning. An avid admirer of the charismatic man, she swooned at news of his illness and was a frequent caller to the Polyclinic Hospital where the idol lay. On the last day of his life, the *New York Times* reported that Valentino was "cheered by a letter of encouragement from the wife of Edward W. Browning . . ."

Peaches, like throngs of others, maintained a gloomy vigil as Valentino's death approached, and upon his passing she was inconsolable. As headlines across the world announced Rudolph Valentino's untimely passing, small articles beneath the fold or buried on inside pages informed readers that Peaches Browning was ill.

❖

In the weeks following their summer honeymoon through the Adirondacks, Peaches and Daddy took up residence at the posh Kew Gardens Inn on Long Island, where Daddy had stayed for a time with Mary Louis Spas. Though Peaches was suffering from convulsive-like seizures and uncontrollable spells of weeping, her illness was viewed as more of a nervous condition and not deemed by her doctors to be serious. Like many others, she was forlorn over the death of Valentino, but she was assured that with some rest and a respite from her exhausting social schedule she would be fine.

Daddy Browning was not convinced. At the time, though Carolyn had taken a small apartment of her own in New York, she visited her daughter nearly every day and dined frequently with the couple at their Kew Gardens suite. As the summer waned, Browning grew increasingly concerned over Peaches' condition and begged Carolyn to take up residence at the Inn so she could care for her ailing daughter. "Mrs. Browning had never been ill previous to her marriage," she later swore. "Now at the end of the Summer of 1926, after a few months of married life, she was almost a nervous wreck continuously subject to fainting spells, hysterical outbursts and occasional convulsions." Peaches was falling apart.

❖

Dorothy Sunshine had returned from camp and for a short time resided with her father, Peaches, and Carolyn. Disturbed by what she perceived as an inordinate amount of attention required by Dorothy Sunshine, Carolyn confronted Daddy Browning about her nightly bedtime routines. Carolyn was wary of Dorothy's fondness for embracing her father and lectured Daddy as to the dangers of preadolescent indulgence. Though the child had difficulty sleeping at night and frequently cried for her father, Carolyn insisted that Daddy not respond. Carolyn maintained that she had solely the interest of this little girl at heart, and perhaps she did. What is absolutely clear is that while Dorothy Sunshine lived with her father she would use every available weapon to keep him from the arms of "Mother" Peaches.

❖

Despite a relaxation of her busy social and shopping routine, Peaches showed no signs of improvement. By the end of September, she appeared on the verge of a complete physical and emotional collapse.

❖

On October 2, 1926, not six months after her now infamous marriage to Daddy Browning, Peaches loaded trunk after trunk with her belongings—some thirty thousand dollars' worth of newly acquired clothing, accessories, and jewels—and, with her mother, directed a lumbering parade of doormen and bellboys through the lobby of the Kew Gardens Inn to a waiting car outside. "Money isn't everything after all," she was heard to say as she walked from the building, and out of the life of Daddy Browning forever.

The initial reality of Peaches' departure hit Browning hard. He understood that things weren't completely right with his bride, but he never seemed to anticipate that she would actually leave him. He issued a statement to reporters insisting that there was no quarrel and that the parting was to be temporary. Peaches, he claimed, had gone away with her mother for a few days for some rest and relaxation. "I love my wife from the bottom of my heart," the statement concluded. A less charitable employee of Browning, upon viewing what was left of the couple's Kew Gardens suite, muttered to the papers, "She took everything but the radiators and the varnish on the floors."

Instantly, the three New York tabloids clamored for every detail of the breakup while a breathless public anxiously awaited each morsel that the papers could feed them. *PEACHES QUITS BROWNING; NEAR COLLAPSE AT MOTHER'S,* trumpeted the *Daily Mirror. PEACHES QUITS*

DADDY BROWNING, cried the *Daily News.* The *Graphic* memorialized the response of the *GRIEF-STUNNED BROWNING.* As Peaches Browning steadied her tattered nerves and a bewildered Daddy considered his next move, a wide-eyed Emile Gauvreau grinned with lusty anticipation.

❖

Agitated and distraught, Daddy Browning waited impatiently for word from his estranged wife, all the while publicly professing his desire that she quickly return to him. Browning had no idea where Peaches had gone and rumors were running rampant. Had she and her mother fled to Canada? Were they seen at nearby Long Beach? Had Peaches signed a contract for her stage debut in Chicago? Wild speculation churned through the papers.

When a bill for a recent purchase from a Fifth Avenue shop landed on his desk, Daddy knew she was still in town. He put out various statements in the papers begging his wife to contact him and pleading for reconciliation. He pledged his love to Peaches and he promised her rewards if she would return to him. Peaches' unequivocal response came several days later in the form of a scathing exclusive exposé appearing in the *Graphic,* under the name of Frances Heenan Browning, entitled "Why I Left Daddy Browning."

❖

Emile Gauvreau understood that it was considerably easier to reach circulation figures than it was to maintain them. Though readership of the *Graphic* had dramatically escalated after Peaches' *Honeymoon Diary* series, the numbers had gradually backed off since then and the editorial staff was looking for the next phase of the story. When word surfaced that Peaches was about to make her exit from the Kew Gardens love nest, Gauvreau knew two things: first, that Peaches would have a story to tell, and second, that she would soon be needing money. He was right on both accounts, and when Peaches and her mother sought out Gauvreau in the days following their departure from Daddy Browning, he was instantly at her side with a team of eager writers.

> My dream of love has turned into a hideous, revolting nightmare. I had to run away. My health, my future and my self-respect were at stake. My nerves were shattered. But can I forget? When I think of the terrible hours I spent—in the night. When I think of the peculiar look in

his eyes sometimes! When I think of what happened in his moments of abandon. Anything is better than the horrors of those haunting days and nights.

In a carefully crafted blistering attack that appeared not only in the *Graphic,* but also through syndication in papers across the country Peaches dismantled any chance of saving their marriage. "My dream of happiness with Edward West Browning is ended," she wrote.

Peaches maintained that Browning was not the generous philanthropist that he was so often portrayed as in the papers, but rather that he was a stingy miser. She declared that much of the jewelry he gave her was costume, and that her daily shopping allowance was barely enough for her to survive on. "I have yet to receive from my husband the costly things he promised me." She indignantly refuted statements claiming that *she* had proposed to Browning and emphatically maintained that it was Daddy who *begged* her to marry him for days. "I thought I was too young," she claimed. "But he insisted so much; and I really did love him then."

She denied reports that her mother had slept in the couple's room and insisted that Daddy wanted her mother to stay with them through most of their marriage. "I really wish now that my mother had been with me every minute," she lamented. "I would have been a very different girl now." The issue of motherhood ran throughout the series. Peaches denied rumors that she didn't want a baby, and vituperatively pointed out that Browning had lived with his first wife for eight years without producing a child. The implicit assault on his virility was clear. She bemoaned Browning's constant thirst for the limelight. "Nothing humiliated me more than Mr. Browning's craving for publicity. It is an overwhelming obsession with him," she wrote. Her versatile ghostwriters crafted her the perfect phrase for her wretchedly public marriage: "I was like a bird in a gilded cage, only the cage was not so gilded . . ." She only wished *she* had thought of that line.

❖

Gauvreau knew quiet well that the Peaches' narrative begged a response, and he was only too happy to accommodate. He turned his head in the direction of Daddy Browning—and by now, Daddy was ready for a fight.

In matters of the heart, Browning's judgment seemed childlike—if not downright foolhardy—at times. Though he had been openly lambasted in the newspapers and viewed by many in the public as a laughable buffoon, he plowed full speed along his chosen course of questionable conduct with an air of innocent naivety. The degree of the man's actual innocence is, perhaps, an open question. However, one should make no mistake that deep inside, Edward Browning was a businessman and extremely capable of protecting his personal interests.

Though he genuinely appeared to love his wife and to have been quite dejected when she left him, it was a natural response for Browning's business side to take over when he felt that those interests were threatened or his character besmirched. He had become very adept at projecting himself in the newspapers as the helpless victim in situations where he was under attack. Now, as the subject of his wife's unrelenting public assault, Daddy Browning would let the world know what life with Peaches *really* was like.

"My Marriage was IN NAME only," he shot back at his detractors (via the *Graphic,* naturally). "From our very wedding night Peaches has denied me my rights as a husband." "From the very first night she has always slept with her mother," he continued. "I don't want to say anything unkind, and even now I won't call my mother-in-law names, but she proved to be no dove of peace." Infuriated by Peaches' subtle reference to his prolificacy, an angry but unabashed Daddy announced, "In her story she charges that mine was a strange and weird love, and intimates that I have lost my virility. I am willing to submit to examination by any reputable group of physicians and they will prove that I am as virile and potent as a youth of 20." "I wanted, oh how I longed for a CHILD OF MY OWN," he protested.

Though furious to the core, Browning was also saddened that his marriage was over. Despite the harshness of Peaches' article and the anger of his response, the man was deeply hurt that his wife would say such things about him and couldn't understand how events had gotten to where they had.

Browning continually appealed, via the newspapers, for his wife to return to him, promising that whatever it was she lacked in the marriage, he would make up to her. He felt, however, that he had no choice but to correct the false impression that Peaches had publicly created about him. He objected to any statement that the jewelry he had given to his wife was cheap or inauthentic. He proudly displayed expensive bills authenticating the rare gems and diamonds that he had purchased, asking, "Does one pay that amount of money in cash for paste diamonds?" and he openly scoffed at the idea that he hadn't taken care of his bride as promised. "My wife weighed 135 pounds when I first met her . . . When she left me she weighed 165 pounds without her coat." He claimed that Peaches never wanted to be a mother, asserting that to her, having babies was something common people did. She would rather go to nightclubs and ballrooms, he insisted, than to start a family.

Getting to the root of the problem, Browning maintained that it was a total lack of privacy that shattered his marriage. "The whole trouble is that my wife's mother wanted to be with both of us day and night." "The mother would not leave us alone, and finally she took her daughter away." Francis Dale, Browning's lawyer and confidant, explained the woes of Peaches and Daddy "as just another case of too much mother-in-law. It's the old story of the murdering of the goose that laid the golden eggs."

During the next week, Peaches and Daddy fired salvo after vicious salvo at each other through the New York press. Competition between the tabloids became so fierce that rival papers would reportedly plant spies in the enemy ranks, seeking to scoop unknown angles on the story. Paranoid sweeps of pressroom personnel would result in the discovery of enemy emissaries who would be violently and summarily dismissed. Later in the day those same individuals could be seen tossing bales of competitor's newspapers, originally destined for New York newsstands, into the East River.

Each of the tabloids claimed exclusive narratives from the combatants and foisted lurid headlines and bylines at a willing public: *"'PEACHES' LIKE ICE, SAYS BROWNING," "PEACHES PANS HER DADDY," "DADDY RAILS AT PEACHES," "NIGHT CLUBS, NOT BABIES, ALL PEACHES WANTED."* The *Graphic* even published a large close-up picture of a sobbing Daddy Browning dabbing a handkerchief to his moist eyes. In typical *Graphic* style, Gauvreau had his art department paint huge pellucid tears streaming down Browning's ashen face. In sharp contrast to the screaming tabloid treatment of the story, the *New York Times* preferred the simple and informative *"BROWNING BLAMES HIS MOTHER-IN-LAW."*

Perhaps feeling slighted by the Brownings' relationship with Emile Gauvreau and the *Graphic,* the *New York Daily Mirror* maintained a decidedly rancorous tone against the Brownings, virtually from the beginning of the courtship. In the *Mirror's* October 7, 1926 piece entitled *"BROWNING UNMASKED,"* the tabloid, in a rare fit of introspection, argued that the matter did not constitute "honest news," though they went with the story in virtually every edition. "It is ridiculous publicity, and all three are wallowing in it," the paper claimed. And then they let loose:

> It is evident that "Peaches" and Mrs. Heenan mean to get much notority [sic] out of this separation. The girl has been on exhibition most of her life, especially in the last seven months. Her barrel-like legs, her over-plump figure, and her bovine features have haunted many a newspaper that has made capital out of her "romance" . . .
>
> Edward W. Browning sold the story of his love for "Peaches." He didn't write a line of it, of course. He wasn't capable of it. He can write little outside of business letters jacking up the rents of his unfortunate tenants and outstanding mortgages.
>
> Browning is almost insane on publicity. He loves nothing more than to see his name in the newspapers . . . The story is really a character study of three persons. First you have a vain, foolish, stingy, cold, old man; a man who went through a Steinach operation some few weeks ago in an effort to regain his long past youth. Not only has he a passion for self-exploitation, but he has always had a passion for young girls, a dangerous passion.

Beneath that paragraph was a drawing of Browning paddling a little girl, a reference to the claims of Mary Louise Spas, long a darling of the *Mirror.*

> Browning consciously stages himself all the time. He is a showcase. He is a talking machine with a Browning record on it. He even stages and displays his wife that she may reflect publicity on him.
>
> Newspaper men—including the present writer—have written columns about "Bunny" and "Peaches" and "Mama" in the firm belief that they were writing news. They were all saps, including this writer . . . But then, until recently, they couldn't believe that any normal human being could want such publicity as Browning has been given. They didn't believe that any full grown man would want to paint himself as a love-sick moon calf bleating and slobbering over little girls. They didn't believe any man over 50 would want to make himself

ridiculous and obnoxious and disgusting, just for publicity . . . [T]his is just a little piece for the scrap book of a clown, a washed out old man whose mouth waters when he looks at little girls. And he can clip it out and paste it up with clippings that tell what a lovely old dodo he is. And some day perhaps he will show it to another little girl—perhaps before he paddles her.

That evening, the *Daily Mirror* was served with a summons in a suit for libel brought by Edward West Browning. The paper used it as an opportunity. The next day, in announcing the lawsuit brought against them, the *Mirror* defiantly reprinted the offending passages of the article about the man they now mockingly referred to as Edward 'Paddler' Browning.

❖

The escalating feud of Peaches and Daddy Browning overshadowed virtually every other news item of the day and before long the circulation of *all* the tabloids had increased to record levels. Emile Gauvreau, in response to the bedlam, posted the following memorandum to the copy room bulletin board:

> The circulation of the *Graphic* has reached the point where it is tearing the guts out of the press. This has resulted from my policy of sensationalism. Any man who cannot be yellow has no place on the staff.

❖

As he celebrated his fifty-second birthday, Daddy Browning worked long into the night assisting Francis Dale in the preparation of his lawsuit against Peaches for legal separation.

Stanley Walker called it "part photograph and part nightmare." The com-posograph technique was perfected by the *New York Evening Graphic* and used to capture events where news-cameras couldn't be.

CHAPTER XIV

A BASTARD ART FORM

"Oh, snow and rain are not enough!
Oh, we must have some brand-new stuff!"

—DR. SEUSS,
Bartholomew and the Oobleck

THE ASSISTANT ART DIRECTOR OF THE *NEW YORK EVENING GRAPHIC* PROVED to be both intrepid and imaginative. Under the tutelage of this enigmatic wizard, the paper's art and photographic department constantly hummed with mysterious activity. This wizard was the unassuming but intensely creative Harry Grogin, and his brew the diabolically innovative marriage of art and photography that was destined to usher in a new chapter in newspaper history.

❖

Harry Grogin's curious contribution to the world of tabloid journalism began amid another controversial marriage that had found itself on newsstands throughout New York near the end of 1925. Leonard "Kip" Rhinelander, a member of a wealthy and prominent white New York family, had fallen in love with and married Alice Beatrice Jones, the working class daughter of English immigrants. Inquisitive news reporters didn't wait long to begin researching the background of Kip's unlikely bride. It was quickly learned that not only was the couple from widely divergent socioeconomic backgrounds, but that Alice's father was of mixed racial ancestry. Within four short weeks of the couple's wedding ceremony, despite the protests and threats from the Rhinelander family, scurrilous newspaper headlines began to appear decrying Alice as "colored" and condemning the marriage as a scandalous betrayal of social norms. Before long, Rhinelander's father was insisting that his son begin legal proceedings against his wife to annul the union. The obedient Kip, of course, complied.

At the time, New York did not have an outright legal ban on interracial marriages, and thus Rhinelander could not claim the marriage to be automatically void in the eyes of the law. Rather, he contended that Alice had misrepresented or concealed her true race, thereby fraudulently inducing him to enter into the marriage. Consequently, the overriding factual issue in the case was to be the racial makeup of Alice Jones Rhinelander. Initially, Alice's argument was that she was in fact white and that the investigations into her background were erroneous. At trial, however, she abandoned this claim, and argued that since Kip had seen her naked body many times prior to marriage, he had accordingly known of her "colored" features when they married, and nonetheless voluntarily entered into the union. Race, she declared, could be visually established.

The salacious nature of the testimony in the Rhinelander case was the mother lode for New York's tabloids. When the court hesitatingly allowed Alice's petition for the jury to view the primary physical evidence in the case—Alice's nude body—the world was promised one of the most anticipated moments in journalistic history. Alice was to disrobe before the jury to display her racial features.

The *Graphic* and virtually every other New York tabloid salivated at the chance to exploit this priceless turn of events. Each sent a squad of photographers and writers to the courthouse, ready to record every titillating moment and every shocking detail. They came armed with enough flash powder and photographic plates to record a Shakespearean play. Back in the hectic pressrooms, anxious photo editors and layout directors made frenzied preparations for the groundbreaking photos of a courtroom drama unlike any that had come before.

The revelry was short lived. To the dismay of the *Graphic's* editorial staff, the presiding judge, perhaps predictably, barred the news photographers from the courtroom, asserting that he was not going to put on a burlesque act for them. The *Graphic's* pressroom was filled with an air of gloom and annoyance, and Emile Gauvreau began preparations for his written coverage of the story.

Harry Grogin was anything but resigned. He viewed the judge's denial as a challenge—an opportunity—to outwit the system with his own ingenuity. If actual photographs of the gripping scene wouldn't be available, why couldn't he *recreate* the scene through his own innovative methods? His mind swimming with ideas, Grogin dashed to Gauvreau's office. "The hell with photographers!" he shouted. Grogin explained that if Gauvreau could provide him with a model, he already had enough photographic material on hand to recreate the tense court-room scene through a combination of artwork and photographs.

Gauvreau set things in motion and within an hour a showgirl by the name of Agnes McLaughlin, who was appearing in Earl Carroll's *Vanities,* stood in Harry Grogin's studio with a promise from Gauvreau that he would make her immortal. In his book *Sauce for the Gander: The Amazing Story of a Fabulous Newspaper,* Frank Mallen, a staff-editor of the *Graphic,* described what happened next: "Grogin photographed her as he imagined the Rhinelander bride would appear almost naked in court, and as she subsequently did, as though by his remote direction. Then he superimposed her on another composite of a courtroom scene he had already prepared by putting real faces on posed bodies. He reduced and enlarged the various photographs so that everything was in true propor-tion in the composite. He did it with such finesse that few could believe it wasn't an actual reproduction just as it had come out of the camera, despite the confession in the caption that it was a composite."

Grogin even added a brownish tint to the girl's body for realism and Agnes sued the *Graphic* over that detail. She ultimately lost her case, but overnight the *Graphic* had become a sensation by creating and publish-ing "the most amazing thing that ever appeared in a newspaper."

The Rhinelander composograph appeared on the front page of the *Graphic* and instantly circulation leapt from 60,000 to several hundred thousand, while nervous editors from competing tabloid papers simply wrung their hands in frustration.

Gauvreau had made newspaper history and revolutionized the *Graphic.* "The 'composograph' opened a new chapter in the history of tabloid journalism," he would write. "It was now possible to make what appeared to be photographic illustrations of any scene anywhere without being present. If I wanted to show the King of England taking a bath and scrubbing his back with a long brush, I would take an actual photograph of a gentleman on my staff going through this hygienic pro-cedure. Then, I would superimpose the features of the King on my reporter's face. This treatment of photography opened up a new field with extraordinary possibilities. Employing the human figure itself, it was more convincing than a mere drawing."

Soon Harry Grogin was depicting any and every shocking sex scandal or crime he couldn't get an actual photograph for. This sometimes had untoward results. While recreating the hanging execution of Gerald Chapman in April of 1926, Grogin placed a noose over the masked head of a *Graphic* staff reporter and slung the rope over a steam pipe running across the ceiling. The reporter, bound at the hands and feet, stood on a chair as other employees of the paper, staged as prison officials, looked on. As Grogin called to the reporter to bend his knees for realistic affect, somehow the chair kicked away and for an agonizing moment in time, he dangled as the real Gerald Chapman did. Like a cougar leaping toward its prey, Harry Grogin dove across the room and grabbed the reporter by the legs, saving his life. From that time forward, when Grogin or one of his people ventured out of the art and photographic department looking around for subjects, the *Graphic* staffers and employees would duck beneath their desks or casually steal away into the nearest corridor.

The *Graphic* never pretended that their composographs were real photos—they were always labeled as artistic renderings—but the public enjoyed every one of them and bought up the paper in record numbers. The response was not unanimously positive, of course. Perhaps from a sense of moral outrage (or, more likely, born of professional jealousy), some in the newspaper industry frowned upon the technique, and controversy ensued. Stanley Walker, in his 1934 book, *City Editor*, summarized the general feeling among journalists, decrying the composograph as "part photograph and part nightmare, a bastard art form . . . completely lacking in integrity."

❖

As the saga of Peaches and Daddy Browning erupted into the tabloid papers, Emile Gauvreau formulated a plan to record the separation proceedings as no one else dared. Gauvreau's composographs would not only succeed in catapulting the *Graphic's* readership to record heights, they would also embroil the paper in a First Amendment battle—a battle that would ultimately land him in the criminal courts of New York City.

The Westchester County Courthouse in White Plains, New York.

CHAPTER XV

INTO THE COURTS

*"What therefore God hath joined
together, let not man put asunder"*

Matthew 19:6
King James Bible

RUMORS THAT PEACHES AND HER MOTHER HAD PAID A VISIT TO THE FAMED New York trial lawyer Max Steuer were brewing, and the newspapers were carrying provocative quotes from Carolyn that Peaches intended to start legal action against Daddy Browning for separation. Publicly, Browning continued to profess his willingness to reconcile with his wife, and appeared content to argue his case through the *Graphic* and the other New York tabloids. He gave no clue as to any intention to engage Peaches in a legal battle and was even quoted as saying that "if a person cares for any one he doesn't sue them." Browning expressed his ongoing hope that Peaches would return to him—right up to the moment when his lawyers obtained an order from the Supreme Court of New York for the appointment of a guardian *ad litem* over Frances Heenan Browning for the sole purpose of serving upon her a summons and complaint for separation. The marriage that had been cursed from the start would now be laid before a courtroom and a country, both of which were destined to stand in sober judgment of this ill-fated couple.

❖

In 1926, when Daddy Browning landed the first legal blow, the remedy of divorce was not available to him. Prior to 1969, the State of New York did not recognize any grounds for divorce other than adultery, and if the facts of a particular case did not bear out that charge, divorce was not an option.

While a claim for actual divorce between Peaches and Daddy was not possible, as neither could allege that the other had been unfaithful, the law did provide the remedy of legal separation. Practically speaking, the difference would be miniscule—in both situations the parties would be physically separated and the law would recognize that separation while also granting financial orders. Legally, however, there was a vast difference. In a suit for separation, regardless of the ferocity of the proceedings or the success of either of the parties, they would walk out of that courthouse the same as they walked in—as husband and wife. The marriage would not be *legally* dissolved. Peaches and Daddy, therefore, would remain bound to each other even after their separation, albeit in an altered condition of matrimony.

The issues consequently presented to the Brownings were twofold: First, were there sustainable grounds upon which the court could grant a separation? And second, and perhaps of most import, if the court were to grant a legal separation, what would be the financial resolution of the parties? Put another way, the case could be distilled into two main interests—reputation and money. Once the first was sacrificed, the second could be secured.

In the time of Peaches and Daddy, New York statutory law provided that either spouse might obtain a judgment "separating the parties from bed and board" for any of the following causes: 1. "cruel and inhuman treatment;" 2. "conduct . . . as may render it unsafe and improper" for either spouse to cohabit with the other; or 3. "abandonment." Sufficient evidence of any or all of these causes was required before the court would issue a judgment for separation. The complaint filed by Daddy Browning merged all three grounds of the statute and alleged:

> That since their marriage the defendant has treated the plaintiff in a cruel and inhuman manner and has repeatedly committed acts of cruelty upon Plaintiff . . .
> That the defendant and her mother, Carolyn Heenan . . . have been for a considerable period of time uniformly brutal and abusive and have applied abusive epithets to this plaintiff...and by reason of the premises this plaintiff believes it is entirely unsafe and improper for him to live and cohabit with said Defendant.
> That although the plaintiff has always conducted himself toward the said defendant as a faithful husband, the defendant disregarded her duties as a wife and without plaintiff's consent has been willfully and continu-

ously absent from the plaintiff since the 2nd day of October, 1926, without any cause and justification therefor and with intent not to return.

That the said plaintiff and defendant were living at Kew Gardens, in the County of Queens, State of New York, at the time the said defendant abandoned this plaintiff.

❖

"Life has been full of surprises lately," observed a seething Peaches. She had been preempted by Daddy Browning and was none too happy about it. Now, the metaphorical gloves were off and Peaches appeared ready for battle.

Though Max Steuer had refused to take Peaches on as a client, he did refer her and Carolyn to his son-in-law, Henry Epstein, who had begun private practice in Manhattan several years earlier. Epstein, a small, scrupulously groomed gentleman with a close-cropped dark moustache, was a former schoolteacher and had a reputation for competence and integrity. Though he knew the case would be a momentous undertaking and would occupy the majority of his time going forward, the soft-spoken Harvard educated lawyer was anxious to move out of the shadow of his high profile father-in-law and thought that Peaches Browning might afford him that opportunity. Epstein only wondered what the price for that opportunity might be.

Henry Epstein, circa 1931

Because Peaches was a minor, a guardian *ad litem* had to be appointed for the purpose of accepting service of Daddy Browning's summons and to oversee defense of the case. Upon Browning's contention that Carolyn was not a proper and disinterested person to act in such capacity, a justice of the Supreme Court sitting in Putnam County appointed an unrelated New York attorney by the name of Otis Rockwood to act as Peaches' guardian. Henry Epstein's first official act of defense was to petition the court to remove Rockwood and to substitute Carolyn Heenan as Peaches' guardian for all legal purposes. That accomplished, he filed an answer to the complaint, which denied every material allegation of Browning's case. Then he went on the offensive.

Epstein was well aware that the high profile nature of the case would result in immense public and press scrutiny, and that the nature of his client's defenses and claims would prove to be scandalous. In his conferences with Peaches and her mother, Epstein had become uneasy with the nature of the allegations they were levying against Browning. He knew, however, that in order to defeat Browning's claim and, more importantly, to persuade the court to issue economic orders advantageous to Peaches, he must portray his client as the victim of abhorrent behavior at the hands of a wealthy miser. To properly represent his client, there was simply no way to be gentle. In a scathing ten-page counterclaim, Peaches would demand a separation from Daddy Browning on her own terms.

Browning's initial case was filed in the Putnam County Clerk's Office in Carmel, and though Peaches' counterclaim in defense of that case was likewise filed in Carmel, it was also asserted as a *separate* action against Browning, filed in White Plains with the Westchester County seat of the Supreme Court, where she now demanded that the trial take place. Unlike the venue rules of today, there was no requirement in 1927 that New York matrimonial trials be conducted in a county where either or both of the litigants resided. As a result, a confused, and often unjust, scheme of forum shopping frequently ensued where litigants were free to choose whichever court they felt would most likely give them the best chance of victory. The court in White Plains had recently given Alice Jones Rhinelander a positive result by denying her husband an annulment (which ultimately led to a financial settlement for Alice), and Peaches and her lawyer theorized that Alice's success might lay the groundwork for a similar result for Peaches in the same court.

Henry Epstein was not so concerned with the choice of venue as he was with the nature of the allegations. He could only shudder when he envisioned the evidence that would be required to support his client's shocking claims. Satisfying the statutory requirements, the counterclaim alleged that Browning had treated Peaches in a "cruel and inhumane manner" and had conducted himself so "as to render further marital life and cohabitation...improper and dangerous" to her life and limb. She then set forth fifteen separate and highly explicit instances, the cumulative effect of which she claimed produced "an hysterical, nervous condition, causing the defendant to faint repeatedly, to lose sleep, to be unable to sleep, to be unable to appear in the open air without becoming an object of public ridicule and jest, to suffer physical and nervous collapse, rendering further and continued life and cohabitation with the plaintiff impossible, improper and dangerous to the life and health of the defendant." In essence, Peaches was admitting that she had abandoned her husband, but claimed that she was *forced* to do so. In what seemed to be an afterthought, a final allegation, which added little to the previous litany of Browning's alleged offenses, claimed that Browning was "suffering from a form of sexual abnormality."

❖

Upon learning of the counterclaim that was filed by Peaches, Browning left the Cold Springs residence where he had been staying since his wife's departure and took a room on the fifth floor of the Hotel Riviera in Newark, where he remained in seclusion. When intrusive news reporters uncovered his location and began asking questions, he adamantly denied that he was attempting to avoid Peaches' legal pleadings. His visit to the hotel, he maintained, had no significance.

❖

One afternoon in early July of 1926, when the Brownings were still flashing smiles and one-hundred-dollar-bills throughout Manhattan, Peaches received a call from Daddy asking her to come to his office to meet someone. She had heard her husband mention the name before, and though she was not anxious to make the acquaintance of Marian Dockerill, she did as her husband asked.

When she arrived at the office, she found her husband tripping about himself beseeched with admiration for the rouge-encased middle-aged woman seated at the foot of his desk. Instantly, Peaches was struck by an overpowering perfume before being utterly distracted by an actual snake that the woman wore about her neck. Peaches hesitated by the doorway as her husband fawned over the peculiar woman. After bidding his wife enter, Browning explained to the bewildered Peaches that Dockerill had the ability to perform mystical life readings and that she possessed the key to everlasting youth. Amidst Browning's toothy grin and affirmative nods, Dockerill gave Peaches a small Buddha Statue and invited her to her apartment for a visit. Daddy implored the reluctant Peaches to befriend the woman and follow her advice. With a polite nod, Peaches looked at her watch and reminded her husband that she was due at a luncheon by one o'clock and had to run.

Whether or not Daddy Browning actually knew it, Marian Dockerill was deeply involved with an occult sect called the Secret Order of Tantriks, which espoused the wonders of sexual magic. Dockerill was a devotee of the leader and soon became the self-professed omnipotent High Priestess of Oom, spreading the belief of sexuality as a form of religious experience. If Daddy Browning had any clue as to these other occupations of Marian Dockerill he adamantly denied it, but in the summer of 1926 he *had* established a relationship with this woman and he implored his young wife to partake.

After leaving her husband and engaging in a tit-for-tat battle in the tabloids of New York, Peaches Browning made an offhand comment about Marian Dockerill as the leader of a weird love cult that appeared in her *Why I Left Daddy Browning* series featured in the *Graphic*. On October 22, 1926, while Peaches and her attorney busily strategized over the separation suit, word came that Marian Dockerill had begun legal proceedings against Peaches for libel and was seeking $150,000 in damages.

Dockerill's bumbling lawyer could not get the suit beyond the initial technical phase of filing. He appeared astonishingly unaware that *truth* was the ultimate defense to libel—in 1928 a True Life confession authored by "Marian Dockerill, High Priestess of Oom" and entitled "My Life in a Love Cult, a Warning to All Young Girls" appeared on newsstands throughout New York. Peaches, however, understood Dockerill's suit for what it clearly appeared to be—an effort on the part of Daddy Browning to divert attention and resources away from the main event.

❖

Warmed by Peaches' current legal woes, Daddy Browning was pleased at the prospect of outlasting his estranged wife with the benefit of his unlimited money and brazen temperament. His joviality was not to last long.

Marian Dockerill

Having had little success with Bird Coler, Anna St. John now turned her efforts to regain custody of little Dorothy Sunshine upon the more receptive ears of Vincent Pisarra of the Children's Society. She had watched with icy suspicion as Daddy Browning stumbled his way through one scandalous story to the next, and now, with the recent well-publicized troubles plaguing his every move, she thought Browning to be a particularly unfit father.

Anna retained a lawyer in the effort and arranged a conference with Pisarra, who was still smarting from his fruitless attempt to prevent the Peaches and Daddy wedding. Pisarra promised Anna that he would investigate the matter and expressed confidence that with sufficient evidence he could prove to a court that Browning was not a fit guardian for the child. Anna's lawyer boasted, "We are going to take every means in our power to remove this innocent child from the decadent influence of Browning."

An enthralled Peaches pledged to Anna whatever assistance she could provide.

To the Editor of The New York Times:
Atlanta, Ga., October 19.—Browning and Peaches are suing for separation; we hope they will be happy. Now, if the newspapers will just get a divorce from both of them the whole of America will be happy.

Yours for new cases,

WILL ROGERS

As the initial pleadings in the Browning separation case were filed and the issues joined, the inevitable next step was the fixing of alimony *pendente lite*. That step came on November 1, 1926, when Henry Epstein filed a motion requesting that the court order Browning to pay temporary alimony to his client pending trial in the amount of $4,000 per month, together with a $25,000 legal fee, and an additional $15,000 for costs of litigation. In support of the motion, Epstein submitted a lengthy affidavit executed by Frances Heenan Browning providing a detailed account of her celebrated marriage, and closing with the following statement:

I do solemnly appeal to this Court of Justice that I am Mr. Browning's wife, innocent of wrongdoing; that I am the victim of a marriage with an abnormal man; that I am attacked with a law suit charging me with cruelty and desertion; that I must defend this action because it is based upon false accusations. While defending this action I am entitled to live comfortably as Mr. Browning accustomed me to. I am informed that it is proper that I should live in the manner in which my husband can support me. I ask this Court to allow me the means of living properly: of defending myself in as efficient a manner as my husband seeks to attack me. To enable me to retain as able counsel and to prepare adequate proof; I ask the means of being able to prepare my case and prove it. May it please the Court to grant the relief which I here ask.

In affidavits opposing Peaches' motion, Browning's lawyers simply called it a shakedown.

When faced with Peaches' motion, Daddy Browning instinctively reached out to the newspapers. He called together reporters at his office and protested his wife's robust spending habits. He reminded them that during their short marriage, he had spent in excess of $30,000 on his bride, and he issued to them a formal, albeit incomplete, listing of the gifts he had given her. The next day, in papers from Manhattan to Seattle, a list of "knick-knacks" that Peaches' papa bought her was perused by avid readers:

Two hundred bunches of flowers.
Fifty boxes of candy.
Twenty baskets of fruit.
One ermine coat.
One fox trimmed coat.
One Russian sable coat.
One "other fur" coat.
Sixty dresses.
Fifteen vases to hold flowers.
One fox neckpiece.
Three ensembles.
One hundred and seventy-five "odd coats."
Twenty hats.
Thirty pairs of shoes.
Tennis and golf outfits.
One hundred photographs of herself and Browning.
One dozen frames.
One expensive ostrich fan.
Twelve hair ornaments.
Eight fancy bags.
Two leather trunks.
One Teddy bear doll which played music.
One hundred small souvenirs.
Lingerie, handkerchiefs, cigarette cases, lighters, vanity cases, hose and . . .
Heaven knows all.

"They used to think it was a great joke to give taxi drivers a $5 bill," Browning lamented.

On November 15, oral arguments on the question of alimony were heard in White Plains before Judge Joseph Morschauser. A crowd that rivaled that at the Rhinelander case had gathered around the courthouse in anticipation and anxious court attendants had to cordon off a lane to allow Peaches and her lawyer entry. As the hearing began, Henry Epstein gave a brief outline of the case, stating in general fashion that Browning's actions had made continuation of the marriage impossible. When Epstein suggested a private reading by the judge of the supporting affidavits rather than to recount the graphic details in open court, a relieved Judge Morschauser thanked him. To support the large request for alimony and counsel fees, Epstein then provided an outline of Browning's vast financial holdings and pointed out that his client, Mrs. Browning, had no resources at all.

In opposition, Francis Dale relied on an affidavit provided by Edward Browning, which predictably played down the value of his assets and played up the spending habits of his wife. Browning did not personally appear at the hearing and surprisingly, Francis Dale spoke very little on the actual merits of the motion. He stated that it was not his client's intention to oppose a *reasonable* allowance for counsel fees and alimony, but that he wished to avoid a protracted pre-trial process that could be unnecessarily delayed at Browning's expense. He requested, and was granted, a commitment for the soonest possible trial date, not later than January. At the close of arguments, Morschauser indicated that he would take the matter under advisement and report his decision as soon as possible. Before leaving the courtroom, he extended an authoritative bony finger at Peaches and commanded, "In the meantime there are to be no new hats, new coats, nor new dresses."

Seven days later, Judge Morschauser's handwritten order allowing Peaches alimony in the amount of $300 per week and counsel fees in the amount of $8,500 was issued. Upon reading the affidavits submitted by the parties, Morschauser concluded that the lurid details of the matter should not, at least for the time being, be subject to public view, and he ordered that the papers in the case be thenceforth sealed to all but the attorneys of record.

❖

While the Brownings fought their legal battles in the courtrooms of New York, the *Graphic* and virtually every other tabloid newspaper continued to monopolize on the exploits of the eccentric couple. Though Emile Gauvreau's infamous composograph had not yet been applied to the Browning case, he worked in close contact with both Peaches and Daddy in publishing their respective stories and cheerfully printed the positions and views of each. Gauvreau wrote of the process, "If the statement be not labeled a vanity I have been the confidante of both of the parties . . ."

Daddy Browning, however, soon became dissatisfied with the vast amount of press that he believed Peaches was garnering in the *Graphic* and other newspapers, and he prevailed upon Gauvreau to shine more of the spotlight in his direction. In a direct response to Peaches' *Why I Left Daddy Browning* series, the *Graphic* published a highly pre-advertised multi-chapter tell-all confession entitled *My Own Story of My Life and Loves by Edward West Browning* through the latter part of November 1926. With headlines such as *Women Caused Sorrow Says Browning* and *My Love Life with Peaches,* Daddy Browning revealed in this exposé his private thoughts and views on the women of his life, and, more importantly, was given a platform from which to refute what he thought were falsehoods placed before the public by Peaches and others. "No fish, after being stranded and suddenly thrust back again in the water, was more in his element . . ." wrote Gauvreau after the series.

❖

On the afternoon of December 11th, a sturdy but otherwise unremarkable gentleman strode through the entrance of Daddy Browning's West 72nd Street office. He introduced himself to the secretary as a salesman of holiday wares and requested a moment of Browning's time to show him some Christmas card assortments. The doubtful secretary asked the man to have a seat as he disappeared behind a closed door and announced the guest to his boss.

After an hour's wait, Browning made his way from his private suite and politely began looking at the man's holiday selection. After a moment or two the man reached into his leather satchel and produced a blue-backed legal document. "Speaking of Christmas sentiments," he said, "look at this one!" Startled, Browning retracted as the salesman jabbed the document into his hand and made his way for the door. Pausing at the threshold, the man turned back to the bewildered Browning and added, "And you be sure to have a Merry Christmas." The salesman was, of course, a process server, and the document, a summons and complaint that announced a lawsuit filed against Edward West Browning by none other than Mary Louise Spas.

❖

Judge Morschauser denied repeated attempts by persistent newspaper organizations to gain access to the Browning court documents, noting that the slush involved in the various pleadings should not be publicized until the actual testimony was heard. In a similar move, he refused the motion of Browning's lawyers for a Bill of Particulars that would have forced Peaches, prior to the actual trial, to itemize and explain every fact to support her rather lurid counterclaim. Finally, he denied Henry Epstein's request to conduct a pre-trial examination of Edward Browning to ascertain the extent of his financial holdings. "This is going to be a trial in the country and country methods will be adopted," said Morschauser. "Carmel is a fine little town and this trial will be handled openly and with fairness to everybody concerned."

By January 24th, as the courtroom doors would close on the first day of the trial, Judge Morschauser's pre-trial attempts to preserve decorum would seem naïve.

❖

Mary Spas had been living, as before, with her parents in Astoria and had been stewing in a pot of anger since her sorry episode with Browning in 1925. She had considered bringing suit against Browning but always hesitated, fearful of the publicity that she knew such a case would generate. Enraged by what she now described as "his disgraceful articles" in the *Graphic*, however, Mary made up her mind to bring her claims.

The complaint, the contents of which were widely publicized, alleged that late one evening in August of 1925, when Mary was staying with Browning at the Kew Gardens Inn, she was aroused to find an "improperly clad" Browning in her apartment, and that he "violently laid hands upon [her], and wantonly and viciously assaulted and mauled [her]." The complaint further alleged that Mary was then locked into her apartment and was further restrained in her liberties so as to become a virtual prisoner. Browning, the complaint charged, later took a revolver from his pocket, pointed it at Mary, and declared that he would kill her and her parents should she reveal to the District Attorney investigating the adoption proceedings what had occurred in the Kew Gardens Inn apartment. Lastly, it was alleged that Browning compelled Mary Spas to sign a document at the conclusion of their adoption annulment hearing, the nature of which she was not aware. She claimed that as a result of Browning's actions she had suffered nervous shock and mental anguish and she demanded $500,000 in damages.

"I'll fight this suit to the bitter end," cried Browning. "Not one red cent will I pay Mary Louise Spas, let alone $500,000. Why, it's preposterous." Browning was outraged over the public attacks on his character and though he was already plotting a vigorous defense to the case, he sought to portray himself in the papers as the blameless and weary victim as he had so effectively done in the past. "If I live through this I shall win out, but I am very, very tired of life. I am discouraged with life," he said wearily. "Money means nothing to me. But my character is sacred and by Heaven I'll fight for that! . . . [A]s there is a God in Heaven I am innocent of all their accusations. Can I say more?"

As Browning's legal problems began to accumulate, so did his level of panic. The court system was not foreign to him and the process did not intimidate him, but the attacks by Peaches and now Mary Louise Spas were personal and went to the essence of his character. He began to lose weight and his moods became more erratic than ever. His temper flared and his demeanor was visibly glum. He announced that his Christmas had been ruined and that his plans to outfit the poor children of the city with new clothing had to be cancelled because of his legal woes. He was clearly bending under the strain and the tension was beginning to take its toll. What Edward Browning didn't know was that he had yet further unpleasant surprises ahead.

When apprised of Browning's new legal problems with Mary Spas, Peaches was overjoyed. "Maybe people will believe me now," she said. And then, like a child competing for the best summer vacation tale in school, she added, "Wait until all my story comes out at my separation trial. . . . Mary's experiences with Mr. Browning don't begin to compare with mine."

What was at stake for Peaches and Daddy Browning was nothing short of their financial and social survival. Each understood the huge sums of money in play and the ruin to both reputation and credibility that could result from their now infamous hostilities. They knew that they would be defined for the rest of their lives by the outcome of the next several months. They were, quite simply, fighting for their place in history.

Browning and his retinue leaving the courthouse.

CHAPTER XVI

BROWNING V. BROWNING

> *"I do now solemnly and deliberately state to this Court that I have been a true and loyal wife to this plaintiff throughout the period of our marital life."*
>
> —Affidavit of FRANCES HEENAN BROWNING
> November 1, 1926

> *"The case, therefore, depends entirely upon the credibility of the parties to the action and their testimony must be weighed with the greatest care."*
>
> —JUSTICE ALBERT H.F. SEEGER
> Browning v. Browning, 220 N.Y.S. 651, 1927

A PELTING RAIN ON DECEMBER 31ST, 1926 DID LITTLE TO DAMPEN THE holiday spirits of New Yorkers as the typical throng made its way to Times Square to usher in the New Year. "Parties Merry and Wet," reported the *New York Times*, which went on to lament twenty-three persons who were admitted to Bellevue hospital "pepped up" at the festivities on the forbidden "doctored liquor." One thousand extra foot-police tried in vain to disentangle the city's worst traffic jam ever recorded, while revelers bearing horns, rattlers, and feather-tipped canes poured from hotels and theaters and tussled quite literally into waiting taxis to make their way to the bustling celebration. The Midtown district was thus overcome by one of the "greatest outturnings" the city had ever witnessed, as the rollicking mob roared its welcome to what would later become known as "The Year the World Went Mad."

John Mack was not in the mood for celebration on that New Years Eve. Though he had attended an early dinner on the town with his wife, she could see that his mind was a thousand miles away and when he

John E. Mack, circa 1930

suggested that they forgo their later plans she smiled and agreed. A few weeks earlier, Mack had been recruited by Francis Dale to act as Edward Browning's trial counsel, and the task was proving to be a monumental one.

The tall and gangly Mack, who looked more like a southern states-man than a Manhattan litigator, deprecatingly described himself as a "farmer who dabbled in the law." Though he was often seen sporting a Civil War-era string tie and a Texas crew-cut, those who opposed him in a courtroom quickly learned not to be deceived by his country lawyer appearance. He was a capable and fearless trial lawyer with an impressive record of success.

With the intensity and purpose that would become the hallmark of his career, John Mack cut his teeth in the law as a two-term district attorney and became highly skilled and well connected in the New York political arena. He was widely credited with personally persuading a young charismatic lawyer by the name of Franklin Delano Roosevelt to enter his first political campaign in 1910. Later, Mack would deliver FDR's nomination speech for the presidency of the United States at the Democratic National Convention in Chicago.

Having entered a law partnership with Charles Morschauser, the brother of Judge Joseph Morschauser, Mack became a well-known litigator in New York, representing several high profile clients who, in turn, brought notoriety and success to the practice. When Francis Dale prevailed upon the measured and precise Mack to represent Daddy Browning in his separation trial, it was an instant boost for Browning's cause.

As 1927 began, however, the details of the case that John Mack had now accepted worried him almost as much as they worried his new client. With the overload of publicity that Daddy Browning and his odd state of affairs now commanded, how, Mack pondered, could he ensure that his client would receive justice with impartiality? It was a question that would haunt him throughout the trial.

❖

Peaches and Daddy and their respective attorneys contested virtually every preliminary aspect of the separation case. There was agreement on nothing, not even the location of the proceedings. Daddy had filed his claim in Putnam County, while Peaches had filed her counterclaim in Westchester County. Neither appeared willing to transfer their side of the matter into the other's tribunal, and neither would waver as to form of trial. In a negotiated accord brokered by Judge Morschauser, it was finally stipulated that the trial would be conducted in a rare bifurcated fashion, split between the two locations—Browning's claim to be heard in Carmel and Peaches' in White Plains.

The one thing that both parties *would* ultimately agree upon was that neither could take the chance on a jury. They reasoned that the pool of potential jurors for the case had been so thoroughly polluted by the very public charges and countercharges levied by and against each of the parties that no prospective juror could realistically be chosen who had not previously decreed either of the parties to be hero or villain. A jury trial was simply out of the question. The final determination of the fate of Peaches and Daddy would rest, therefore, with the Justice of the Supreme Court of New York, who with the remainder of the legal entourage, would be forced to travel the snow-covered roadways between Carmel and White Plains to adjudicate the destiny of this troubled marriage. The trial was set to begin on January 24, 1927, in the picturesque town of Carmel, New York.

Smarting from the devastating success of the Brownings' firsthand accounts in the *Graphic*, the *Daily Mirror* pounced again. In another biting series of articles, which began in the January 3rd edition under the first page headline of *BROWNING'S CULT,* the paper claimed to be "telling the truth about Edward West Browning's relations with the little girl members of a high school sorority."

The self-confessed basis of the series was a chain of affidavits acquired from investigators retained by Peaches for use in her upcoming trial. Through a list of unnamed sources, the *Mirror* denounced Browning as "the high priest of a 'cuddle cult'" and accused him of a long course of "spooning parties" and of kissing and petting young girls in the back of his Rolls Royce. On one occasion, claimed the article, "Browning 'petted' five little girls on a single automobile ride, the girls sharing his caresses apparently without jealousy." The *Mirror* could not cajole a comment from Henry Epstein, who bristled at the series, but the ever-attentive Vincent Pisarra was quoted in the paper as having been consulted on the matter, and was apparently adding the *Mirror's* findings to his ever-growing file against Browning. Stating the obvious and surely expecting another lawsuit, the *Mirror* observed, "Mr. Browning will probably not appreciate this series of stories."

❖

Whether it derived from a sense of legal obligation or perhaps as a sober and intelligent act of avoidance, Judge Morschauser, the brother of John Mack's law partner, recused himself as the presiding justice on the Browning case and enthusiastically passed that honor to Judge Albert H.F. Seeger, whose upcoming docket just happened to have been clear. A rugged and vigorous sportsman, the iron-gray Seeger was well known for his arduous work ethic, his enthusiastic love of life, and his robust sense of humor. Seeger would call upon each of these qualities in the coming weeks.

Prior to his judgeship, Seeger maintained a law practice in Orange County, New York and employed several young law clerks in his office. A favorite yarn in the area legal community recounted one afternoon when Seeger departed the office early leaving his clerks to mind things. The clerks, not expecting Seeger to return, invited many of the local law students to the office for an afternoon of smoking and idleness. In fact,

Seeger did return and upon viewing the spectacle inquired wryly, "to what good fortune do I owe the visit of so many young people?" The students, all at a loss for words, shifted uncomfortably about and glanced nervously at each other, until finally one young student bowed his head and answered, "to your absence sir." Seeger hired the boy the following week for his truthfulness.

Another episode from his tenure as a New York Supreme Court Justice also attests to his wit and judicial temperment. Seeger was called upon to rule on a dispute between contestants in a Miss Yonkers beauty pageant. In denying the petition of the alternate based on questions as to the actual age of the winner, Seeger ruled, "Motion denied regretfully, without costs: *no taxes on beauty*." The case that Judge Seeger now found himself at the center of would test his keen sense of humor like never before.

In his first official act as presiding justice of the Browning case, Judge Seeger issued an order banning cameras from the courtroom during the trial. He was sending a message, he hoped, that *this* trial was not to become the media sensation that he had seen others become. Cameras or not, Judge Seeger's message would be embraced by few.

❖

Daddy Browning, no doubt, did not appreciate the *Mirror's* attempt to interject itself into the dialogue of the case, nor its blatant effort to sway the results of the proceedings against him. Perhaps absorbed in the rigors of litigation or his myriad other exhausting problems, Browning did not sue the *Mirror* again for libel. In point of fact, it appeared that the public paid little attention to the *Mirror's* series, preferring instead to focus on the upcoming trial rather than to wallow in unproven matters of the past.

One old friend of Edward Browning did, however, read the articles with engrossed preoccupation, and for good measure she cut them out and pasted them to her cupboard. Her name was Renee Shapiro and just days before the scheduled start of Browning's separation trial she brought a lawsuit against the man with whom she had conspired three and a half years earlier to bring down Charles Wilen and Nellie Adele Browning.

The suit alleged that in the course of her dealings with Edward Browning, he had attacked and assaulted her, causing the usual and requisite suffering of mind and body. She claimed $100,000 in damages.

Francis Dale characterized the claim as another "ridiculous attempt to gain sentiment favorable to the suit brought by Mrs. Frances (Peaches) Browning." John Mack could only shake his head and hope that Judge Seeger did not read the papers.

❖

For weeks the peaceful and bucolic village of Carmel had prepared for the onslaught that would accompany the Peaches and Daddy separation trial. Every detail of preparedness touching nearly every citizen of this small country town would be carefully considered in an effort to manage the rigors of the expected invasion. Six special wires were connected for Western Union operators, and several additional trunk lines bound for the city were installed by New York Telephone Company. Janitors of the County Courthouse dusted off the old oil painting of *Mary and Her Little Lamb* that adorned the lobby, while the Carmel Board of Supervisors placed an additional $20,000 of fire insurance and $100,000 indemnity on the building in anticipation of the increased risks and liabilities that the trial presented. New benches and chairs were squeezed into the recesses of the courtroom, expanding its capacity from two to three hundred, and seats were allotted by Sheriff Stevens to each of the forty-plus newspapermen covering the trial, as was a stern warning to heed Judge Seeger's prohibition of cameras in the building.

In an effort to avoid arousing the interest of the village minors, the topic of the Browning case was broached at none of Carmel's five churches on the Sunday morning before the trial. The headmaster of the Drew Ladies' Seminary issued orders that none of its 125 female students would be allowed off campus during the trial for fear that some unspeakable morsel of forbidden testimony would reach young and tender ears.

Every available hotel and boarding house room in the snow-clad village had been reserved far in advance, and to the dismay of the many reporters, photographers, and curious spectators who had made their way to the tiny seat of Putnam County, prices for whatever rooms that did remain had been driven skyward. Even a bewildered Judge Seeger found that the only room available to him contained three beds and if he wanted to stay there alone, he'd have to pay the price for all three.

The village of Carmel boasted a population of about eight hundred and was no stranger to visitors from the city. For years, Lake Gleneida, located in the center of the small hamlet, provided a summer respite to vacationing New Yorkers anxious to flee the steaming heat of the city streets. In January of 1927, however, the lake was covered with a crystal glaze. The country road that meandered from its icy shores was dotted with white colonial houses, each trailing a plume of fireplace smoke that filled the streets with the scent of smoldering pine.

Carmel's peaceful aura notwithstanding, plenty of residents welcomed the Peaches and Daddy spectacle with curious and open arms. Finally, inhabitants of this tiny farming community would pick up their morning newspapers, sip their home-brewed coffee, and cast their proud eyes upon nationwide stories beginning with the phrase "Dateline Carmel." On the day before the trial was set to start, correspondent Damon Runyon, whose coverage of the case was carried by the wire services, aptly summed up the mood: "Anyway, Carmel is all agog—in fact, I might say it is all agoggogga—over the events of tomorrow. The court house is in apple pie order, the telegraph wires are tuned in to the Queen's taste, and your correspondent's typewriter is well oiled."

❖

On the morning of January 24, 1927, Daddy Browning's peacock blue Rolls Royce rumbled down the snow covered Main Street—the *only* street in downtown Carmel—and settled before the grand façade of the Putnam County Courthouse. The square, white-frame colonial structure was built in 1814 in the Greek Revival style and renovated in the early 1920s after a fire damaged a portion of the building. Great pillars stood prominently at the front of the two-story structure and two sets of four symmetrically aligned windows, shielded on the interior by white dotted Swiss curtains, flanked the heavy wooden front doors.

Inside the newly remodeled second-floor courtroom, two large wooden desks lay at the foot of the ornately carved judge's bench and were surrounded by an oak-grain bar beyond which only lawyers and witnessed were permitted. New green benches augmented the seating capacity and the smell of fresh touch-up paint was evident throughout. Though the ceilings were low, it did not negate the majestic quality of the courtroom which, according to at least one observer, "could rival that of many a large city."

Early on the first day of the trial, a crowd of three hundred curious spectators gathered outside the courthouse while hundreds more scrambled to claim seats inside. A wall of photographers that had massed along the steps leading to the building snapped to attention at the first sight of Browning's celebrated car and the crowd squinted in the blinding glare of sunlight reflecting harshly off the fallen snows of Main Street.

As he stepped from the rear of the limousine, a cheer rose from the horde and a stern faced Browning paused and stiffly posed for photographers, smiling only when asked. He wore a dark blue business suit lined with white pinstripes and a black overcoat edged in velvet. In his right hand was a back leather case with the initials *EWB* broadly painted in scarlet on the front. Francis Dale and John Mack were already inside the courthouse joined by four other lawyers that made up Browning's legal team. Browning made his way into the building and was quickly ushered into a small sheriff's office on the first floor where he huddled with his lawyers. He hardly noticed the arrival of Peaches.

The trains were running a bit late from the city, but as the 9:15 lurched into Carmel station a small crowd gathered. Peaches Browning, accompanied by Carolyn Heenan and Henry Epstein, hurriedly made her way from the train and into a waiting taxi. Attired in a blue dress, a close-fitting matching hat, and a sable coat decorated with orchids, a beleaguered Peaches managed only a forced smile as her attorney gently shuttled her through the swarm toward the County Courthouse. The diamond pin that she wore on her lapel sparkled in the bright sunlit morning, as did the diamond pendant about her neck. In sharp contrast to Daddy's warm reception, the spectators quietly stared as the trio politely posed for the photographers and then disappeared through the courtroom doors.

Epstein hurried his young client beyond the sheriff's office where Daddy and his entourage conferred, and up the stairs to their place at the defendant's table in the crowded courtroom. Peaches was visibly frightened and did all she could to hold back her tears.

Judge Seeger briskly entered the courtroom from the adjoining rear chambers and took his place on the same bench where the Revolutionary War patriot Enoch Crosby, immortalized by James Fenimore Cooper's *The Spy*, sat as justice of the peace in Special Sessions. Seeger scanned the overflowing courtroom and glanced once more at the relevant pleadings of the court file. A crowd of over three hundred spectators and newspapermen found seats in the now buzzing gallery while an additional hundred stood anxiously against the side and back walls.

A moment later, Daddy Browning, surrounded by his crack legal team, was propelled into the courtroom like a prizefighter. He held his fedora in his hand as he walked, his dark eyes carefully avoiding those of his opponent. A burst of cheering and applause rose from the back of the room and quickly spread forward. The eyes of every person in the gallery fixed upon the man they had come to see. The show had begun. Daddy Browning turned slightly, and with a robust smile bowed like an actor in a Shakespearean play.

Judge Seeger slammed his gavel on the bench. "If there are any more outbursts such as that, the courtroom will be cleared!" As the judge spoke, Browning's cunning eyes met with those of his young wife for the first time since the previous October, and then he grinned. Peaches quickly turned away and slumped in her chair. Large tears welled up in her eyes and rolled down her flushed cheeks as she fumbled about her handbag for a handkerchief. Carolyn, who was seated beside her, attempted to console her daughter. Though Daddy turned away, the grin remained on his lips.

As the court came to order, Henry Epstein preemptively rose and in a low, resolute tone requested the Judge's indulgence of a preliminary matter of business. The trial and all of its proceedings, he said, should be conducted in secrecy away from the public and the press. He argued that the nature of the testimony that he intended to offer in support of his client's claim would be of such a nature as to make its public airing inadvisable. He stated further that an open and public trial might affect witnesses' abilities to testify truthfully. In reality, of course, Epstein was attempting to spare his client the shame of seeing the humiliating details of her marriage smeared across the front pages of American newspapers.

To the surprise of nearly everyone in the courtroom, John Mack then rose in agreement to the motion, claiming that public decency demanded that the details of the proceedings be suppressed. Browning himself had personally pushed hard for an open trial and the complete vindication that he believed it would bring. He reasoned that since he had been so lambasted by Peaches in the newspapers, a public trial would be the only way for him to clear his name and restore his reputation. In the end, however, he was persuaded by his counsel that the risks of a public hearing were simply too great and that Epstein's motion should not be opposed.

Judge Seeger considered the plea. "Ordinarily," he began, "I would grant such a motion at once," adding that he had in fact received correspondence from a "women's club" imploring him to keep the trial private. "But it seems to me," he continued, "that heretofore no effort to avoid publicity has been seen in this case." Then, with a hint of sarcasm in his voice, he asked rhetorically, "Why all the secrecy at this stage of the game?" He informed the gathering that he would reserve judgment on the matter until the following day, but that this day's business should proceed as planned. An audible sigh of relief could be heard from the enrapt gallery.

❖

Having elected to dispense with opening statements, Judge Seeger requested that John Mack proceed directly to his first witness. Mack's sole objective during the Putnam County Court phase of the trial would be a relatively simple one: to make out a *prima facie* case of abandonment. He merely needed to prove that Peaches left Daddy Browning, without any intention to return. To accomplish this, Mack first called to the stand one Edward P. Kearney, Browning's chauffer, who had also been given the charge of driving Peaches and her mother from store to store and event to event during the short marriage.

Kearney testified that he was actually employed by John S. Guishaw of New York, who, to the astonishment of the murmuring crowd, was the owner of Browning's trademark—and, apparently, leased—Rolls Royce. Directing Kearney's attention to the events of October 2, Mack then asked him to describe what he had witnessed. The stocky coachman shifted with unease in his chair and stated that on the day in question he had met the Brownings and Mrs. Heenan at the Kew Gardens Inn and had been directed to transport Daddy Browning to his downtown office. As Browning left the car, Carolyn then instructed Kearney to return to the Inn, and upon arrival she further told him to bring the two empty trunks at the rear of the car into the apartment. He testified that Peaches and her mother then filled each of the trunks with clothing, jewelry, and other women's wearables from the apartment and exited the building, each holding extra coats over their arms.

"Did they leave anything?" Mack asked.

"I don't think they left a thing," responded Kearney.

"Did she say anything as she left?"

"Yes, she said 'Money isn't everything. I am sick and tired of it all.'"

After a brief and rather ineffective cross-examination by Henry Epstein, the witness stepped down from the box amidst a smattering of applause from the gallery. As he returned to his seat, Kearney shot an inquisitive glance to Daddy Browning, who nodded approvingly.

John Mack then called a bald man named John P. Gorman to the stand. He identified himself as one of several secretaries employed by Edward Browning. In a short inquiry, Gorman testified that he had been asked by Browning to listen in on another extension to a telephone conversation that Browning had with Carolyn Heenan shortly after October 2nd. Browning, it came out, often had his employees monitor otherwise private calls for the very purpose that Gorman, now sworn as a witness, clearly understood.

"What did you hear?" asked Mack, without objection from Peaches' counsel.

"I heard Mrs. Heenan say, 'You can't talk to Peaches. My daughter is through with you, Mr. Browning, and she is not coming back.'" With a pleased look, Mack stated that he had nothing further of the witness.

Again, Henry Epstein spent little time on cross-examination and upon Gorman's departure from the stand; John Mack announced to the court that the Plaintiff rested. Epstein then made the obligatory motion to dismiss that he knew would be denied, followed by a request that the trial be adjourned to the following day at 10:00 am in the Westchester County Courthouse in White Plains. Having previously agreed that Peaches' defense and counterclaims would be proffered in White Plains, Mack nodded and Judge Seeger granted the request and closed the proceedings amidst audible groans of disappointment from the crowd. Both Peaches and Daddy peered quizzically at their respective counsel and each was gently reassured that all was in order.

The first day of the trial had lasted no more than an hour, but Daddy Browning, through his counsel, had set forth sufficient evidence to prove that Peaches had abandoned him within the meaning of New York law. The village of Carmel, and virtually everyone else who had followed the case, was totally dissatisfied with what they had heard on day one—or more accurately stated, what they hadn't heard. There had been no steamy testimony at all. The public and the press began to worry that the case would not live up to its grand advanced billing. Damon Runyon wrote of the proceedings at Carmel, "I must warn Daddy and Peaches that the great American Public will not tolerate many more pale performances such as they gave this morning."

Among his many idiosyncrasies, Browning would become a raw foods enthusiast, which earned him the name the "Grass-eater." In the court proceedings, Peaches would accuse him of being "sexually abnormal."

CHAPTER XVII

A MAN OF PECULIAR CHARACTER, TASTES, AND IDEAS

> *"Your correspondent's manly cheeks are still*
> *suffused with blushes as he sits down to write*
> *of a few peeks into the bridal chamber of dear*
> *old Daddy Browning and his Peaches."*
>
> —DAMON RUNYON
> January 25, 1927

NEWSPAPER ORGANIZATIONS ACROSS AMERICA HELD THEIR COLLECTIVE breath as Judge Seeger deliberated whether to exclude them from the remainder of the Peaches and Daddy separation trial. Press treatment of the parties, meanwhile, had turned decidedly scoffing.

"Peaches should diet or exercise, or something, to get rid of her surplus flesh," wrote the *Daily Mirror.* The *New York World* described her as "an overripe girl of fleshy build and doll-like, almost expressionless features . . ." and later, as "the tenement girl bride." A news writer for *Universal Service* wired the following description of Daddy Browning to papers throughout the nation: "This flabby, gray-haired, half-century gay Lothario has put himself over with the multitude in a way that is worth $50,000 a year to any theatrical manager...The cheeks hang like those of a walrus. The mouth is full, loose and heavy. The eyes pop when he is disturbed and the pouches under them puff out . . . His hands apparently have not had intimate relations with soap and water for a long time."

Emile Gauvreau, however, had no axe to grind. Unlike the embittered *Mirror* and several of the writers for the news wires, Gauvreau was not interested in hurling insults at the parties or inciting public opinion for or against the Brownings. His primary concern in covering the trial was to capture, in the most uncensored and sensational manner possible, every nuance and detail of the case, with the sole objective of—what else?—increasing the circulation of the *Graphic*.

As the Brownings commenced their courtroom tussles, Emile Gauvreau unleashed his first composograph of Peaches and Daddy to the glee of delighted readers. In a variety of ingeniously positioned photographs and superimposed faces, a defensive Daddy Browning, dressed in formal bedchamber garb, is seen dodging a pillow hurled by the pajama-clad Peaches, who kneels on the mattress of a four-post bed in the imagined boudoir of the feuding couple. For the first time in history, readers of a newspaper were allowed inside the marital bedroom of a man and his wife.

Gauvreau cared little if the judge excluded the press from the courtroom or not. Whatever details he lacked he would get directly from the parties and the rest he would surmise. Emile Gauvreau's graphic depictions in the coming days of the clash between Peaches and Daddy would be described as "the most daring that have ever been seen in New York Journalism."

❖

On January 25, the scene of the separation trial shifted from the farmlands of Carmel to the crowded city streets of White Plains, New York. The fourth rendition of the Westchester County Courthouse had been completed just two years earlier and was widely recognized as one of the most modern and efficient government buildings of its day. Spanning nearly two hundred feet along the city block of Main Street, the courthouse rose seven stories from a concrete foundation. The building bore a slight resemblance to the *Lincoln Memorial*—it was faced with white granite and twelve fluted Ionic columns, each nearly forty feet in height, placed evenly along the front of the second story. Travertine marble encased the interior walls, and a central rotunda rising the full height of the building was brightened by a glass-covered skylight.

Four ornately decorated courtrooms, paneled in quartered oak and equipped with the most modern lighting and acoustical garnishes, were arranged on the second and fourth floors of the building, and were accessed by oversized stairways of Napoleon Grey marble. From the steps of the original incarnation of the Westchester Courthouse was heard the first reading in New York of the Declaration of Independence on July 11, 1776, making White Plains the "birthplace of New York State."

Early in the day, voracious crowds began to mass along the city streets outside the white marble steps of the courthouse. Skittish policemen struggled in vain to keep jammed motor traffic and trolley cars from stalling, while hordes of the curious encircled the area. At the first sight of Daddy Browning's car, photographers climbed atop the mired vehicles for a clearer vantage, and cheers went up from the crowd as he stepped out of the Rolls Royce. The brightness of Daddy's flushed face was exceeded only by the brilliant colors of his extraordinarily wide necktie. "Wait a minute boys," he said with a broad smile. He then removed his hat, fished through his pocket for a comb, and ran it though the thinning locks of his white hair. Thusly prepared, he gazed lovingly into the cameras and posed for each and every one of them.

Judge Seeger had clearly come to a decision on the secrecy of the trial. The gallery was crammed solid. Those who couldn't find seats stood three to four deep along the walls, while others scrambled atop radiators and window ledges. Upon observing the scene, Judge Seeger admonished the horde that they occupied their makeshift perches at their own risk. It was reported that in the mania to gain seating in the courtroom, some frenzied mothers had actually abandoned crying babies in their carriages outside of the building. Damon Runyon said cynically, "We have the great moral spectacle in this modern civilization of a legal hearing involving a gray-haired old wowser and a child-wife attracting more attention than the League of Nations."

Prior to the commencement of testimony, Judge Seeger affirmed that the hearings would, in fact, be conducted openly and in the view of the public. Citing the policy that legal proceedings should be held open to scrutiny, especially in cases of great public interest, he posited that to deviate from that policy in this case would create a suspicion that the parties were being favored because of their wealth and prominence. He expressed doubt that the Brownings could be prejudiced by an open hearing, considering the amount of detail that they had already submitted to the newspapers, and he took issue with Henry Epstein's argument that the presence of the press would discourage witnesses from truthfully testifying. To the contrary, he affirmed that witnesses would be "less likely to swear falsely when they knew that what they were saying was being taken down and made known to the world." "Taking all things into consideration," he concluded, "I think it is better for these parties and the public that the hearings should be open to the public."

Albert Seeger was guided by principled common sense. He concluded that simple *justice* required an open hearing—and he viewed that justice as poetic. Motivated not only by the rule of law, but also, perhaps, by a modicum of spite, he reasoned that the Brownings, who had daily volunteered their lives to the press, should not now be permitted to exclude that press for their own selfish gain. He would not allow these individuals, in the name of money and power, to obtain the benefits of publicity without sharing in its burden.

"HOWEVER," Seeger cautioned, "I intend to make a ruling that young girls shall not be permitted to enter the courtroom, and the officers will see to it that that rule is enforced." With that, the doors to the courtroom were swung open and several adolescent females—perhaps older than Peaches herself—were led from the proceedings, protesting their age with every step.

In all the commotion, few noticed as Peaches, Carolyn Heenan, and Henry Epstein discretely slipped into a side door of the courthouse. Peaches, wearing the same blue dress and matching hat as the previous day in Carmel, took her place with her lawyer at the Defendant's table and readied herself for the grueling day of testimony that she knew lay ahead.

❖

Henry Epstein had met with his client at various times prior to the trial to organize his case and to prepare her for her coming testimony. As he sat with Peaches in his office, his mind was constantly evaluating her as a person and as a witness. She was most assuredly mature for her young age and she could articulate her thoughts in a clear enough manner. But would she present herself as a credible witness, and, perhaps more importantly, could she arouse the sympathies of the trial judge?

She was visibly unnerved about the trial and she was easily provoked to tears. Epstein knew that a show of emotion on the witness stand, in a case such as this, was not necessarily a bad thing, but he worried whether she could control that emotion and express the details of her story. He knew, though, that despite the risks she had no choice. Since Peaches was the sole witness to many of the events that Epstein sought to prove at trial, she was indispensable to the case and regardless of her tender age and frayed nerves, she had to testify.

The demeanor and believability of his client was only part of Henry Epstein's problem. The actual *facts* of the case, as applied to the law, presented his real challenge. The settled law in New York stated that a wife was not bound to remain with her husband when his treatment of her was such as to "impair her health, safety, and peace of mind." If she left her husband under these circumstances, she could not be found guilty of abandonment. Guided by this principle, it was Epstein's intention to portray Daddy Browning as an unbalanced and deranged personality whose actions drove his client to the brink of physical and emotion breakdown. He had to prove that Peaches was left with no choice but to leave her husband.

❖

At trial, John Mack would undoubtedly allege that whatever conditions Peaches was shown to be suffering from existed well before her marriage to Edward Browning. To refute this, Henry Epstein called Peaches' family physician, Dr. Edward S. Cockle, as his first witness.

In a short series of questions, Epstein developed that Cockle had treated Peaches prior to her marriage to Browning and that he noted no physical or nervous conditions at that time. He stated that in 1924 he removed the girl's tonsils and found her to be in such good health that he opted to perform the procedure under local anesthesia only. He then testified that when consulted at a later date following the girl's marriage, he found her to be suffering from anxiety and nervousness. Epstein had thus produced at least some evidence that whatever ailments Peaches endured did not preexist her marriage.

As Doctor Cockle stepped away from the box and returned to his seat, Henry Epstein whispered earnestly to Peaches, "Just pretend it's a conversation between the two of us." He then rose to his feet and called Frances Heenan Browning to the witness stand.

❖

She rose timidly and made her way to the box at the left of the judge's bench, managing a nod and a weak smile to Judge Seeger as she passed. Then swearing on the Holy Bible that the testimony she was about to give would be "the truth, the whole truth, and nothing but the truth," she was seated.

From the gallery, the unmistakable click of camera shutters was heard, and an annoyed Judge Seeger commanded the court deputies to confiscate the offending cameras and remove the photographers for the duration of the trial. Written accounts were acceptable, but Seeger would hold strong against photographs. Even as three news photographers were led from the courtroom, the shutters of other cameras unambiguously announced their flagrant contempt of the judge's orders.

Henry Epstein paused at the table for a moment to look at his notes. Then he approached the witness. Carolyn Heenan, seated in the front row of benches, shuddered as the crowded gallery hushed and leaned forward almost in unison. Epstein calmed his client with a reassuring smile and began, "Mrs. Browning, you are the defendant in this action?"

"I am," she responded.

A series of preliminary questions followed to acquaint the court with the witness—and to acquaint the witness with the process. Address. Age. And then slowly, deliberately, Henry Epstein guided Peaches back to her initial meeting with Edward Browning on the evening of March 5, 1926, at the Hotel McAlpin, and through the whirlwind courtship that followed. As she answered the questions, she toyed nervously with her diamond wedding band and smoothed back her blonde hair. With each passing response, however, she seemed to gather poise and confidence. One observer wrote of Peaches' testimony, "Her English was good and she surprised everyone by her choice of words and her ability to define her meaning. Only once or twice did she use a crude or slangy expression. She affected a broad accent, in which the a's rolled out with the most approved Boston value. Her voice was throaty and not unpleasant."

Having set the stage, Epstein embarked upon the task of exposing Daddy Browning's eccentric behavior and the manner in which it was revealed to Peaches. As he inquired about the various affairs that Peaches attended with Browning during their courtship, he directed Peaches' attention to the events of Saint Patrick's Day, 1926. She related that on that evening, Browning had taken her to a dance at the Majestic and then two more at the Waldorf and the Plaza. "He must have had hundreds of green handkerchiefs, which he kept pulling from his pocket, one after the other," she recalled, "and as the ladies would ask for it he would give it to them. Then, as they turned back he would pull out another one . . . It was very, very odd. He amused lots of people that way."

Epstein's inquiry then shifted to the mysterious acid attack upon Peaches and the specifics of her treatment and recovery. Though this portion of her testimony was highly anticipated, it was relatively brief and offered little in the way of explanation of just who was behind her injuries. It was shortly thereafter, she stated, that Browning proposed marriage. "I said yes. I would do anything to get of the city."

Browning's offbeat sense of humor would immediately begin to grate at Peaches' nerves. She testified that he would bring home huge boxes of very odd things, such as spoons that bent in the middle and rubber eggs and balloons and dolls and little white tablets that, when placed at the end of his lit cigar, would produce a large snowflake when he puffed on it. He used these items, Peaches lamented, in dance halls and dining rooms and would even have the trick spoons and fake eggs sent to other tables at hotel cafes during breakfast. "And was he very amused by this?" asked Epstein. "Yes," she replied, "nobody else was . . . It caused me very much embarrassment."

Peaches complained bitterly that her true desires were time and time again thwarted with Daddy's inane attempts at humor. When she asked for a pet, Browning brought home three little clay puppies and a pink frilled teddy bear, each of which Epstein marked as an exhibit and introduced as evidence. When she asked for a roadster to drive about the countryside, he bought her a toy car. "I was very much surprised because I don't play with toys any more; I thought I had gotten over that stage," she said.

When the topic turned to having children, Peaches told the court that she had expressed her loneliness to Browning and that perhaps having a baby would fill that void in her life. "Mr. Browning said he never wanted children . . . and when I told him I was so alone, I got lonely during the day, he said he would get me a Japanese princess; that they were very cheap and he could get one for almost nothing sent over from Japan . . . I could walk along the streets with her and it would make wonderful publicity, and she would be my companion." Judge Seeger hid a broad smile behind his hands and, sensing this, the gallery burst into laughter, to the delight of Daddy Browning and his lawyers. Peaches shifted uncomfortably in her seat while Carolyn glared angrily at the judge.

In an effort to further illustrate Browning's mindless and attention-craving sense of humor, Epstein then directed Peaches' testimony to the African Honking Gander episode that had so peeved the young bride.

Q. "And did he bring it into your apartment?"
A. "Yes."
Q. "Did the African Honking Gander leave the apartment clean?"
A. "Did it leave the apartment clean? No, very unclean and the chauffeur had to clean it up after."

Q. "Did [Mr. Browning] express any displeasure?"

A. "Oh no."

Q. "Did he seem to be pleased?"

A. "Yes, he thought it was funny."

Q. "Did he laugh?"

A. "Of course he laughed."

Q. "Where else did you go with Mr. Browning and the goose?"

A. "He took me to Long Beach on Sunday with the goose."

Q. "Where was the goose when you and Mr. Browning were in the car going to Long Beach?"

A. "It was in the trunk case in the back; the trunks were removed and the goose was honking in the back of the car."

Q. "You went all the way to Long Beach that way?"

A. "Yes."

The courtroom again erupted into laughter, but an undaunted Henry Epstein methodically proceeded, describing event after eccentric event, the cumulative effect of which, he hoped, would establish cruel and inhumane treatment.

Until then, Daddy Browning gazed rather mockingly at his opponent and his lips arced into a pale smile as if he were enjoying the proceedings. Enjoyment would quickly become indignation, however, as Peaches began to reveal hints of Daddy Browning's dark side.

❖

The first indication of Daddy Browning's unseemly conduct occurred early in Peaches' testimony. She stated that while they were courting, Daddy took her to see a theatrical production entitled *A Night in Paris*, which she described as "quite a nude show," and that later he brought her a book filled with pictures of nude women. This behavior, she said, continued well into their marriage.

"He used to stop at newsstands and buy all the nude magazines and bring them home."

"Did he ask you to look at them?" asked Epstein.

"Yes, he did," she answered. "I refused, because those things never interested me."

After soliciting a lengthy narrative of Peaches' wedding day, Epstein then hesitatingly turned to the events of the wedding *night*. Browning shifted uncomfortably in his seat, as did Peaches, who was now ringing her hands with tension. Epstein furrowed his brow and once again pleaded with Judge Seeger to clear the courtroom. Firm in his resolve, however, Seeger refused the plea and ordered the flustered lawyer to proceed. Epstein paused, dabbed a handkerchief to his now sweating upper lip, and stammered into the matter.

Q. "Did you have an apartment of your own with Mr. Browning that evening?"

A. "Yes, we did."

Q. "Were you physically well at this time?"

A. "No, I was not." [Affidavits submitted prior to trial stated that Peaches was menstruating at the time of her wedding night.]

Q. "Where did you undress?

A. "In the bathroom."

Q. "When you came out of the bathroom undressed, did you have on any bed clothes?"

A. "Yes. I was attired in a night gown and negligee."

Q. "Did you then go to bed?"

A. "Mr. Browning asked me if I would walk around the room without any clothes on, and when I objected he became very, very angry."

At this point in the questioning, large tears welled in Peaches' blue eyes and spilled down her cheeks. In more of a nervous reaction than actual amusement, Francis Dale, sitting at the Plaintiff's table, smiled slightly, and Peaches happened to see it. "I think if Mr. Browning's attorney finds it so terribly funny . . . !" She then buried her face in her hands and sobbed profusely.

Judge Seeger pounded his gavel upon the bench and declared a recess as uncontrollable wailing and convulsive trembling overtook the witness. Carolyn Heenan, now sobbing herself, rushed to the stand and embraced her afflicted daughter, while women in the courtroom cried in convivial sisterhood. Peaches was helped from the box and whisked into an adjoining room, where Carolyn and Henry Epstein consoled and encouraged her. Many in the courtroom starred blankly at the floor while others regarded one another with sad, uncomfortable smiles. Browning counseled with his lawyers on the turn of events.

After a few moments, Peaches was back on the stand and facing new and even more embarrassing questions.

"Did Mr. Browning seek to enter your bed?"

Peaches again appealed to Judge Seeger, who mournfully advised her that she must answer the question. In a barely audible voice, she moaned, "Oh, I can't," but after a moment of strained composure she straightened in her chair and fixed her eyes directly on Daddy Browning, who recoiled.

"Did he enter your bed?" demanded Epstein.

"He did."

Q. "What did you do?"

A. "I refused."

Q. "Did he persist?"

A. "He did."

Q. "Did you consent?"

A. "No, I did not."

Q. "And did he subsequently leave your bed?

A. "Yes; [but] he told me that Mr. Dale said that the marriage must be consummated that night, and Dale said we positively must have sex that night."

Q. "You did not have sex that night with him, did you?"

A. "No, I did not."

Peaches was already on the record with regard to her sexual relations with Browning. In her pretrial affidavit of November 1, 1926, she stated: "That my best recollection is that my husband had sexual intercourse with me every night from April 10th, 1926, when we were married except at such times when I was seriously ill or unwell. That I never refused him intercourse unless it was rendered impossible by reason of my physical condition." When Peaches did refuse intimacies, she claimed that Browning became hot-tempered and querulous.

According to Peaches, Daddy Browning's strange requests that she parade before him in an unclothed state persisted. On a regular basis, she declared, her husband walked around the rooms of their abode naked and implored her to do the same. She testified that at various times he insisted that she present herself at the breakfast table unclad, and when she refused, he pinched and scolded her to such an extent that on one occasion she finally acquiesced, to her utter shame and embarrassment.

There is no question that Epstein's allusions to Daddy's desire to view his wife in the nude were designed to show an aberrant side of the man's personality and, considered in the context of the era, such a tactic would, no doubt, succeed. Add to this equation the constant goading and teasing of Daddy Browning (as testified to by Peaches), and we have the appearance of a man foisting himself on an unwilling and innocent child. By today's standards the act of posing nude before one's husband may not be considered out of the mainstream. In the days of Peaches and Daddy, however, such an act was, perhaps, more likely to have been met with disapproval. Even if it did occur, it was not something that would be spoken freely of—especially where the wife was only fifteen years of age and thirty-seven years younger than her husband.

Calmly and deliberately, Henry Epstein questioned Peaches regarding the peculiar conduct of Daddy Browning. He recognized that no one occurrence made or broke his case, but that each in total demonstrated a systematic pattern of abuse. He thought surely Judge Seeger must come to realize that the sensibilities of any wife, let alone a sixteen-year-old child-bride, would be offended by this unrelenting cruelty.

And on with his direct examination of Peaches went Henry Epstein.

❖

"Did he do anything else . . . that caused you any annoyance?"

Again, Peaches spoke of Browning's affinity for French magazines and pictures of nude women, but now she focused her testimony on none other than the self-confessed High Priestess of Oom, Marian Dockerill. In a tone of complete bewilderment, Peaches swore that Browning brought home many pictures of the "Love Cult" queen in various stages of undress and that he persistently demanded that Peaches strike a relationship with the woman. Though Browning was clearly infatuated with Dockerill, Peaches stated that she did not share her husband's fascination and had no desire to associate with the cult woman.

At that point Henry Epstein pulled a closed folder from within his briefcase and approached the witness stand. Placing a photograph of an unclad Marian Dockerill before Peaches and asking Judge Seeger, "to please keep this from the public eye," Epstein asked the witness if that was one of the photographs that Browning brought home to her. "There were many like that," Peaches replied matter-of-factly.

❖

Focusing in on the practical hardships of her life, Epstein then questioned Peaches about her husband's love for publicity and the daily suffering that it caused her. She described how constant crowds of people made it impossible for her to come and go unmolested between shopping tours and luncheon dates. "We always had a terrific crowd around the place, because everybody seemed to recognize the car, which always stood in front of the store. We were pushed and shoved."

She testified that unrelenting news reporters were a fact of life from the beginning and that Daddy Browning always instigated their appearance. Browning, she claimed, relished the attention and was at his happiest when surrounded by adoring crowds and clamoring newspapermen. He would never allow two parcels to be placed in the same box so as to give the appearance to reporters and photographers that their purchases were larger than they actually were.

On one occasion, Peaches recalled, the crowds had made it nearly impossible for her to receive treatment for her acid burns. Such a large horde of photographers and admirers had followed her to the Fifth Avenue Hospital that they trampled the grounds and the hospital refused her admittance. When she was finally able to obtain treatment from a city doctor, she said, Browning ranted and raved about the size of his bill and refused to pay it.

While she was confined to her home recovering from her burns, it was Browning, she insisted, that called a bevy of photographers to her bedside, to take pictures of the immense Easter Egg that he had presented to her. "I refused first," said Peaches, "but he was very persistent." After the marriage, Peaches testified, reporters had actually taken up residence at the Hotel Gramatan to cover the couple's every movement at a moment's notice. When confronted with various published pictures taken of her during that period, Peaches admitted that she had posed for many of them but insisted that each was at the request of her indefatigable husband.

Peaches repeatedly expressed distaste for the interviews and first person stories that appeared in the *Graphic* and other New York tabloids all at the behest, she claimed, of Daddy Browning. In particular, she protested the story printed under her husband's name in the *Mirror*, entitled, *Why I Married Peaches*, in which Browning claimed that *she* had proposed to him.

"Was it true that you proposed to Mr. Browning?" asked Epstein.

"No, it was not true."

Even the *Peaches Honeymoon Diary* series that ran in the *Graphic* shortly after her marriage was initiated by her husband, complained Peaches. In all respects, she represented herself as an unwilling participant in Daddy Browning's insatiable quest for publicity.

Thus far, Henry Epstein was pleased with the examination of his client. She had managed to articulate herself in a credible manner and with just enough emotional tilt to arouse sympathy. She had endured the portion of the testimony that she had most dreaded and she presented herself well as the victim of an unrelenting, albeit rather bumbling, monster.

Rubber eggs and nude magazines, however, would get Henry Epstein only so far. He would now have to show that Browning's actions went well beyond playful annoyance, and into the realm of madness.

❖

The fairytale Browning union, as choreographed by Daddy in mainstream American media, was filled with nothing but happiness and love. The reality, as Peaches now put forth, was dramatically different.

As direct examination continued, Epstein skillfully led his client to an occasion early in the marriage when the couple was spending time at the Cold Spring residence. Peaches testified shakily that Browning's demands for her to walk around nude had become more and more insistent.

This time Browning's insistence turned to rage. "I started to cry, and I was sitting on the side of the bed, and he grabbed ahold of the back of my neck and pushed me to the floor and said 'Boo' in a very loud voice, which frightened me very much, and I screamed."

Browning always kept the bedroom door locked and bolted, she said, and upon hearing the screams, Carolyn and her friend Catherine Mayer came running up the stairs, pounded on the door and demanded that it be opened. When Browning did open the door, an hysterical Peaches came bursting out and into her mother's arms. After a night of uncontrolled sobbing, she returned to Browning's bedroom at the persuasion of her mother, only to find him compulsively pacing the floors and chain smoking cigarettes. Browning hadn't slept a wink.

The abuse continued. The same repugnant requests persisted virtually every night and through their honeymoon journey into the Adirondacks. Peaches testified that on one occasion on their honeymoon, Browning locked her in the hotel room and refused to let her out when she refused his requests. She stated that throughout the marriage, he repeatedly forced her to view suggestive photographs of Marian Dockerill and other nude women, and when she declined to do so, he became enraged and forced the pictures into her face. In her pretrial affidavit, Peaches articulated her growing revulsion of Daddy Browning:

> At certain times Mr. Browning's actions when we were about to retire to bed shocked me into a state of hysteria. He would approach me nude and solicit physical contact unnatural and unknown to me. I could do nothing but turn away with horrible nausea, causing me to become very ill. I never consented to nor permitted such contacts. These actions together with his acts of cruelty and his desires and all of the incidents of our life heretofore have indicated to me and have convinced me Mr. Browning is sexually abnormal; that he is suffering from some incurable neurotic sexual troubles . . .

❖

The question of what "unnatural" acts Peaches Browning might have been referring to in her affidavit is an interesting one. Whether Daddy actually did suffer from "neurotic sexual troubles" is a matter of speculation, but again the issue must be viewed in the context of the era. It is possible, as the affidavit suggests, that the physical contact Daddy sought was perhaps normal adult behavior, but "unnatural" and "unknown" to Peaches. One might speculate Daddy had suggested something like oral sex. Peaches' statement furthered her contention—true or not—that she was an innocent and inexperienced child who suffered at the hands of an unrelenting sexual predator.

This was far from the end of Peaches' damning testimony. Upon returning from their honeymoon trip and taking up residence at the Kew Gardens Inn, Browning's actions allegedly became more appalling. One evening Peaches had quietly retired to bed. Daddy, however, compulsively walked the floors late into the night. She drifted into sleep only to be abruptly awoken by a harsh grinding sound. As she opened her eyes and gained her awareness, she observed Daddy Browning sandpapering a shoetree at the foot of the bed.

"What time of the night was this?" asked Epstein.

"*All* night," was her response.

Having little choice but to cradle the pillow over her ears, Peaches finally began to fade into sleep. Before long, however, she was jerked awake by yet another jarring noise. She testified that in her bewilderment, she sensed an object hurtling toward her. Browning had thrown two telephone books in her direction; the first slammed on the floor, jolting her from sleep, while the second almost struck her. Browning had laughed maniacally, and Peaches had huddled under the blankets. Too terrified to sleep, Peaches kept her eyes glued upon her husband, whom she now observed bounding about the floor on his hands and knees, clad in multicolored pajamas and spewing unintelligible dog-like sounds to his own utter delight.

After a time, Browning's mutterings mercifully died down and Peaches slowly drifted back into sleep. At about three o'clock in the morning, however, she awoke with a scream, as the shrill sounds of an alarm clock that had been perched next to her ear pierced through her head. "I told Mr. Browning I couldn't stand it any longer; I had to get out." She climbed from the bed and proceeded to get dressed. As she put on her hat and coat, Browning sheepishly asked where she was going, and then he fell to his knees and with tear-filled eyes begged her not to leave him. "He . . . told me he never would act that way again and apologized, and I consented to stay then."

The strain, however, was becoming unbearable according to Peaches, and Daddy Browning's activities had begun to take a physical toll on her. "The next morning I woke and had this terrible attack."

❖

Epstein had to prove that Peaches had suffered impairment to her health, safety, and peace of mind at the hands of Daddy Browning and to do so he needed medical evidence. The testimony of the doctors who treated Peaches was to come, but Peaches herself could testify on the point. She recounted the morning following her strange and sleepless night at Kew Gardens.

"As I walked towards the breakfast table, my nerves were absolutely under no control at all . . . and my arms were twitching, and I sat down and I fainted . . . I had bit my tongue and gone into convulsions." The spell didn't last very long but Daddy Browning was unnerved. She had suffered from various spells and attacks of fainting before, but Browning had never seen one of this severity. He sent for a doctor and contacted Carolyn whom, according to Peaches, Browning beseeched to take up residence at the Inn so she could take care of her daughter. She testified that her episode was of such intensity as to convince Browning that she was going to die at any day.

Peaches was seen at that time by Dr. George Blakeslee, who assured them all that she was not going to die, and preliminarily identified

Peaches' problems to be related to stress and anxiety. He suggested that she get out of the house more often, stay out of the newspapers, and avoid excitable situations.

Despite Dr. Blakeslee's orders, Daddy Browning's poor conduct continued, according to Peaches. On the very evening of meeting with the doctor, she testified, Browning had come home in a reckless and cantankerous mood, and, producing a bottle of bootleg liquor from his jacket, exclaimed that he was drunk. A moment later, she said, he called her into another room, though Carolyn was within hearing, reached into his hip pocket, and threatened to kill both Peaches and himself.

Peaches knew that Browning always had a shotgun alongside of his bed in Cold Spring, and otherwise carried a pistol either on his person or in his various apartments. She now became terrified that Browning intended to use that pistol and she screamed in horror. Carolyn ran to the telephone and threatened to call the police, and Browning instantly fell to his knees, begging her not to do so. Carolyn slowly returned the receiver to the phone and Browning collapsed on his bed in a fit of tears.

❖

Peaches had been on the witness stand for nearly four withering hours. She was pale and exhausted and had not yet even begun the ordeal of *cross*-examination. A nearly purple-faced Daddy Browning glared at Peaches and frequently conferred with John Mack over this or that point of her testimony. What Browning had no way of knowing was that the worst was yet to come.

Henry Epstein reviewed his checklist of topics and, as he neared the end of his inquiry, he unfurled perhaps the most explosive revelation of the day.

❖

After Peaches' convulsive fainting spell, Daddy Browning refused to sleep in the same bed with his wife for fear that to do so would induce further attacks. He slept instead in the parlor adjoining the bedroom, while Peaches and her mother stayed in the master bedroom. At about that time, Browning's adopted daughter, Dorothy Sunshine, had come to spend time with her father prior to her return to boarding school and had been given another small room also adjacent to the main bedroom.

As Henry Epstein began his next line of questioning, he was seen to close his eyes for an extended moment and his breathing appeared to quicken. "Now at any time while Dorothy was sleeping in the next room and Mr. Browning in the parlor did you ever hear Mr. Browning during the night go into Dorothy's room?"

John Mack leapt to his feet. "Objection, Your Honor! I fail to see how this questioning is relevant to the issues at hand!"

Seeger screwed up his face as if he were chewing on a lemon and informed counsel that he would allow the inquiry. Peaches looked Henry Epstein square in the eye and said, "Yes. Many times." A veil of silence shrouded the courtroom.

"At what hours?"

"Two or three o'clock in the morning."

"How often did he go into Dorothy's room?"

"Well, about three or four times a week."

With that, Henry Epstein announced that he had no further questions.

Left to right: Peaches, Daddy, Dorothy Sunshine, Carolyn.

CHAPTER XVIII

A WOLF
IN SHEEP'S
CLOTHING

"We wanted to keep out of the dirt, but
they started it, now let them watch out!"

—JOHN MACK

AS THE TALL AND ANGULAR JOHN MACK MADE HIS WAY TOWARD THE witness stand to begin his cross-examination of Peaches Browning, he presented an immediately obvious contrast to the soft-spoken Henry Epstein. Though he was not exactly unfriendly in his style, Mack approached the witness with an air of dynamism and condescension that at once angered and intimidated Peaches.

John Mack's objective in the cross-examination would be simple and evident from the start. Mack had made the calculated decision not to attempt to rehabilitate his own client. Instead he would tear down the character of the witness who testified against that client. Browning, he theorized, would restore his own reputation later in the trial. For now, Mack would set out to prove that Peaches was not the chaste and innocent young girl that she had portrayed herself, but rather a worldly vixen with tainted motives.

Mack, however, could not let stand fresh in the judge's mind the explosive charge that Peaches had made regarding Browning's relations with his own adopted daughter. Abandoning any pretext of sensitivity toward the witness, Mack attacked Peaches' interpretation of Browning's conduct.

Peaches stated that Dorothy could not fall asleep at night until Daddy Browning "rubbed" her. She insisted that this, and other things that Dorothy had told her, led her to the conclusion that Browning had "debauched" the child. Listening to the testimony, Browning suddenly threw his head back and laughed with incredulity at the charge.

"Do you know what *debauched* means?" demanded Mack. It meant, Peaches replied, to teach a person to commit an unnatural act. "Well, do you think it unnatural to rub a little girl to sleep?" Peaches did, and she told the court so.

❖

Mack then sought to establish for the court the extent—and limitations of—Peaches Browning's virtue. "Now prior to your meeting the plaintiff you were a young girl fifteen years of age . . . and not used to the ways of the world?" She stated, of course, that she wasn't—"not in that sense of the word." Much of Peaches' testimony on direct examination was designed, after all, to show that she was of tender age and innocent mind. Mack would now force her to defend that claim.

He began with a daunting series of questions designed to show that despite her tender age, Peaches was no stranger to a date. "I had gone out with the boys," she admitted.

"How many different boys had you gone out with before you met Mr. Browning?" Mack inquired.

Peaches had no choice but to be truthful on a point that could be so easily corroborated. "Many boys."

Q. "Two or three times a week?"
A. ". . . I would go out two or three times a week."
Q. "With different boys?"
A. "Yes."
Q. "Go to theaters?"
A. "Yes."
Q. "To movies?"
A. "Yes."
Q. "To dances?"
A. "Yes."
Q. "To restaurants and had dinner with them?"
A. "Yes."

Mack then questioned Peaches about specific gentlemen who had courted her and the places they had taken her to. Having a somewhat unclear memory of particular events, she was then directed to a certain diary that she had kept during the period prior to her marriage. The diary was not at that time introduced as evidence for consideration by the judge, but rather was used simply to refresh the recollection of the witness as to various points of her testimony. Peaches was made aware prior to trial, however, that the diary might be needed and she was instructed to bring it to the proceedings, which she did.

As Mack handed the diary to Peaches, he asked her if it was the original. She swore that it was.

❖

Over the stunned gasps from those viewing the trial and the repeated objections of Henry Epstein, an undaunted John Mack steered his interrogation forward.

Q. "Now, I understand that never before had you been nude in the presence of any man?'

A. "Never."

Q. "And when you married Mr. Browning you never intended to be nude in his presence, did you?"

Sensing that Mack was attempting to corner her, Peaches drew a trembling breath and peered at Henry Epstein for assistance that he was powerless to give. After a brief pause she pleaded, "I never intended to walk around the rooms and sit and eat dinner so."

"Did you *ever* intend to be nude in his presence?" demanded Mack.

"Well, to a certain extent, yes," she said, without hesitation.

"And you knew what married life meant, did you not?

"Yes."

"And in the seclusion of your own bedroom you were afraid to have your husband look at you naked?"

Peaches' cheeks were now scarlet. "I wasn't exactly afraid, I was just never brought up in that spirit," she said in a near whisper.

Mack then suggested that Browning's prodding of Peaches to display herself naked was motivated by nothing more than admiration of a man for his wife. "He was rather proud of you, was he?"

"I don't know if you would call that pride or not."

Mack was annoyed by this quip. "He was getting you photographed outside all the while, wasn't he?" Peaches pointed out with impressive panache that Browning was having his own photographs taken as well.

Pressing the theme, Mack attempted to develop that it was likewise Browning's pride in his wife that led him to send Peaches on shopping sprees to buy expensive clothing and jewelry. Browning had also spent large amounts of money outfitting his bride and Mack wanted the judge to hear it from Peaches directly.

Q. "Did he buy you any diamonds?"

A. "Yes, he bought me a wedding ring and an engagement ring and a bracelet for my birthday."

Q. "What did he pay for the wedding ring?"

A. "He paid $200."

Q. "Did he buy you one for $1500?"

A. "He bought an eight-karat stone for $1500."

Q. "Did he buy you any other?"

A. "Yes. A bracelet for my birthday."

Q. "How much did he pay for that?"

A. "$2600."

Peaches noticed that Judge Seeger had discretely raised an eyebrow of astonishment as she recounted the sums that Browning had paid for her rings and bracelets. She thus quickly added that much of the jewelry that Browning bought for her was fake and imitation that she considered worthless.

"So much that anyone knew they were fakes—just by looking at them?" asked Mack.

"Pos-i-tive-ly!" came the answer.

❖

With feigned empathy, John Mack then questioned Peaches about the circumstances of the acid attack and asked if she believed that Daddy Browning actually had someone go into her apartment for the purpose of attacking her in this manner. "I have suspicions to that effect," she said, rather snootily. When pressed on the subject, Peaches could offer no explanation as to why she thought Browning would do such a thing, but she adamantly stuck to her position.

Q. "The doors were all locked?"

A. "Yes."

Q. "You know there was a complete investigation made by the detectives who were there and they could find nothing?"

A. "I do."

Q. "And you now believe that he was instrumental in having your face disfigured?"

A. "I think he was in some way, yes."

Q. "Did you find any burns on the bed linen or bed clothes?"

A. "No."

Q. "Or on your night dress?"

A. "No."

Peaches could offer no further elucidation on how the attack had occurred or in what manner Daddy Browning may have been involved.

❖

In an effort to debunk Peaches' claim that she was averse to public attention, Mack introduced into evidence her entire *Why I Left Daddy Browning* series. As Peaches attempted to identify each of the stories at Mack's insistent request, Carolyn Heenan could see that her daughter's nerves were again fraying. She approached the witness stand and requested a seat next to Peaches. "I want to be near Babe in case she breaks down again," she said to the Judge, who nodded approvingly.

Mack elicited that the exposé had appeared under Peaches' name, with her express permission, and under written contract with the newspaper. She had, of course, been paid for the articles, and had willingly provided the information contained in each of them. Peaches was then asked to identify a variety of photographs that appeared with the series, including one of her in a meager bathing suit, which she hesitatingly admitted posing for. Mack's clear implication was that a woman who sincerely professes discomfort in being naked before her husband would not be willing to pose almost naked for a newspaper.

Though Mack tried, Grogin's initial composograph of Peaches and Daddy in their boudoir was ruled by Judge Seeger as inadmissible. Henry Epstein winced as Peaches then demonstrated her knowledge of photojournalism, explaining to the court the not-so-subtle differences between a composite rendering (a la Harry Grogin) and an actual photograph.

Peaches, it had been demonstrated, could work with the press about as well as her publicity-starved husband.

❖

As Mack's cross-examination began to wind down, he abandoned any effort to conceal his contempt for the witness. His smile was never broader than when he raised the issue of the African Honking Gander.

Q. "And the gander did the usual thing for a goose—he soiled the floor?"
A. "Yes, he did."
Q. "And Browning laughed at that?"
A. "Yes,"
Q. "And that hurt you very much."
A. "It didn't hurt me, no."
Q. "It caused you great pain and anguish?"
A. "No; it didn't cause me great pain and anguish."

Through his sarcasm, Mack was making the clear point that Peaches' sensibilities on the matter—and thus other matters by implication—were bizarre and unreasonable. He recognized that whatever her responses to the questions were, they would bind her. If she claimed that the event had caused her great anguish, it would appear that she was humorless and overly emotional. If she answered that it didn't cause her pain and anguish, as she did, it argued against the very premise of her case.

Peaches testified that she "hated the goose," and to the delight of the entire courtroom, Mack asked, "You didn't think you *married* one of course?" Mack then presented her with a photograph that had been taken of her with the goose and he elicited an admission that, although she disdained the bird, she had willingly posed for pictures with it. "I did pose for that picture," she sheepishly admitted.

Q. "And did that cause you great pain?"
A. "No."
Q. "Great humiliation?'
A. "No."
Q. "That didn't bother you at all?"
A. "Yes. My friends thought I was foolish.
Q. "And that hurt your feelings very much?"
A. "Of course it did."
Q. "It humiliated you?"
A. "It did."

Sensing advantage in the absurdity, Mack then focused his questioning on the toy animals that Browning had bought Peaches when she asked for a pet. "Did that humiliate you too?" he jeered. "That had nothing to do with you leaving him, did it?"

"It got worse," she sobbed.

"You mean the three pups got worse or—"

At that moment Peaches burst into angry tears and scolded, "No, Mr. Mack, this isn't a joking sensation for me!" The courtroom erupted with crowing laughter and Judge Seeger demanded order.

As John Mack turned his back and walked away from the witness stand, he was heard to say, "It may not be, but some part of it is for me, Mrs. Browning, I will be perfectly frank with you."

❖

After nearly five hours of grueling testimony, Peaches was visibly relieved to step down from the witness stand, and leave the courthouse. She was relatively pleased with her testimony and had received the compliments of both her mother and her attorney. Something, however, still bothered Peaches, and as evening turned into night, that bother became panic. Not knowing what to do, Peaches sent for Henry Epstein, who in a very short time was sitting with Peaches and her mother, in the parlor of their Manhattan apartment. Epstein searched his client's tear-filled eyes and asked, "What is it, Frances? What is troubling you?"

Peaches reprimands the infamous African Honking Gander as Daddy looks on in amusement.

CHAPTER XIX

AN
ADMISSION

*"I always say, keep a diary and
someday it'll keep you."*

—MAE WEST

HENRY EPSTEIN, A DEEPLY PRINCIPLED AND ETHICAL MAN REALIZED HE HAD
no choice but to risk his entire case in order to do what he knew was
right and proper. At the start of the second day of trial in White Plains,
he rose to his feet and timidly requested permission to make a statement
to the court on the record.

"Last evening after leaving the courthouse," Epstein began, "I was
told by the witness . . . that the diary that she produced yesterday, was
not the exact and original diary which she had kept prior to her marriage. I then asked her if she had the original diary and she said that she
did." The now blushing Epstein continued, "I deemed it my duty as an
officer of this court to inform the court of the fact, and I ordered her to
produce the original diary today, so that the whole truth might be presented." Epstein then handed both diaries to Peaches, who was back on
the witness stand, and had her identify them.

"Why did you do it?" he asked. She peered at him with sheepish and
embarrassed eyes and explained that the original diary contained the
names of certain boys with whom she had spent time, and whose iden-
tities she had hoped to keep from the court record. She accordingly
rewrote the diary with those names redacted.

"Were the boys mentioned in the original diary boys that you had
made love to, and that had made love to you?" ventured Epstein.

"They were," she sobbed.*

---

*Be careful! The words "made love" in the day of Peaches and Daddy
Browning carried a much different connotation than they do today.

John Mack, looking very much like the proverbial child on Christmas morning, rose to his feet and again approached the beleaguered witness. He requested of the stenographer a copy of the court transcript from the previous day and he read aloud Peaches' false testimony regarding the diary. Peaches could feel the heat rushing to her face as Mack then asked if she had lied as to the authenticity of the diary she had submitted to the court. The answer, of course, was yes.

Up to that point, neither of the diaries had actually been offered into evidence for consideration by the judge of their contents. John Mack, however, now insisted that they be marked as exhibits and admitted as evidence. Epstein retorted that the diaries only contained entries dated prior to the marriage and thus were not relevant to the issues at hand. Mack fired back, "Your Honor will find in the diaries, unless I am mistaken, and I am satisfied that I am not, the writings of this young lady to show that she was a woman of the world, even though young. They are extremely important as bearing upon her story that she was an innocent girl at the time of her marriage, and knew nothing of the usual marriage relations."

Peaches, now crimson with rage, leapt to her feet and shouted, "I was a good girl when I married!" Henry Epstein tugged at his client's arm, imploring her to sit down, while many in the courtroom gasped in astonishment.

"They are part of the *res gestae*," Mack continued, raising his voice over the clamor, "and bring into Your Honor's mind, in my opinion, the conviction that the story which this lady told on the stand is, under all circumstances and all the evidence, unbelievable."

Judge Seeger slammed down his gavel in an effort to regain order and informed John Mack that he doubted whether the diaries had any bearing to the primary issues of the case. It was his inclination, he continued, to exclude them from evidence unless the parties cared to submit briefs on the subject for his later consideration. The judge then instructed Henry Epstein to proceed with his next witness.

As John Mack returned to his seat, he glanced at Daddy Browning with a smirk on his face. The substance of the diaries, he knew, was not the salient issue. It was, instead, the damaged credibility of Peaches Browning that no doubt would endure in the Judge's principled mind.

CHAPTER XX

CREDIBILITY, CORROBORATION, AND CORRUPTION

> *"I heard a thud, and loud voices, and of course I started to run. I said 'something is the matter with Frances' and I ran to the door, and it was closed."*
>
> —CAROLYN HEENAN
> Direct Examination; January 26, 1927

HAPPY TO MOVE ON, HENRY EPSTEIN CALLED TO THE STAND CATHERINE Mayer, the friend of Carolyn Heenan who stayed with her at the Cold Spring residence after the wedding. The heavyset Mayer ambled to the stand and adjusted her glasses, fearful that her failing eyesight might somehow disqualify her as a credible witness. It would be what she *heard*, however, rather than what she could see, that Catherine Mayer would be called upon to recount.

The purpose of Mrs. Mayer's testimony was to corroborate Peaches' claim that early in the marriage Browning had thrown her to the floor and frightened her to such an extent that she spent the night with her mother. Mayer testified that on the occasion in question, she heard a loud thud from the couple's third floor bedroom, followed by a scream that she identified as coming from Peaches. Upon running up the stairs, she and Carolyn encountered a locked door and demanded that Browning open it. When he did, she stated that an hysterical Peaches ran out of the room and into her mother's arms, where she stayed for most of that night.

Epstein called his next witness, Carolyn Heenan, to the stand.

She wore a dark blue dress, accented with touches of white, which fit snuggly about her rather wide hips, and a tight fitting black hat that was stylishly skewed to one side of her head. She appeared matronly and unflatteringly stout, and upon taking her seat in the box, she smiled weakly at her daughter, and then glared at Daddy Browning.

As Epstein began his questioning, it was immediately apparent that she shared little of whatever poise and acuity her daughter had displayed in the same seat. She hesitated and stumbled even over preliminary questions of background, and inappropriately wavered between a low expressionless voice and a phony hammed-up tone. Epstein knew he would need to quickly make his points and move on.

Carolyn testified about her daughter's courtship with Daddy Browning and of his efforts to persuade her to entertain his serious intentions. "Every time he came he said that he wanted to do something nice for my daughter," she said. "He took letters out and showed them to me, what a nice gentlemen he was—that many girls would love to marry him." She confirmed that Browning had indeed sent his secretary John Aldrich to speak with her to verify Peaches' true age, and she freely admitted that the aggressive actions of the Children's Society was the catalyst for the hastily planned wedding arrangements.

Immediately following the wedding, lamented Carolyn, she could see that Browning and her daughter were already quarrelling. She described an occasion where Peaches had cut out from a local newspaper certain pictures of her and Daddy that she wanted to keep for a scrapbook. Browning insisted that she give him the pictures for display in his office and the two argued over them, until Browning ultimately, threw them on the floor, exclaiming, "Take them, I don't want them."

Browning commonly scolded his bride, Carolyn went on, and on one occasion she heard him shout at Peaches, "You're no good—you ran around with other men." Perhaps Carolyn Heenan wasn't clever enough to realize the damage this particular revelation did to her daughter's character, but her statement did tend to show Daddy's Browning's poor treatment of Peaches. Not convinced that he was succeeding with this line of questioning or in controlling Carolyn's testimony, Epstein moved on.

Corroborating Peaches' and Catherine Mayer's statements regarding the evening that Browning struck Peaches to the floor, Carolyn described the loud thud from the bedroom above and the scream to which she and Mrs. Mayer responded. She then recalled her daughter's sobbing statement, "He wants me to sit on the side of the bed naked all the time, and parade around the floor."

Later that evening, Carolyn had approached Browning and asked, "Oh Daddy, why can't you be happy?" His chilling response, according to Carolyn, was, "Listen, if we are ever separated, there is not a judge in the land that will believe you. They buy my lunches while I freeze the poor people out . . . The newspapers will keep me on the front pages, and you will be in the dirt like the other Mrs. Browning . . . Do you know your daughter proposed to me?" During this part of her testimony she stared directly at Daddy Browning with an angry scowl on her face.

Carolyn insisted that Daddy Browning wanted her to come live with the couple, first at the Gramatan Hotel and then later at the Fairfield and Kew Gardens Inn. "He said, 'Mother, you must come and stay with us. I have to be at the office, and [Peaches] must have care. Somebody must be with her.' I said, 'Mr. Browning, I do not want to be hanging around with you and Frances.' He said, 'That is all right now, I will get you a room . . . and you will come right up here, Mother.'"

"He called you 'Mother?'" asked Epstein.

"Yes," she said, as Browning, who was, in fact, nine years older than the witness, shifted uncomfortably in his chair.

It was at the Fairfield Inn that Carolyn observed many lewd photographs and French magazines that she claimed Daddy Browning had brought home for viewing with his wife. "He brought one of the lady whom he admired very much," she said. "Mrs. Dockerill."

Carolyn stated that near the end of September, when Dorothy Sunshine had come to stay with them, she had noticed that Peaches' nervous condition had worsened, and she begged Daddy Browning to bring the girl to a doctor. She corroborated fully Peaches' testimony that on the evening they had gone to see Dr. Blakeslee, Browning had come home in a fowl frame of mind and began slamming doors and shouting at Peaches. He took a "vial" of whiskey from his pocket and "he appeared very nervous and highly excited." Carolyn then testified that Browning, "put his hand back in the pocket as if he was going to take out a gun and he [said], 'I am going to kill you and myself, Peaches.'" Epstein had now introduced corroborating evidence of Browning's alleged violent tendencies.

During this period, according to Carolyn, Browning had refused to share a bed with Peaches for fear, he claimed, that she would have another spell of convulsions, and that this refusal continued even after Dorothy Sunshine had left for boarding school. Though Epstein carefully avoided any reference to impropriety on Browning's part with regard to his adopted daughter, Carolyn's pretrial affidavit, which had of course been read by Judge Seeger, stated:

> It is with great reluctance and hesitation that I bring the name of this young child into this unfortunate matter. She is about twelve years of age and fast approaching full physical development. The actions and statements of this little girl wholly innocent of wrongdoing as yet and of Mr. Browning towards this little girl convinced me that my daughter's husband is sexually abnormal and that a careful analysis of his attentions to Dorothy Sunshine would reveal this.

Henry Epstein walked slowly from the stand and paused at the Defendant's table to examine his notes. After a brief moment, he turned to John Mack and said, "Your witness."

❖

Mack rose and approached the witness box with a broad smile on his face. After establishing that Daddy Browning had supplied Carolyn with a generous monthly stipend of her own during his marriage to her daughter and eliciting Carolyn's admission that, prior to the marriage, her daughter had been out with many young men and even appeared on occasion before them in a bathing suit at the beach, he then devoted the balance of his inquiry to the evening that Browning had allegedly threatened to kill Peaches.

"Was he drunk?" asked Mack.

She wasn't sure.

"How old are you?" he asked.

"Do I have to tell?"

"Do you mind?"

"No. I'm forty-three years old."

Mack then asked whether Carolyn had ever seen a drunken man, to which she responded she had, and then she added that Browning had acted "a little like he was drunk" on the night in question.

"What sort of bottle did he have?" asked the lawyer.

"It was kind of a vial. It was about a two ounce bottle," she said.

At this, the courtroom erupted into laughter, as did both John Mack and his heartily entertained client.

"Did he stagger?" offered Mack in his most mocking tone. "Did he stagger like this?" The lawyer fell about the room in his best hooch hound impression.

"*Just* like that," she said curtly. Then Carolyn looked squarely at John Mack and scolded, "Now Mr. Mack, this is not play. I don't want to play with you," to which Mack responded through his laughter, "You can't play with me anyway—I'm married!"

Henry Epstein had heard enough. He sprang to his feet and protested Mack's tone to the Judge. Seeger, apparently enjoying the questioning, answered that he could not control Mack's demeanor and in any event he would rather that the mood of the day be light as opposed to angered. He then added that if Mack's voice became objectionable he would intervene.

"My voice could never be objectionable to her," quipped Mack.

In point of fact, John Mack had crossed the line with this remark. Judge Seeger had the right and power to admonish the lawyer, but in failing to do so missed an opportunity to properly assert his own authority as well as to preserve the decorum of the courtroom. And in the coming days that decorum would be challenged in ways Judge Seeger could not have imagined.

❖

It was now time to offer evidence bearing directly on Daddy Browning's character and credibility. Epstein believed that his next two witnesses would do just that.

On the Saturday evening before the opening of the trial, Marion Tussey, a longtime friend of Peaches, received some unwanted visitors. Her landlord had called up from the first floor of the Manhattan apartment house and asked if she would come down to discuss some matters pertaining to the building. She peaked in the mirror, patted her auburn bob, and trotted down the stairs. When she reached the landing, however, she could see several gentlemen waiting there for her—and one of them was Daddy Browning. Marion hesitated and then slowly made her way down the rest of the staircase.

As word had spread of the upcoming trial, Marion could almost guess what was about to happen. Daddy Browning and a lesser member of his legal team met her at the bottom of the stairs and handed her a document which was, of course, a subpoena (and the required five dollar fee) commanding her appearance on January 26, 1927, at the Westchester County Courthouse in White Plains.

"I'm a ruined man if you do not help me, Miss Tussey," pleaded Browning. He knew that Tussey, who was slightly older than Peaches, had accompanied the girl on many nights about the town. He was convinced that she could bolster his claim that his wife was not an innocent child or repulsed by matters of a sexual nature. Had Tussey not attended nude parties given by the Heenans prior to the marriage, and hadn't she at one point accompanied Peaches to a clandestine doctor for an illegal operation? And wasn't Mrs. Heenan running a call house from her apartment, and weren't there games of strip poker that she had witnessed?

Marion Tussey looked at Daddy Browning with incredulous eyes and, denying knowledge of any such matters, she demanded that he leave the premises at once. Browning gathered his winter scarf around his neck, peered at Tussey, and said, "If you retrieve your memory, as I think you can, I will make it right for you. You will never need for anything."

Browning's prodding of Marion Tussey had clearly backfired. No sooner had Daddy and his cohort left her apartment than she was on the telephone to Peaches and her lawyer. In the afternoon session of January 26, Henry Epstein called Marion Tussey to the stand. She happily swore under oath as to Browning's attempt to buy her testimony. In so doing, however, Epstein may unwittingly have placed Browning's allegations as to Peaches' own conduct—contested as those allegations were—right into Judge Seeger's lap.

In a similar effort to show that Daddy Browning had endeavored to manipulate or manufacture witnesses for his cause, Henry Epstein then called one Arthur Le Duc to the stand. Le Duc was a reporter for the *New York Evening Journal* who had covered the Peaches and Daddy story rather extensively from the beginning. Browning had clearly taken note of the relationship that the reporter had struck with his wife, and he wondered if perhaps there was something more than a professional association in their contacts.

Le Duc testified that after the couple separated, Browning had contacted him and asked him if he had not, in fact, kissed Peaches on the occasions when they were together. Le Duc denied ever having done so, and though he did acknowledge conducting an interview of Peaches while she was in bed, he insisted that it was not by either's choice—she was confined to bed recovering from her burns—and that other reporters were present at the time.

As was the case with Marion Tussey, Browning's contacts with Arthur Le Duc proved to be more harm than help to his cause. Henry Epstein rested his case, and Judge Seeger announced an agreed upon four-day adjournment of the trial to give the parties a much-needed breath. Daddy Browning was left to ponder his tattered reputation.

Gauvreau and Grogin's famous "Woof! Woof!" composograph appeared in the *New York Evening Graphic* above the caption "When Peaches Refused to Parade Nude!" In a telegram to Judge Seeger, John S. Summer, Secretary of the New York Society for the Suppression of Vice, wrote "Your unfortunate decision to make a public show of the Browning trial has resulted . . . in a flood of filthy published matter . . ."

CHAPTER XXI

THE REVEL
OF FILTH

"When a man begins to make type mumble unintelligible words or when he begins to cut the heads off of photographs of news subjects and paste them on the bodies of half-clad human figures, thus to create lewd and obscene images, seeking to justify such abominations by characterizing them as representing scenes from real life, there is a question whether that individual does not deserve the kindly ministrations of the psychopath."

Editor & Publisher
February 5, 1927

WITH EACH DAY OF THE TRIAL, EVEN THROUGH ITS SHORT ADJOURNMENT, the newspaper coverage had become more and more audacious. Even before Peaches had stepped down from the witness stand at the completion of her testimony, knicker-clad schoolboys working for voraciously competitive news organizations were shouting their respective headlines on street corners throughout New York and across the nation. *"PEACHES SHAME! CONFESSES HER BRIDAL NIGHTMARE," "PEACHES FLAMING YOUTH," "BUNNY CRAZY!"* shouted the *Mirror*. *"PEACHES ON STAND TELLS HOW DADDY MADE LOVE, COURT BARS YOUNG GIRLS," "PEACHES' SHAME STORY IN FULL," "RAH, DADDY! HAIL PEACHES," "PEACHES ADMITS HIDING NAMES OF BOY LOVERS . . . GIRL WIFE QUIZZED ON MARITAL DEPRAVITY,"* ran the *Graphic*.

The pause in the proceedings did little to dampen the fervor of the reporting. During the four-day adjournment of the trial from January 27 through the 31, the news coverage became more frenzied than ever. Wild speculation as to upcoming trial strategies and prospective witnesses led newspapers to print bizarre statements—some true, most not—regarding the case. Fueled by rumor, innuendo, and ill-advised announcements and interviews given by the Brownings and their lawyers, some papers stated that Browning would be subpoenaing one hundred witnesses in the coming days to testify on his behalf. They conjectured whether Dorothy Sunshine might be one of them. They asserted the existence of a mystery witness who would travel some two thousand miles to deliver explosive evidence, and they maintained that Peaches' telephone wires had been tapped.

Statements by William Heenan accusing Browning of having offered him $5,000 to turn against his daughter and testify on Browning's behalf were printed widely. Following up on the inferences of the Marion Tussey testimony, some papers made fierce accusations about Peaches and her mother having taken part in sex orgies and strip poker games, and speculated wildly about the contents of her diary and whether Judge Seeger would allow its admission as evidence. Many stories asserted that Henry Epstein was considering calling an alienist—a psychiatrist, in modern terms—to the stand for the purpose of assessing Daddy Browning's mental health and having him committed to a mental institution if so recommended.

In what may in fact have been the most credible claim of all, some newspapers declared that an outstanding figure would testify that the date, time, and circumstances of Peaches' departure from Daddy Browning had been engineered and choreographed by news reporters employed by the *Graphic* as a publicity stunt. Finally, the generally highbrow *New York Times*, apparently starved for inside information on the case, performed some crack investigation and reported that the African Honking Gander, which so tormented Peaches Browning, was actually owned by a Mrs. John H. Greaves of 3566 Southern Boulevard, Staten Island. Mrs. Greaves denied rumors that motion picture concerns had made overtures to film the bird, and stated that even if she had received such offers she would have rejected them. "The bird has been through enough already," said Greaves, according to the *Times*.

❖

During the separation trial, nothing in print or illustration compared to the concoctions of the *New York Evening Graphic*. Gauvreau and Grogin unleashed a series of composographs that at once delighted, entertained, offended, and outraged. The *Graphic* would, quite simply, test the era's definition of obscenity.

On the evening of January 26, 1927, just after the first full day of trial, Emile Gauvreau placed upon the front page of the *Graphic* his magnum opus. In a historic coalescence of artistic renderings and ten actual photographs, Harry Grogin had depicted the bedroom scene of Peaches and Daddy Browning in a farcical moment of marital rage. Above the printed caption—"*When Peaches Refused to Parade Nude!*"—Grogin placed the pajama-clad Daddy Browning, fists clenched above his head, opposite the shrinking Peaches, who, with thick legs fully exposed, held a towel over her barely clothed body in a protective pose. Prancing on the beautifully adorned elevated bed was none other than the African Honking Gander with the exclamation, *"HONK! HONK! IT'S THE BONK!"* hovering above its mouth in a word bubble. Another word bubble, inspired by Peaches' testimony, came from Browning's mouth: *"WOOF! WOOF! DON'T BE A GOOF!"*

Within hours of its release, the phrase, inane as it was, would catch fire. Children playing on the streets and in ball yards yapped the ridiculous rhyme at one another and soon it was appearing in vaudeville shows and musical comedies. The *Graphic* ran a *WOOF! WOOF!* contest, seeking the public's best Peaches and Daddy aphorism. Gauvreau himself claimed that his own boy hurled the chant back at him in childish defiance. "I boxed his ears," wrote Gauvreau.

Circulation of the *Graphic* instantly shot off the charts, and Gauvreau, liking what he saw, demanded more. Harry Grogin and his staff worked day and night producing other freakish curios for successive editions of the paper. On January 28, the front page of his *Graphic* once again bore a composite depicting another scene straight from Peaches' testimony. In the same bedroom setting, Browning, still clad in pajamas but now donning an Arabian headdress or *ghutra*, taunts his young bride with a toy doll, while Peaches, dressed in the same skimpy nightie, is now defensively sprawled on the floor with an expression of horror, amidst lewd photos of woman. *"YOU'LL HAVE TO BE SATISFIED WITH THIS BABY DOLL!"* shouts the lunging Browning, and in the background the African Gander again squawks, *"HONK! HONK! IT'S THE BONK!"* The *Graphic*, always subtle, captioned the image "Mad as a scene from the House of Usher."

Other composographs followed. One popular image portrayed Peaches and her mother, playing a game purporting to be strip poker with two men and two other ladies. Another showed a formally dressed Browning amorously posed over a reclining Peaches with the meddling Carolyn Heenan leaning against the closed door of the room, cupping her hand to her ear struggling to hear what is happening. No person or element described in the trial was immune, and Gauvreau delighted in the uproar that his creations were stirring.

The last of Harry Grogin's odd masterpieces depicting the Peaches and Daddy marriage appeared on February 1, 1927, above the caption *"A Smooth-Working Sheik."* The couple was again shown in their boudoir with Daddy, this time dressed as a Caliph in full Arabian attire with boots, striped cape, and turban and mantle, diligently sandpapering a shoetree, while Peaches, again in a revealing night dress, sits in a chair

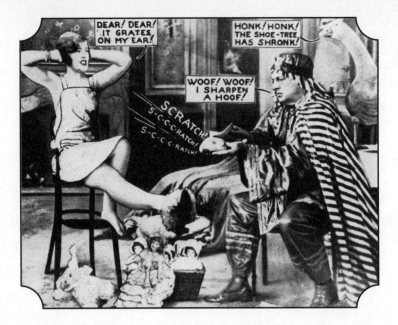

with her hands over her ears. Toys and dolls are strewn all over the floor, and again the Gander makes his appearance, screeching, "HONK! HONK! THE SHOE-TREE HAS SHRONK!" Daddy, focused on his work, is saying, "WOOF! WOOF! I SHARPEN A HOOF!" and Peaches moans, "DEAR! DEAR! IT GRATES ON MY EAR!" One commentator wrote, "Nothing more sensational or fantastic ever appeared in that or any other newspaper."

❖

For those who had hoped for a closed trial, the *Graphic's* composographs represented the quintessence of the worst-case scenario. The backlash was as severe as it was inevitable.

John S. Sumner, Secretary of the New York Society for the Suppression of Vice, fired an angry telegram to Judge Seeger. "Your unfortunate decision to make a public show of the Browning trial," he wrote, "has resulted . . . in a flood of filthy published matter, including imaginary pictures to illustrate lewd incidents of the Plaintiff's story, especially in the so-called tabloid press. It is no answer to say that the publishers may be prosecuted for publishing lewd matter. Hundreds of thousands of copies of these filthy detailed reports have been issued and will be issued if you stand by your decision for publicity." Shrugging off the criticism, Seeger simply referred Sumner to the text of his previously issued opinion regarding the policy of the law against secrecy of trials. He then leaked the telegram to the press.

The protests reverberated far beyond the courthouse. In a "wave of editorial revulsion," newspapers across the nation stood up and objected to the public airing of the Browning trial. In Florida, the *St. Petersburg Times* announced that it would publish no more details of the case, stating that it was not so much a moral question as a "sanitary measure" that drove its decision. In New England, the *Boston Traveler* ran a bold type editorial on its first page, apologizing to its readers for "having embarked on a course that led to depths beyond the wildest stretch of the imagination." In a statement that was echoed in newspapers throughout the country, the editorial continued, "The revel of filth that has been indulged in by the contestants at law has passed beyond all limits of decency, and a further publication of the details the *Traveler* feels is a menace to the morals of the community." Even the *New York Daily News,* perhaps as an admission that the *Graphic* had beaten them at their own game, came out with an editorial favoring limited censorship. "In this Peaches-Daddy Browning trial some of the publications reporting it have gone so far beyond the line of decency as to seem insane."

The backlash was not limited to self-censorship of the press. In Yonkers, New York, the Commissioner of Public Safety issued an order to news dealers to cease selling the *Graphic* or risk revocation of their newsstand licenses. Though the *Graphic* sought an immediate injunction against the commissioner, the courts ultimately upheld the order as a proper application of the statutes against obscene publications. In churches across the country, jeremiads were delivered against the evils of the Browning case and the impropriety of open court divorce hearings. In his Sunday morning sermon in the Bedford Presbyterian Church in Brooklyn, Reverend S. Edward Young told his flock that Judge Seeger bore great responsibility for promoting "the most flagrant pictorial and news debauch ever put before the youth of this or any other land." And in a speech before the canned food industry's American Can Association in Atlantic City, Will Rogers, Mayor of Beverly Hills, California, was quoted as saying, "All we're getting now, three times a day, is peaches, mush, and applesauce."

❖

The trial and its coverage had one more unintended consequence. Anna St. John announced that she did not believe the charges of Peaches Browning as they related to her former adoptive daughter, Dorothy. However, she and her husband thought it best for their other child that they not take Dorothy back, even if Vincent Pisarra should have her removed from Browning. As though Dorothy were damaged goods, St. John added, "Dorothy was a fine girl when she left us. I had taught her all the finer instincts."

Peaches (circa 1927) - At trial John Mack declared, "We propose to show that this young woman was accustomed to being unclad and had been intimate with young men before her marriage."

CHAPTER XXII

A WOMAN
OF THE
WORLD

"Probably the biggest draw line in the Browning trial, is the repeated use of 'Is Peaches a woman of the world?' It piques the curiosity of the young and stimulates the imagination of the old. It is the keynote that makes the Peaches-Bunny show the biggest box-office attraction of the day."

—New York Daily Mirror
January 29, 1927

ON JANUARY 31, 1927, THE BELEAGUERED LITIGANTS ELBOWED THEIR WAY through the bellowing crowds back into the Westchester County Courthouse. Overnight Peaches and Daddy had become part of the popular culture and the American lexicon.

The area surrounding the courthouse had taken on a carnival atmosphere and mobs of people—estimates as high as three thousand—turned out to be a part of history. Street vendors pushing heavy wooden carts braved the bitter cold and peddled little toy dogs, teddy bears, and model cars such as those described by Peaches in her testimony. Merchants advertising Peaches and Daddy song parodies sold phonograph records and sheet music by serenading passersby like Christmas carolers. Spectators gobbled up at least fifteen different musical spoofs, among them "Who Picked Peaches Off the Tree?"and "You Are Old, Daddy Browning!" The simple lyrics of the pop hit of January 1927—a song called "Crazy Words, Crazy Tune"—became easy prey for clever wordsmiths eager to satirize the trial. Across America, college boys and flappers alike were strumming their ukuleles and crooning the words:

What did Peaches Browning Say
In the court the other day?
Vo-do-dee-o
Vo-do-dee-o-DO

Up at White Plains the other day
What did Peaches Browning Say?
Vo-do-dee-o
Vo-do-dee-o-DO

Throughout New York, daily newspapers carried spoofs and contests lampooning every detail about the couple. In the *Graphic*, a cartoon entitled *A La Carte* showed Daddy Browning looking at a menu on which was printed the word "Peaches." In the next frame, Daddy is seen shoving the plate away, saying, "I ordered Peaches and they turned to prunes!" The waiter responds, "I'm sorry, sir, the crop has been very poor lately. . . ." And in the *Mirror*, an offer of payment was made for "Bunny-Peaches Wisecracks:" "BUNNY is going to marry Siamese twins! Why? He's tired of PEACHES and wants a PAIR (PEAR)."

Across America, young women were wearing articles of jewelry similar to that worn by Peaches during the trial, and a gander necklace craze began to take hold. Flappers from Newark to San Antonio hung imitation geese around their slender necks and mail-order businesses worked overtime shipping their novelties air postal.

By early Monday morning, as the trial resumed, a solid wall of spectators extended from the front of the courthouse, across the sidewalk, and out onto Main Street, despite teeth-chattering temperatures. Policemen and deputies struggled to hold their ground as ferocious grandmothers, flappers, and housewives stormed the courthouse grounds. Teems of women tested security personnel to their capacity and there was frequent and certain bedlam when police hands inadvertently came in contact with forbidden feminine territory.

Inside, the throng clogged every artery of the building, fighting up and down staircases and swarming through corridors. In the mayhem, one of the large oak doors to the third-floor courtroom was torn from its hinges and the masses poured in like water rushing into a void. "The crowd filled every foot of space," wrote the *Times*, "some girls even sitting on window ledges and climbing on the backs of seats and chairs. The room seemed to slope up the sides where they perched, like a tiny amphitheatre around a clinic." Even Judge Seeger was forced to ask himself whether perhaps a private hearing might, in fact, have been the better choice.

❖

The day began with a point of contention, again surrounding the proposed admission as evidence of the altered diary of Peaches Browning as well as several letters allegedly authored by the girl prior to her marriage. John Mack announced that he wished to submit a brief on the issue and again claimed that the disputed material bore relevance to the case. Henry Epstein rose to register his objection, and Seeger interrupted, "Gentlemen, I will save you the argument about this matter—the diary is excluded." Peaches shifted in her seat and nodded in approval.

Seeger then asked John Mack about the letters he sought to introduce. "The defendant wrote them to a girl friend before marriage, Your Honor. They show that she is a woman of the world. One of them tells of a game of strip poker!"

Again Epstein objected to the letters, claiming that since they were written before the marriage, they were immaterial to the case at hand. Whatever they indicated about Peaches' character, how could that lessen the degree of cruelty she had suffered during her marriage?

Mack retorted, "She comes here and claims her nerves are shattered on account of her husband's treatment. If Your Honor persists, I will show that this woman has a past! We propose to show that this young woman was accustomed to being unclad and had been intimate with young men before her marriage." The gallery seemed to inhale in unison. Peaches wept bitterly, despite the consoling hand of her mother upon her back.

Mack argued that even if the letters did not have direct bearing on the issue of cruelty during the marriage, they did tend to show Peaches' lack of credibility. How could she have been traumatized by Browning's conduct when she was, in fact, mature and experienced far beyond her years? These letters, he argued, would demonstrate that maturity.

Seeger was not persuaded. Though he indicated a willingness to consider *some* limited evidence of Peaches' premarital conduct so long as that evidence stayed within the bounds of decency, he ruled the letters inadmissible.

The ruling was inconsistent on its face. Seeger had already entertained much evidence involving Peaches' past and the relevance of that evidence was undeniable. Proof that she had willingly engaged in the conduct that she now claimed shocked and traumatized her would go straight against her credibility. Browning had earlier expressed his dismay that women were unfairly favored in the courts and now his concerns appeared to be validated. Amidst audible sighs of disappointment from the packed courtroom, Seeger declared, "I don't think it will help me very much to go into the lives of either of these persons before their marriage. I think I can decide this case on the basis of actions during the marriage."

Then commenced the morning's parade of witnesses.

❖

Mack's first objective—impeaching Marion Tussey's credibility, and convincing the judge that Browning had never tried to bribe her—focused on the Saturday evening when Daddy Browning handed Marion Tussey a subpoena. After a short reexamination of Tussey, Mack called Marion's landlord, Bondy Croner, to the stand. Croner, a petite, well dressed bald-headed gentleman of about seventy, testified in a thick German accent that Marion had, in fact, told him that she had personally seen Peaches Browning in a series of rather compromising positions with men prior to her marriage. Croner then stated that he was present when Daddy Browning handed Marion a subpoena, and he denied that Browning ever offered her a bribe or said that he would "make it interesting for her" if she were to testify for him. Under cross-examination by Epstein, however, Croner admitted that it was he who called Daddy Browning on the Saturday evening in question, to tell him that Marion was home and available to receive a subpoena.

Mack's next witness was Croner's housemaid, Margaret Leu, who stated that she was present during conversations between Marion Tussey and Mr. Croner, and that she could corroborate that Marion told him of several compromising premarital situations involving Peaches Browning. Epstein brought out that Leu was dependent upon a weekly salary from Croner.

Bonder's wife, a garrulous German woman with rimmed glasses and a boisterous voice, was next to testify. Despite repeated reprimand by Mack and Judge Seeger, Mrs. Bonder sought her oratory fifteen minutes of fame, constantly protesting, "I must tell you how it happened . . ." The gesticulating Mrs. Bonder confirmed her husband's story in total. She stated that Browning made no offer of money to Marion Tussey, insisting that he, in fact, said nothing at all. "There he sat and never said a word," she persisted. Even as she left the witness stand and walked past reporters, she could be heard muttering, "never opened his mouth."

❖

John Mack then turned to his second objective of the morning: demonstrating that Peaches did not detest the limelight as much as she had implied. Through a series of witnesses, all employees of a news syndicate that handled the national publication of stories originating in the *Graphic*, Mack intended to prove that Peaches Browning, contrary to her testimony, engaged in and profited from newspaper coverage.

Leslie Fullenwider, a slim young man with a Southern drawl, testified that his company had worked with Peaches and Gauvreau in assembling the material for both the *Honeymoon Diary* and *Why I Left Daddy Browning* series. He stated that he had been in contact with Peaches in October, shortly before she and her mother left Browning's Kew Gardens residence. "She told me that Mr. Browning was unbearable." He testified that Peaches negotiated and signed the contracts and was paid $1,000 for each of the exposés. "Peaches didn't write the stories herself," he admitted, though she did go over them and approve of their content. Fullenwider further stated that Peaches voluntarily posed for pictures that appeared with each of the stories, and only once hesitated, when she wasn't feeling well. John Mack then had the court stenographer mark as a collective exhibit a large stack of newspapers—*Graphic* issues in which Peaches' first-person stories appeared—and introduced them into evidence.

It was evident from Fullenwider's testimony that he had no axe to grind on the stand and that he favored neither party. On cross-examination, therefore, Henry Epstein did not attempt to impeach the witness as untrustworthy, but instead focused on the stories that his office had syndicated for Daddy Browning. Then, a stunned courtroom gasped as Epstein asked, "Did Browning ask you to testify that you had kissed Mrs. Browning?" It was a shot in the dark. Epstein knew that Browning had contacted the reporter Arthur Le Duc and had made a similar inquiry of him. The shot was a good one and it hit the bull's eye.

"Well, Browning said to me, 'You and Peaches have engaged in osculation, haven't you?'" replied Fullenwider. Laughter rang out from the courtroom; even the witness was giggling.

"What did you say to Browning?" asked Epstein.

"I laughed—it was so ridiculous. I hadn't kissed Mrs. Browning."

❖

With distinctly mixed results thus far, John Mack then endeavored to accomplish his third goal of the morning—to rehabilitate Daddy Browning's pulverized character. To accomplish this, Mack turned to the employees and workers of the Kew Gardens Inn.

An eye-catching waitress by the name of Belle Edwards testified that she had served the Brownings on various occasions and found them to be a very happy couple. "He bought her lots of flowers," Edwards said.

Frank Golden, the headwaiter at the Inn, also found Browning's treatment of Peaches to be exemplary, but he balked when asked how generous a tipper Daddy Browning was. He rung his hands and stumbled on his words. "I ah . . . er . . . oh . . . ah . . ." In an effort to break the moment of tension, Judge Seeger looked benevolently at the witness and said he needn't answer if he didn't want to. Then with a broad smile, Seeger added, "You won't have to give them up if you tell!" Even Golden was laughing as he stepped down from the box.

Other witnesses, including residents of the Inn and the manager, testified in kind as to Browning's attentive and friendly manner towards his wife, and to how well dressed and happy she always appeared. On cross-examination, Henry Epstein asked of one of these witnesses, "You wouldn't expect a man to beat his wife in public, would you?" Upon Mack's objection, Judge Seeger responded in laughter, "Yes, it would be improper to beat your wife in public."

❖

Henry Epstein passed the lunch hour with Peaches and her mother, commenting on the results of the morning testimony. Meanwhile, a strange young man who had previously slipped unnoticed into the back of the gallery now huddled with John Mack and Daddy Browning behind the closed door of a private office in the bowels of the courthouse.

Judge Seeger called the afternoon session to order and, with every expectation that the afternoon's testimony would be as good-natured as the morning's, he directed John Mack to proceed. Mack turned his attention to the dark and stocky young man with whom he had spent his lunchtime. "The Defendant calls James Mixon to the stand."

Dressed in a tired blue serge suit typical of that worn by college men of the day, Mixon walked slowly to the stand, fixing his gaze straight ahead. Daddy Browning cast an admiring gaze on the lad. Henry Epstein and Peaches watched quizzically as Mixon ambled his way to the witness box and settled laboriously into the chair. Large dark circles hung under his eyes, as though he had not slept in days. "He had a black, beetled brow and rather a snarly expression," wrote Damon Runyon. "He did not state his age, but I would guess it as in the mid-twenties." As Mack began his preliminary questioning of the witness, Peaches leaned over to Henry Epstein and whispered, "I've never seen this man."

Mixon stated his name and address and told the court that he was born in Louisiana. He said that he knew Peaches from before her marriage, having met her at the Strand Roof dance hall, and that they had thereafter struck up a short friendship. Peaches angrily whispered her protests to Epstein, who was preparing himself for the worst. Mack then fired a series of questions at the witness, each of which Epstein shouted his heated objection to, and all of which Judge Seeger barred the witness from answering.

"Did you give Frances Heenan money with which to buy under-clothes?"

"Did you accompany her to a room in a hotel?"

"Did she take a bath while in the hotel?"

"Did she then come in to where you were, clad in the underwear you had gotten for her, and ask how you liked her?"

"Did you and Frances stay over night in the hotel room?"

An excited gasp shot through the courtroom and Judge Seeger demanded, "That's far enough, Mr. Mack!" Peaches stiffened in her seat and tears again welled in her swollen eyes.

Directed to limit his inquiry to matters within the timeframe of the Browning marriage, Mack then asked the witness if he had spoken to Peaches at any time since April of 1926. Mixon responded that he had received a telephone call from Peaches to inform him of her marriage and to solicit his well wishes.

"Was it this young woman here at the end of the table?" Mack pointed to Peaches.

"It was," said Mixon.

Peaches leaped to her feet and shouted, "I never saw him before in my life!"

The typically reserved Henry Epstein, now flush with anger, rose and pointed an accusatory finger at Mixon. "Do you see this girl sitting there?"

"Yes."

Peaches glared back at the reprobate.

"Is she the one you are talking about?" demanded Epstein.

"Yes."

Pounding her fist on the table, Peaches again shouted, "He lies! I never saw him before in my life!"

Daddy Browning looked on with amusement as John Mack then asked the witness, "That's the one, is it? There's no question about that, is there?"

"No," said Mixon.

"I never saw him before in my life! He's perjuring himself!" cried Peaches as she stomped one foot on the floor and crumpled back into her seat in a cascade of tears.

❖

Mack's next two witnesses proved that the testimony could get even more provocative.

Through an accent that was so thick as to be virtually indecipherable, an insurance salesman named Roman Androwsky testified to a chance encounter one dark night with two women whom he was able to identify as Peaches Browning and her mother, Carolyn. Androwsky stated that on the evening in question, he was standing on Riverside Drive waiting for an appointment when Peaches and Carolyn took a seat on a bench in front of him and began speaking to each other, unaware in the darkness of Androwsky's presence. Androwsky testified that the woman whom he described as "the older one" asked the other, "Did you really care for Mr. Browning before you married him?" The reply, according to Androwsky was, "Don't be foolish, I could never love an old man, but so far I've got what I want and I'll have more by the time I am through." Then the older one said, "I don't know. You know as well as I do that a lot of people never thought you married Mr. Browning for love. But if you use my method you'll succeed."

After a disorganized cross-examination in which Androwsky confused everyone in the courtroom and perhaps no one more than himself,

Judge Seeger, happy for the respite, excused the witness. With James Mixon's testimony fresh in mind, credibility seemed to be a long lost friend.

Mack's final witness of the day was Lee Swint, who had been a longtime friend of Francis Dale and was Browning's personal body-guard during the time of his marriage to Peaches. Swint testified that he had spent a great deal of time with Peaches and her mother and that he knew them quite well. He recounted several instances in which Peaches used vile and inappropriate language and he stated that he had person-ally seen both Peaches and her mother in a drunken state at a party given by Carolyn at her apartment. Swint then added doubt to Peaches' claim that Browning was violent toward her. With a generous smile, Swint quoted Carolyn Heenan as saying, "I watched that old fart like a hawk. If he had ever hurt her, I'd have broken every bone in his body."

"Did Mrs. Heenan ever say anything to you about what she would do if this suit were lost?" asked John Mack.

Swint raised his eyebrows and nodded emphatically. "Yes, she said, 'If I lose this case I'll kill the judge, Dale, and the whole bunch of them,'" to which Judge Seeger and the entire courtroom responded with a burst of unrestrained laughter.

In the levity of Swint's testimony, perhaps the most damaging exchange of the day was lost in the moment. Swint testified that in a conversation with Peaches and her mother shortly after the separation from Daddy Browning, he asked Carolyn why she ever permitted the marriage to begin with. As Carolyn began to answer that Browning had been such a fine gentleman early on, Peaches interrupted, according to Swint, and exclaimed, "Cut your kidding. You know why I married that old bozo. I married him for his jack!"

A rare kiss—according to Browning. "I asked her if she would act with me as man and wife. . . . She said 'If you mention that I will go to my mother!'" Note the check that Peaches holds up as a present from Daddy.

CHAPTER XXIII

NON PAYMENT
OF KISSES

"You are a sane man, aren't you?"
—JOHN MACK

BY THE FINAL DAY OF TRIAL, IT SEEMED TO THE CASUAL OBSERVER THAT Peaches and Daddy had pretty much sullied each other to a virtual draw. Though Browning had clearly been bruised and buffeted, he had yet to complete his defense, and neither side seemed to have created a dramatically more favorable impression on Judge Seeger than the other. They would now have only one remaining opportunity to deliver a decisive blow.

Mack opted to begin with witnesses who he hoped would buttress the battered reputation of Daddy Browning to the court and in the public eye. Each witness swore either to the good name and character of Daddy Browning, or to their particular perception of the couple at this or that time or event. To a person, the witnesses consistently depicted Daddy Browning as a fine and charming husband who treated his wife in an exemplary fashion. "He was always petting Peaches and speaking to her in endearing tones," insisted one witness. "I thought Mr. Browning was most courteous to Mrs. Browning and his mother-in-law," observed another.

Henry Epstein conducted only a short cross-examination of each witness, hoping only to point out that a marriage is not always as it may appear on the surface or as portrayed to the world. As for Browning's character, Epstein well knew that for every person willing to testify that the man had a heart of gold several others would gladly swear that he did not. Judge Seeger needn't endure such a litany of testimony, and Epstein trusted that enough evidence of Browning's odd character had already been presented.

John Mack believed that over the last day and a half of testimony he had delivered a harsh blow to the integrity of Peaches Browning and had also begun to rehabilitate the tarnished credibility of his client. Mack had one last card to play, however.

He fixed his gaze on Daddy Browning, who steadied himself with a deep breath. Mack announced, "We call Edward West Browning to the stand."

❖

Daddy Browning was no stranger to a witness box. Through his many years in the rough-and-tumble business of New York real estate he had found himself embroiled in all levels of litigation and had been called to testify in many cases. As he made his way to the stand on February 1, 1927, however, Browning's complexion flushed a shade of crimson that would have brought alarm to those who didn't know him.

He was dressed in a fine blue business suit with a colorful scrambled egg pattern necktie and, as always, three fat cigars stood prominently in the outside breast pocket of his coat. Though he was visibly tense, he was ready for the opportunity to tell his side of the story. "He settled himself in the witness chair and faced Mr. Mack with an air of welcome expectancy," wrote the *Times*. "He has an unusual face. It is long and puffy in unexpected places. His nose is long, his eyes are prominent and shiny as if continually about to water. Under pouty and full lips he has a small chin."

As the questioning began, Browning habitually ran the fingers of his left hand inside the rim of his collar and tugged at it as if gasping for air. At the start, he rapidly answered his attorney's questions with such pro-lixity that he often bordered on incoherency, but gradually he calmed and settled into a rhythm of clarity and purpose. "His New York accent," wrote Lester Cohen, "made the guys at Fulton fish market sound like noble Romans."

John Mack began his inquiry with the couple's initial meeting at the Hotel McAlpin. Browning immediately contradicted his wife's version of the events of March 5, 1926, and insisted that it was Peaches who aggressively pursued him. "Miss Heenan walked right up to us," he said. "I thought she knew all the girls, and one of them introduced me to her, and she asked me to have a dance with her before I left . . . She [gave] me her telephone number, and her house number, and wanted to know if I would come and see her . . ." When asked how soon after their initial meeting the couple again communicated, Browning stated, "She called me up. I got a message at the office . . ."

As if to defuse the obvious pink elephant in the room, Mack then queried, "How old are you, Mr. Browning?"

"Fifty-two," came the answer.

According to Browning, Peaches initially gave her age as twenty-three and then reduced it to twenty-one. He confirmed that he sent his manager, John Aldrich, to meet with Peaches' mother and learned that Peaches was, in reality, not quite sixteen.

Browning related that as the relationship began to take hold he tried to persuade Peaches to go back to school. He stated that he gave her money for that purpose, only to later learn that the money was used for clothing and other frivolities. Peaches, he complained, did not reenroll in school but instead applied as an extra at the Earl Carroll Theatre. "I told her it was no place for a young girl," claimed Browning.

Peaches had testified that early in their courtship she had begun to see Browning's odd public behavior surface. When asked about his alleged antics on St. Patrick's Day 1926, Browning admitted that in the mood of the holiday he had purchased and placed into his pocket maybe ten or twelve green silk handkerchiefs to hand out to people at the dances they attended. "I defy anybody to place *several hundred* handkerchiefs into their pocket!" he wailed.

Mack then directed his client's attention to the acid burning incident. Browning stated that when he arrived on the scene, he was dismayed to find that Carolyn, a trained nurse, had done virtually nothing for the girl. Browning had been the one to take action, directing Mr. Aldrich to contact a doctor while he hurried to the drug store to obtain some absorbent cotton and bandages.

"What was then said about the police?" asked Mack.

Carolyn protested his suggestion to call the police, Browning went on with showy incredulity. "Mercy don't do it; we don't want anybody to know about it," she had said (according to Browning). He testified that Carolyn would not allow him to use the phone to call the police, so he directed his chauffeur to drive up Broadway, find a phone, and alert the police to what had happened.

"Did you at any time suggest not calling the police?" asked Mack.

"No, I did not; I wanted to right away!"

"Did you have anything to do with this acid burning on this girl?"

"Absolutely nothing!"

A murmur suffused the courtroom. The newspapers and the public at large had speculated greatly as to the circumstances of the acid attack, and it was highly anticipated that some explanation or culpability for the event would be revealed at trial. With Browning's testimony, however, it had become disappointingly clear that little else would be learned about the attack, and that its origin would remain a mystery.

Browning testified that after the acid incident, Carolyn lamented that she couldn't properly oversee her daughter's recovery since she had to work during the days. Browning told her that she needn't worry, that he would support her, and he offered her $50 per week for this purpose—$15 more than what she earned as a nurse. Shortly thereafter, Browning stated, he was paying the Heenan's rent and providing money for furniture and food as well.

At about this time, according to Browning, Vincent Pisarra of the Children's Society was poking around and making threats to remove Peaches from the care and custody of her mother. "She would die without her mother," testified Browning. He hired two attorneys to assist Carolyn in her fight against Pisarra, but he soon realized he would need to take further action. "I said she would make a wonderful wife, and it was the only way to save her from going into an institution," said Browning.

❖

Mack guided his witness through the events of the wedding day and into the wedding night, for which arrangements had been made for the couple to dine and lodge at the Hotel Gramatan. Browning asserted that his marriage was kissless right from the start. As he spoke, Peaches watched him closely and whispered to Henry Epstein, who busily scribbled notes upon his writing tablet.

Browning testified that when the couple retired the evening of their wedding, Peaches informed him that she was feeling unwell and thus could not consummate the marriage. Though he had been displeased, Browning vehemently denied any persistence on his part after she made her condition known to him, and protested any suggestion that he had somehow forced or cajoled his wife into relations when she didn't want them.

At the Cold Spring residence a few days after the wedding night, Peaches was feeling better and he again raised to her the question of sex. "I asked her if she would act with me as man and wife." To Browning's dismay Peaches again refused his affections. "She said 'If you mention that I will go to my mother!'" Angered by his wife's rebuke, Browning testified that he took her by the arm and said that she needn't bother.

He would bring her to her mother. "She seemed to be provoked when I did that and threw her feet out, and went on the floor . . ." said Browning sheepishly.

"Did you at that time strike her?" asked John Mack.

A: "I certainly did not."
Q: "Or threaten her?"
A: "Absolutely not!"
Q: "Or throw her on the floor?"
A: "No sir."
Q: "Did she scream?"
A: "No sir."

Peaches' sexual rejection continued throughout the marriage, Daddy went on angrily. "She repeatedly repulsed me. We talked about it, but she didn't want children." Peaches always had another excuse to avoid romantic contact, he claimed. "First she had the burns . . . and the mother was there, you know . . . Her mother lived with us half the time."

By the time the couple arrived at Kew Gardens, Peaches had expanded her justifications for avoidance. She claimed, according to Browning, that sex would bring on "the jerks," or epileptic fits, as Browning referred to them. She knew that her husband feared that greatly. "And the time before that it was not wanting to spoil her figure . . . and she was young, and then a number of times she kept saying she would, provided I bought her more things, and finally when I bought her about $6,000 worth of stuff . . . she promised to then, and then her mother came right down and didn't practically leave us. I don't think I had a word alone until she left. I couldn't get her to one side, hardly to whisper in her ear."

At Kew Gardens, Carolyn became unbearable, according to Browning. "Her mother came right in and said that she wasn't going to leave her. She got right in bed, and I took another room." At this, the courtroom erupted in laughter.

Browning spoke mournfully of his desire to have children. Because of his age, he said, he considered his marriage to Peaches his last chance to start a family. "I lived in the hotels, and I wanted to have children and a home of my own, naturally . . ." But Peaches wanted nothing to do with children. "She said she was young and she wanted to have a good time and she wanted to go to dances and dinners and theatres . . .

She said that it would spoil her figure, and that having children was for poor people . . ."

Mack then asked what else Peaches said about having children. "She didn't want any."

"Did you?" Mack inquired sympathetically.

"I did."

John Mack then asked Browning about Peaches' nervous attacks—the so-called jerks. Browning demonstrated the movements that his wife displayed when these attacks occurred and he described them as epileptic in nature. "She rolled her eyes and bit her tongue and frothed at the mouth . . . and it scared me half to death." He explained that these events occurred after periods of prolonged rest rather than as a result of excitement or agitation, and that he did his best to care for Peaches as they happened, patting water on her head, fanning her, and giving her smelling salts.

Mack then directed his questions to the particular night of abuse about which Peaches had testified.

"The night previous to this attack," Mack began, "had you been throwing telephone books around any room?"

"I never threw telephone books around *any* room."

"Had you set an alarm clock off at her ear?"

Browning threw his head back in laughter. as did many in the courtroom, but upon glimpsing an unmoved Judge Seeger he composed himself. "No sir. Absolutely not."

"Was there an occasion . . . when you got down . . . and you were in your pajamas, hopping around on your hands and knees?" asked Mack. The lawyer's voice was sarcastic, suggesting the charge was obviously ludicrous.

"No sir."

"Did that ever occur?"

"Well, when I was one year old I might have crawled on the floor, but never since," said Browning.

"Did you on one occasion sandpaper shoetrees all night?"

"I did not!"

Browning developed that he and Peaches wore the same size shoe—size 6—and that on occasion they actually shared the same tennis shoes and house slippers. As many in the courtroom leaned over to capture a glimpse of Peaches' feet, Browning continued that when one of Peaches' dress shoes fit too snugly over the instep, he attempted to alter the shoe-

May 15, 1926

```
To The Most Wonderful Prince Charming in all this World,

        You really are my Prince Charming, for you are a true
Prince.
        I love you more than any thing else in all the world.
    I love you for so many reasons.
        First, beacause you are just yourself.
        Next, beacauseyou are so good to me,you try to
give me everything I want.
        I know my Daddy dear has so many bussiness troubles
    and I will always try to makeyou forget your troubles
    and be happy.

                ILl always love my Daddy,
```

Peaches

A love note authored by Peaches and introduced as evidence at trial.

tree in several places so that it would stretch her shoes more smoothly on the inside. "It was just a little piece of sandpaper," said Browning, approximating the size with his hands. "She thanked me for it."

After an unequivocal denial that he ever offered to purchase his wife a "Japanese Princess" or anything of the sort, Daddy Browning then took up the matter of the African Honking Gander. He insisted that it was Peaches who tied the red ribbon about its neck and suggested that they take it for a stroll on the boardwalk of Long Beach. She had happily consented to being photographed with the bird, he claimed, and was eager to show it to her mother once they returned home later that night. Browning stated that he had his chauffer take the bird to the garage for the night and returned it to its owner shortly thereafter.

❖

At the close of the morning session, Mack proffered into evidence three letters that Peaches had punched out on Daddy's typewriter which she had done on occasion, as she waited for him in his office. One such letter read:

Dearest Daddy in all the world. I love you, I love you, I love you. What more could I say to you. As long as you love me nothing else matters. You are the idle (sic) of my dreams. I love you.

Peaches.

After a brief recess for lunch, Daddy Browning was back on the witness stand.

"Did you at the Gramatan, Cold Springs, or any other place ask your wife to sit in the nude, so you could look at her?"

Browning exhaled deeply as if taxed by the very thought. "No, I did not."

Q: "Or to walk around without any clothes on...?"

A: "I did not."

Q: "Or did you walk around in her presence nude?"

A: "I did not! I had two beautiful silk dressing gowns that I wore."

Q: "Did you ask her to eat breakfast without clothes?"

A: "No sir! She was always cold and wore clothes...It would have been impossible!"

Q: "Did you push her and pinch her and make her eat breakfast without clothes?"

A: "Absolutely not!"

About the lewd pictures and French magazines with which Daddy Browning had allegedly tortured his wife, Browning had much to say. The material was, first of all, to do with "artists and models," claimed Daddy, and in no way were the pictures lewd or vulgar. He insisted that it was Peaches who requested that he bring these magazines home, as she thought one of her friends had posed in one of them. "I went and got three and handed them to her, and she turned over the page and showed me this girl's picture which was not nude; it was partly draped, I couldn't tell which one it was; I paid no attention to it."

Q: "Were you accustomed to buying these magazines for your own use?"

A: "I doubt if I ever bought one in my life."

Q: "Did you bring her magazines in which were pictures of nude women and insist that she should look at them . . . or become angry if she didn't look at them?"

A: "It was the other way around; I didn't want her to look at them."

Next, Mack touched upon Daddy's supposed drunken rage on the evening of their appointment with Doctor Blakeslee. Almost rising from his chair in protest, Browning pointed his finger at Mack and roared, "I was never drunk there or anywhere else in my whole life, and nobody ever saw me drunk!" He then added, "If they did, let them come on and say so."

"Did you threaten to shoot [your wife]?"

"I did not. No sir!"

Browning denied that he carried a pistol or that he even had a permit for one during the time of his marriage. He admitted that he did *possess* a weapon but wasn't sure where he kept it, whether at Cold Spring, his office, or at his hotel residences. Mack then asked whether Carolyn called or threatened to call the police on the night in question, and whether he, Daddy Browning, had fallen to his knees begging her not to, as alleged by Peaches and her mother. "No. She never telephoned the police or threatened to telephone the police."

Noting that these events came at a time when Dorothy Sunshine was staying with the Brownings at Kew Gardens, Mack then shifted his questioning to the scandalous accusation that Daddy Browning had inappropriately touched his adopted daughter.

There had been serious consideration amongst Browning's legal team to not even raise the issue on direct examination. Mack believed that he had sufficiently debunked the claim during Peaches' cross-examination and he was willing to just leave it at that. The concern, of course, was that denying the charge further might in some fashion validate it. Daddy Browning, however, would have none of this thinking. He steadfastly insisted that he be questioned fully on the issue and that his refutation become part of the public record. These allegations, he maintained, must be confronted and disposed of.

Mack asked whether Browning had ever gone into his child's bedroom at late hours of the night. "I did not! Never!" shouted Browning. When asked to explain his attentions to his daughter, Browning responded, "Why, she used to kiss me goodnight, and I was very careful about not offending my wife, and I did kiss her on the forehead, but not even on the mouth. And I *never* went into her room!"

"Did you ever, as testified, when the child was going to sleep...rub her backside?"

"That is an absolute lie!" Browning was on his feet in the witness stand again. The courtroom buzzed with excited anticipation and reporters' pens scrawled busily.

"Your answer is you never did?"

"Absolutely not, or any other part of her body, EVER!"

"Did you ever do *anything* improper to the child?"

"No sir! I think more of that child than I do of my own life."

❖

With a resounding rap of the gavel, Judge Seeger demanded that the now raucous gallery be restored to order. John Mack used the moment to again shift the focus of the inquiry.

"Did you buy clothing for your wife?" asked Mack.

"I certainly did!" Browning proceeded to itemize, with detailed precision, a litany of cloaks, coats, dresses, hats, and other items with which he had adorned his wife during their marriage. "Anything she wanted, she could have."

He explained that every morning as they drove over the bridge into the city, Peaches and Carolyn presented a new list of demands. "They wanted a roadster!" And but for Daddy Browning's fear that an open-air vehicle would have brought on the jerks, Peaches would have had one, he insisted.

Browning then explained that his wife had demanded a New York apartment for the couple to call home. He insisted that he would have been happy to have such an apartment, and that he went out and found several possibilities on his own. "Nothing I would have liked better in the world than a home."

"They wanted all sorts of things. One wanted one dog, and the other wanted two, but I couldn't seem to get just what they wanted." He then paused for a moment. "I tried my best."

❖

As the inquiry neared its conclusion, John Mack asked the witness, "Do you remember the 2nd day of October—the day she left?"

He did. He had obtained tickets for a ball in which Peaches was to co-judge a Charleston contest with Gloria Swanson, and later they were to attend the theatre. Arrangements had also been made for a luncheon at the Biltmore Hotel. "I was to call her up a little before twelve," he said.

Mack asked how he traveled on that day and Browning indicated that the three of them drove into the city in his Rolls Royce. He was dropped off at his office. "When I got out I kissed her goodbye."

On that day, as twelve o'clock approached, Browning, as promised, put a call into Peaches to finalize their luncheon plans. It was then,

Browning testified, that Carolyn got on the phone and declared that "Frances isn't coming back to live with you." Dismayed and confused, Browning wanted an explanation. "I said, 'Is there anything in the world that I haven't given her or done for her . . . ? Have I ever said a cross word to her?'" Carolyn answered both of these questions "no," according to Browning. When he demanded what other reason there could be, Carolyn hesitated a moment and declared, "Why, you didn't buy the big apartment on Park Avenue I wanted!"

"Prior to that time did you have any knowledge or intimation that [your wife] was going to leave you?"

"Not the slightest idea."

". . . or that your mother-in-law was going to leave you?"

The courtroom had gone quiet. Browning looked up and his frown transformed.

"I . . . ah . . . er . . . I was hoping so."

❖

"Your whole testimony, Mr. Browning, is a categorical denial of each charge that your wife has made?" Henry Epstein began his cross-examination.

"Every one that isn't true, yes."

Though Browning had been articulate and self-assured throughout John Mack's inquiry, his manner instantly changed as Epstein approached the stand. Suddenly, no doubt by design, his responses became vague and evasive. He frequently used phrases such as "I don't recall," and "I think . . ." when answering, at one point prompting Epstein to throw up his arms.

Browning would also engage in a lengthy discourse when the question required simply a yes or no answer, generating heated exchanges between lawyer and witness. "I would like you to please confine yourself to the question," chided Epstein on one such occasion, prompting Judge Seeger to add, "On cross-examination, Mr. Browning, you must not volunteer anything." Epstein, normally patient, was driven as far as asking, "Do you know what a yes or no answer is Mr. Browning?"

With growing frustration, Epstein attempted to lead Daddy Browning through the quagmire of his finances and expenses. Browning spoke so softly that at one point Epstein shouted, "I can't hear you, Mr. Browning!" to which no audible answer came.

Browning denied he had coaxed his wife to become friendly with

Marian Dockerill and insisted that the woman was a total stranger who had come to him seeking to perform a numerology reading for him.

Q: "Did you bring home any pictures of her?"
A: "She gave us . . ."
Q: "DID YOU BRING HOME ANY PICTURES OF HER?"
A: "Yes."

When Epstein then confronted Browning with a photograph of an unclad Marian Dockerill and asked if he had ever shown it to his wife, Browning snapped, "No! That's a filthy picture. I'd be ashamed to show it if I were you."

"But you weren't ashamed to show it to your wife!"

"Yes, I was—maybe *you* showed it to her! I never saw such a nasty thing in my life. Nasty thing!"

Suddenly, the color washed from Epstein's face. He turned and staggered into his seat. The air in the suffocating building had become fetid; fumes from a stink bomb that had been detonated earlier in the day on the lower floors by a prankster attempting to make comment on the Peaches and Daddy proceedings had finally made their way into the packed courtroom. Judge Seeger ordered the windows opened while other court officers hurried about seeking water and spirits of ammonia for the ailing lawyer. Epstein forced his way through the episode, standing in front of the open window and breathing deeply. Warily regaining his composure he resumed the floor.

With varying degrees of success, Henry Epstein spent the remainder of the afternoon attempting to find whatever holes existed in Browning's testimony. By the conclusion of Epstein's cross-examination, however, Browning remained relatively intact. As Daddy stepped down from the stand, he shot a glare toward Peaches and her mother, and then ceremoniously clasped hands with John Mack and the rest of his now smiling legal team.

Wearing the same blue dress and matching hat that she had worn for the entire five days of the trial, Peaches once again made her way to the witness stand for a brief reexamination by her lawyer. In a trembling voice that betrayed the strain she was under, she formalized for the record her unequivocal denial of ever having laid eyes on James Mixon, and she informed the court that she *never* used the kind of fowl language that Lee Swint accused her of. With regard to the love letters that Mack had introduced into evidence, Peaches insisted that she was directed by Daddy Browning to write the letters. "He said, 'Sit down and write me a love letter,' and he stood right beside me."

❖

The final witness of the trial, Peaches' doctor George Blakeslee, was then read a lengthy and confused narrative of the allegations against Daddy Browning as testified to by his wife. John Mack had argued that Peaches' jerks and other attendant symptoms were caused by a preexisting epileptic condition that had nothing whatsoever to do with her marital relations. On Epstein's examination, however, Doctor Blakeslee concluded, "I think it can be fairly stated that Mrs. Browning's nervous attacks or seizures are undoubtedly due to a very disagreeable environment."

Epstein persisted, "Would you consider, Doctor...further life and cohabitation with her husband under the evidence in this case, to be detrimental to her health?"

"I would."

❖

After a brief flurry of questions from Mack and then Epstein and then Mack again, both sides rested. Judge Seeger opted for written briefs in lieu of closing arguments, but deferred to the parties on that issue. As the courtroom began to empty, Judge Seeger called the two attorneys to the bench and stated, "I know you gentlemen, and you have tried the case like gentlemen and lawyers and I have enjoyed it..." The judge paused, raised one eyebrow, and added, "so far as I could a trial of this kind."

Then, with a rap of the gavel, the trial of Peaches and Daddy Browning came to a close.

CHAPTER XXIV

THE
SUPPRESSION
OF VICE

"When the constitutional guarantee of free press is used, as we are now beginning to see it used as a license to cover the operation of circulation-mad panderers to the lowest appetites of what Mencken calls the great American boobery, the time has arrived for action."

—Editor & Publisher
February 5, 1927

BEFORE DADDY BROWNING EVEN STEPPED DOWN FROM THE WITNESS STAND in the Westchester County Courthouse, a national debate regarding the need for censorship of the press by legal enactment was brewing. The editorial backlash to the whole Browning pageant was well underway; the *legal* backlash, however, was just beginning.

In New York, a conservative movement to clean up the theatrical industry, spearheaded by Mayor Jimmy Walker, had begun. Legislative measures, which provided broad censorship over spoken drama, were threatened and the already harassed theater industry leaped to self-regulate in an effort to avoid further trouble. A so-called Housecleaning Committee composed of producers, actors, and playwrights was forced into action to purify the stage in an attempt to curb the pending legislative effort. The chilling affect on free expression was unmistakable.

Amidst this environment of police raids on Broadway vice shows and sex plays, the New York Legislature sitting in Albany had taken notice of the Browning case and its colorful press coverage. A storm of bills and resolutions found its way onto the floor of the Assembly, and impassioned arguments for against these measures tested that delicate balance between the concepts of liberty and morality.

Among the proposed measures was an amendment to the Penal Code, introduced by a New York City Assemblyman, making it a crime to "publish, publicly print, or disclose" the facts and details of any pending or incipient matrimonial case. A like resolution was presented condemning the printing of salacious testimony in divorce or separation cases. "This testimony," declared the measure, "is a cesspool of human depravity and its publication and dissemination in conversation and the public press demoralizes the youth of the country." The resolution concluded that the people of New York believe in the freedom of the press "but not license of filth." Not surprisingly, none of those bill ever saw the light of day.

The legal backlash was not limited to New York. Similar measures were introduced in states across the country. William David Upshaw, a Georgia congressman, presented a bill to prohibit the details of salacious divorce cases from reaching the public through the printed word. He cited the Browning trial as the catalyst for his wave of reform. Even *Editor & Publisher*, the weekly defender of the American press institution, was so outraged by the vagaries of the *Graphic* during the Browning trial that it called for public restrictions against the paper, if not the industry as a whole.

Throughout the Browning trial, John S. Sumner, the head of the New York Society for the Suppression of Vice, had attempted to persuade Judge Seeger to close the doors of the courtroom to the press. Though veiled in a noble effort to secure the public interest and comply with law, Seeger's motivations in refusing to do so had more to do with his personal feelings about the litigants and his desire that they not be permitted to benefit from secrecy. Unquestionably, Judge Seeger made the right decision in allowing public access to the trial—but for the wrong reasons. His ruling made little mention of the overriding constitutional issues and delicate balancing of rights required in such an analysis, but instead focused on the *appearance* that would be presented by allowing trials of the wealthy to be held privately. The prevailing conservative movements of the day, however, cared little about legal rational. Their concerns lied solely in what they saw as the outrageous content of the trial—the cause and effect of Judge Seeger's ruling.

Seeger's unwillingness to close the trial to the press, and the *Graphic's* consequent audacious coverage of the case, would now culminate in a battle that would go to the very foundations of the First Amendment and the freedom of the Fourth Estate.

The crusade to purify the New York newspaper industry found its early roots in a stalwart Civil War veteran by the name of Anthony Comstock. Not content to limit his zealous anti-vice efforts to the swearing and drinking soldiers of his unit, or later to his fellow workers in the dry goods business, in 1873, Comstock incorporated the New York Society for the Suppression of Vice, inspired by the principles of the Young Men's Christian Association, and guided by a stated objective:

> The enforcement of the laws for the suppression of the trade in and circulation of obscene literature and . . . advertisements, and articles of indecent and immoral use as it is or may be forbidden by the laws of the State of New York or of the United States.

In the early years of the NYSSV, Comstock focused his zeal on the enforcement of anti-abortion laws and the eradication of street pornography. After an early series of sweeping successes, however, the focus of the organization soon expanded to newspapers, magazines, obscene art, and gambling. With the staunch support of New York's elite class, Comstock soon took his crusade to Washington DC, where he success-

Anti-vice crusader and founder of the New York Society for the Suppression of Vice, Anthony Comstock.

fully lobbied for an intensification of the penalties for use of the mails to disseminate obscene materials—the so-called Comstock Act. Unwilling, for obvious reasons, to divulge the specific content of his seizures but eager to publicize his various activities and espouse his agenda, Comstock always reported the number of violators he arrested and the sheer tonnage of books, photos, and other indecent materials destroyed. By the turn of the century, Comstock had become nothing short of a national crusader commissioned, according to many, by the Almighty himself.

Following the death of Anthony Comstock in 1915, the NYSSV announced, to the dismay of book dealers and newspaper publishers, that its work would continue, now under the leadership of John S. Sumner. A Wall Street lawyer by trade, the ruddy-faced and athletic Sumner was considered to be less militant and more genial than his grim-faced predecessor. "Where Anthony Comstock was a berserk lion of purity," wrote *Time* magazine in 1927, "Mr. Sumner dislikes being thought of as a reformer. His smile and forbearance are of the efficient Y.M.C.A. type. With affability, not anger, does he discountenance the evildoer."

Notwithstanding Sumner's reputation for calm forbearance, the NYSSV, in close cooperation with the district attorney, possessed vast quasi-governmental police powers, and it actively used those powers. Sumner focused his efforts on the enforcement of New York Penal Code Section 1141, a legislative provision Comstock had brought about that criminalized the publication of crime news or other objectionable matter. With the fervor of civic duty, Sumner waged war upon any who, in the name of First Amendment freedom or mere entrepreneurial gain, circulated materials that in his view constituted a violation of the law. When Emile Gauvreau's composographs of Peaches and Daddy Browning reached New York City newsstands, it became a matter of only *when* John Sumner would act. On February 4, 1927, he did.

❖

Circulation of the *Graphic* had spiked to nearly 600,000 during the Browning trial. As Gauvreau celebrated his triumph with Bernarr MacFadden, a resolute John Sumner was weathering a storm of complaints from certain segments of the public regarding the paper and its exploits. Just days following the completion of the trial, Sumner stood before a Tombs Court Magistrate seeking a summons for the appearance of Gauvreau, MacFadden, and several other employees of the

Graphic for alleged violations of Section 1141 of the Penal Code.

In 1927, the relevant portion of Section 1141 provided that any person distributing printed material "devoted to the publication, and principally made up of criminal deeds, or pictures, or stories of deeds of bloodshed, lust, or crime" would be guilty of a misdemeanor punishable by imprisonment and/or fine. Oddly, the statute had yet to be applied to a newspaper organization, and thus MacFadden was eager to have the matter settled in the courts for better or worse for the entire press industry of New York. Justifiably concerned about the effect a verdict against them would entail, the *Graphic* would have to fight the "purity hounds," as the paper called them, tooth and nail.

❖

Knowing that capable legal counsel would be essential to their cause, MacFadden and Gauvreau met with William Travers Jerome, who, as former New York District Attorney, had risen to national prominence as the prosecutor of Harry K. Thaw in 1906. What the two didn't know was that by 1927, Jerome was aging and rather disconnected with events of the day. As the two newspapermen revealed their story, the senescent lawyer nodded graciously and patiently listened to every word. It soon became evident however that not only had Jerome never read a tabloid paper in his life, he had never even heard of Peaches and Daddy Browning.

"Let me see the newspaper which carried this material," said Jerome.

Gauvreau produced each copy of the *Graphic* in question and laid them on the lawyer's desk. Jerome adjusted his glasses and peered intently at the material for a few moments. He then looked up at Gauvreau and MacFadden, face devoid of expression.

"Plead guilty," he said.

❖

After securing a more appropriate legal team—led by Max Steuer, the famed trial attorney and father-in-law of Henry Epstein—the *Graphic* succeeded in postponing a hearing on the charges against the paper until March 6. This did not, however, preclude a war of words in the interim.

"The *Graphic* has acted like a small child trying to be nasty," said John Sumner. "Its stories on the Browning case have been simple, inane and foolish, with a strain of dangerous filth running through them harmful to all society. It is a terrible example of the length people will go to obtain circulation for a newspaper. All ethics of the publishing profession have been ignored."

For his part, Bernarr MacFadden enlisted the assistance of New York Assemblyman Frederick Hackenburg, who introduced a bill in the state legislature to abolish the NYSSV by repeal of the 1873 act that incorporated it. On February 9, the *Graphic* then quoted Hackenburg as saying, "Comstockism and Sumnerism have made us ridiculous in the eyes of the world." The paper continued, "The New York Society for the Suppression of Vice, which has had the rich privilege of splitting fifty-fifty on all fines collected through its instrumentality, will have to fight for its very existence before the New York State Legislature."

A day later, the NYSSV filed a lawsuit against the *Graphic* for $100,000, claiming that it had been libeled by the newspaper, and denying that it received any such sums from the levied fines.

❖

On March 6, 1927, a hearing was held in the Tombs Court to determine whether the case would proceed to trial, and on April 26 Magistrate Joseph Corrigan dismissed the charges against all defendants in the case—with the exception of Emile Gauvreau, who was held on $100 bail and ordered to appear for trial in the Court of Special Sessions on the penal code charges in question. All of the parties viewed the matter as a test case of vital import to the newspaper industry. John Sumner was already making plans for similar prosecutions should his case against the *Graphic* succeed.

Magistrate Corrigan remarked that he had never before read a tabloid newspaper prior to his involvement in the present matter, and he added that he hoped never to read one again.

Peaches and Carolyn on their way to court. Judge Seeger's final verdict would change their lives forever.

CHAPTER XXV

JUDGMENT

*"The decision ought to discourage such mar-
riage hook-ups. They're unnatural anyway."*

—Letter to the New York Daily Mirror
March 21, 1927

As JUDGE SEEGER GATHERED THE NEARLY TWO THOUSAND PAGES OF TRAN-
scriptive testimony together with the various briefs, letters, and exhibits
generated during the lengthy trial, the city of White Plains licked its collective wounds. "The fair name of White Plains has been made to
become a byword and a joke upon the lips of stage comedians," lamented the city Ministers Association. The community populace, many of
whom had attended the trial, now outwardly grumbled about the harm
done to their reputation by the now infamous trial.

The practical problems presented by the fiasco were perhaps as dramatic as the perceptual ones. In the wake of the trial, city and county
workmen scurried to clean the dreadful mess left behind by the unruly
mobs and to repair the damage, estimated at over $1,500, that had been
done to the doors, furniture, plumbing, and grounds of the courthouse.
Policemen and deputized court officers all sought payment for long and
perilous hours of duty in the fruitless effort to maintain order during the
case, while county officials, who never conceived of such a dramatic
strain on public resources, squeezed the municipal budgets for funds
with which to pay them.

As the inhabitants of White Plains struggled to reassemble the pieces
of their city, the litigants awaited word of Judge Seeger's decision. On
February 9, Peaches Browning and her mother sailed for Bermuda,
where they sought removal on the warm, windswept beaches of
Hamilton. Back home, Henry Epstein and John Mack were both still
neck-deep in post-judgment matters, exchanging charges, countercharges, and supporting affidavits as if the trial had never adjourned.

Each side accused the other of witness tampering and misconduct during the investigation phase of the trial.

In a hearing conducted to address these claims, Browning's lawyers vigorously denied charges that James Mixon, whose scandalous allegations were all but excluded by Judge Seeger, had been promised $5,000 in exchange for his testimony. The question of Mixon's alleged perjury was referred to the District Attorney of Westchester County, while Judge Seeger indicated that he could do no more than to consider each affidavit "for what they are worth."

❖

As the weeks wore on, fierce speculation over Judge Seeger's final decision seized the press. Predictably, Daddy Browning presented reporters with reams of letters that had been sent to him from across the country in loyal support of his cause. Despite these, Browning gloomily predicted the worst. "You know how it is," he lamented. "A woman always has ninety-nine chances out of a hundred."

By March 8, rumors began to surface that Browning was making plans with his attorneys for the filing of an annulment claim against Peaches in the event of a finding against him in the separation case. Soon after, the *International News Service* wired a nationwide story revealing the generally held opinion that Peaches had won and would be granted a generous allowance of alimony. A day later, the same news service, relying on an exclusive story from the *New York American*, declared that Judge Seeger had completed his decision and that Daddy Browning was the victor.

Irate over the reports, Judge Seeger, whose every step was by now being tracked by rambunctious newspapermen, closeted himself in his chambers and threatened to "pitch through the window" any reporter who attempted to question him about the case. "I have been working night and day on the case," was his official comment, "and will continue to do so until I am ready to file the decision." Referring directly to the story in the *New York American*, Seeger denied that he had even yet finished writing his opinion and he declared the report that Browning had won the case a lie.

Judge Seeger's coyness, naturally, only resulted in a higher pitch of public attention. An hourly watch for court messengers and mail deliveries to the County Clerk's offices of both Putnam and Westchester Counties ensued, and by the third week of March, a near frenzied storm of expectancy surrounded the case and its central characters.

❖

As the first hint of spring air breezed through the farms of Carmel, so came Judge Seeger's decision in the Peaches and Daddy separation case. On March 21, 1927, an unremarkable man wearing a straw hat and a wide necktie pulled his sputtering Nash Cabriolet in front of the Putnam County Clerk's office and, clutching a small satchel in his arms, ran through the front doors of the rustic building. He arrived at the desk of County Clerk Edward Agor out of breath, reached into the bag, and pulled out a sealed and tied legal-size packet. Before Agor had unsealed the envelope, a flock of curious citizenry and boisterous news reporters barged into the building and surrounded the now bewildered messenger and clerk. Instantly, Agor realized what the contents of his delivery were.

He hurried into an adjoining private office and quickly unsealed the package, carefully removing two identical documents from inside, each titled "Memorandum." As he began to scan the blur of words etched across nine typewritten pages, a faint smile came to his lips. After a few moments of digesting what he was able, Agor slowly emerged from the side-office toward the impatiently waiting crowd. Barking instructions not to tear or destroy the document, he posted it to a board near the main counter, and the throng rushed forward to gain their first peek at the judge's opinion.

Shouting out legal phrases and searching for underlying conclusions, agitated reporters scribbled notes on yellow pads and rushed anxiously to telephones to break word of Judge Seeger's findings. Within a few hours, the full decision would be in the hands of John Mack, Henry Epstein, and virtually every newspaper in New York.

❖

Judge Seeger began his written opinion with a brief and competent restatement of the law appertaining to the case, and then added that "a careful consideration of the testimony is required, to ascertain whether the defendant's conduct in leaving the plaintiff is justified, especially in view of the youth of the defendant." Noting that the charges levied by Peaches Browning were almost exclusively dependent upon her *own* testimony, and since only the parties to the case had witnessed most of the occurrences complained of, Judge Seeger concluded that the case depended entirely upon the credibility of the parties. The testimony of each had to be weighed with "the greatest of care." Then, with the efficient and dispassionate precision of an executioner, Albert Seeger, article by article, thrashed Peaches Browning and Carolyn Heenan in a written opinion that survives to this day as one of the most vituperative castigations of a litigant in the annals of New York law.

❖

"Many of the charges of alleged cruelty are too trivial to warrant the belief that, if true, they could in any way have affected the defendant's health or peace of mind," began Seeger. "Nor is there sufficient testimony to establish defendant's charges of abnormal and unnatural acts and practices."

> The weight of evidence is against such charges. The conduct and actions of the defendant in continuing to live with plaintiff as long as she did, continuously accepting his bounty up to the last minute of the time she lived with him, and the fact that her mother remained in the plaintiff's house, enjoyed his hospitality, and accepted his bounty, are entirely inconsistent with the truth of these charges . . .

Seeger then turned to the exemplary treatment that Peaches received during the marriage. "[T]he plaintiff's generosity exhibited toward the defendant and her mother successfully contradict the false charges of penuriousness made against the plaintiff," he wrote.

> He paid large sums of money for medical treatment to numerous physicians, both before and after the marriage. He paid the defendant's mother a sum larger than her earnings before the marriage for remaining at home and nursing her daughter, as well as providing food and other necessaries and paying room rent. While furnishing defendant's mother with rooms in his apartments, the plaintiff also paid her an allowance....During the time that the defendant now accuses plaintiff of ill treatment, he devoted considerable time to the entertainment of his wife, introducing her into good society, allowing her to play golf and tennis, and furnishing her with the implements with which to play. It is true that he permitted photographs of himself and his wife to be taken; but I am constrained to the belief that she did not object there-

to, and that she enjoyed the foolish publicity as much as he did . . .

She enjoyed a life of ease and pleasure during her life with plaintiff, taking her breakfast in bed, and enjoying all the pleasures that money could buy and that the plaintiff could lavish upon her. She gained 20 pounds in weight.

The charges that the plaintiff locked defendant in her room, and that he came home intoxicated and threatened to shoot her while in that condition, are inventions pure and simple, and the insinuations as to improper conduct on part of plaintiff with the young adopted daughter, Dorothy, were groundless and particularly vicious.

Further to his evident opinion on Carolyn Heenan, Judge Seeger observed, "In [the defendant's] acts she is undoubtedly assisted and encouraged by her mother, who is her natural as well as legal guardian."

Addressing the mysterious acid attack head on, as a further example of the incredibility of Peaches and her mother, Seeger reasoned,

It is unbelievable that the acid burns were inflicted upon her while she was sleeping without her knowledge, by a person unknown to her, who escaped through closed doors and closed windows before she was wakened by the action of the acid. Her insinuation that the plaintiff was in some way connected with the application of the acid is false and vicious.

An investigation made by the police demonstrated that the doors and windows of the apartment had not been forced and no traces of any intruder were found . . . No acid was found upon the clothing or bed of the defendant, so that, if the acid was thrown upon the defendant by another person, it was done with remarkable accuracy.

And in a final blow to the character of Peaches Browning, Judge Seeger addressed the altered diary.

She copied her diary, eliminating some entries therein, and undertook to palm the copy off on the court as the original. It is greatly to the credit of her counsel that, when he discovered the fact, he made it known to the court. In short, the defendant and her mother have falsified, exaggerated, and magnified to such an extent as to render their testimony entirely unbelievable.

With a total and unequivocal nod to Daddy Browning's testimony, Seeger agreed with Browning's assessment as to the reasons for Peaches' departure.

> I am satisfied that the immediate cause of defendant's leaving the plaintiff was because she and her mother conspired to compel the plaintiff to purchase or lease a large apartment...as well as to procure an automobile for the personal use of the defendant . . . and also to procure additional and unnecessary clothing, and that the act of leaving was a trick to that end, or that she became tired of her aged husband and preferred alimony to his society.

Daddy Browning did not completely escape Seeger's wrath. One small paragraph in the total opinion was devoted to the false testimony introduced on the plaintiff's part. Referring to James Mixon and Roman Androwsky, the judge wrote that the testimony of each was "false and unworthy of belief . . . had no bearing on the case . . ." and had "wholly failed of its purpose, and . . . been disregarded entirely." "I am satisfied however," continued Seeger, "that the plaintiff and his counsel acted in good faith in the matter. Counsel should be more careful in investigating the character and antecedents of such witnesses before attempting to use them. These witnesses should be prosecuted." Seeger stopped short, however, of the obvious. Perjurous witnesses do not simply materialize; their testimony is coaxed and suborned. The judge noted the untrustworthiness of Mixon and Androwsky, but failed to lay the real blame at the feet of Daddy Browning where it truly belonged for blatantly tampering with the administration of justice.

The opinion concluded with praise for Daddy Browning and his loving treatment of his child-wife:

> The plaintiff may be a man of peculiar character, tastes, and ideas; but the fact that he married the defendant under the circumstances which existed, that he endowed her with his property, lifted her out poverty, and gave her every attention up to the very day of her leaving him, and made arrangements for her entertainment that evening, all tend to show that his intentions toward his wife were good. His treatment of the defendant and her mother was uniformly kind and considerate, but there was no limit to their demands.

In one final jab at Peaches Browning, Judge Seeger laid down the ultimate put-your-money-where-your-mouth-is challenge.

> At the time of leaving, the defendant made statements to the effect that plaintiff's money was not all that was to be desired. If she is sincere, she has a remedy by which she can effectively rid herself of both the plaintiff and his money. The law of this state accords to her a right of action for an annulment of the marriage . . .

In other words, Peaches *could* end the marriage if she wished—and accordingly relinquish all future rights to Browning's estate.

With that, Judge Seeger dismissed Peaches' counterclaim and awarded a judgment of separation "from bed and board forever" to Edward W. Browning.

❖

In the end, it was the cold decisive logic of a judge that separated Peaches and Daddy Browning, but the union was doomed from the moment these farcical individuals laid eyes upon each other. The infatuation of new love captured the quixotic nature of Browning the man, but he *was* a man, and he had chosen a child for his bride. Their interests were as divergent as any could be. They shared nothing in common. The bonds that secure true love were absent from the start.

Did Daddy Browning engage in unnatural acts and conduct that led to the demise of his marriage? Perhaps so. In the subjective world of assessing the credibility of human beings, there is no right and wrong—only perceptions. In the trial of Peaches and Daddy, Judge Seeger found Browning's testimony to be trustworthy. Another judge—another individual—might have concluded otherwise. Trustworthy or not, Daddy Browning must stand rightfully accused of utter and careless stupidity in the courtroom of common sense. His blunders, if not outright unlawful, were downright reckless, and though he stood victorious in a court of law, he would pay dearly for that victory for the rest of his life.

Peaches leaving divorce courthouse

CHAPTER XXVI

THE GOOD
JUDGMENT
OF THIS
CITY

"In closing, it might not be amiss to paraphrase the famous remark of Voltaire—'Though I thoroughly disapprove of what you do, I will defend to the death your right to do it.'"

—REMARKS OF JOSEPH SCHULTZ,
Attorney for MacFadden Publications
Editor & Publisher
July 9, 1927

ON JUNE 15, 1927, EMILE GAUVREAU STOOD TRIAL BEFORE A THREE-JUDGE panel of the Court of Special Sessions, on specific violations of Section 1141 of the New York Penal Code. Represented by Max Steuer and Joseph Schultz, both well-known New York attorneys, Gauvreau's defense centered on two main arguments. First, that Section 1141 was unconstitutionally vague and should accordingly be struck down, and second, if the statute be allowed to stand, that Gauvreau had not violated it.

At trial there was no real dispute as to the facts of the case. The prosecutor introduced the offending editions of the *Graphic* without objection by the defense and Gauvreau's title at the paper was stipulated. The case, therefore, was based purely on the philosophical interpretation of the law as applied to this newspaper.

The essence of Gauvreau's defense came down to whether or not the treatment of the Browning case by the *Graphic*, even if shown to be in bad taste, could warrant a finding that the paper itself was principally devoted to "pictures or stories of deeds of bloodshed, lust, or crime," as proscribed by the statute. On July 1, 1927, the three justices of the

Court of Special Sessions decided that it was not.

Though avoiding the issue of the constitutionality of the statute itself, the court declared, "It would be impossible under the facts and conditions to find the defendant guilty." In a precise and well-reasoned written opinion, the judges stated:

> . . . [W]e might find that the pictures, and perhaps the printed matter, might be, in the opinion of some, disgusting and perhaps not what we believe should be printed in a paper in the City of New York or [any] other place. But still, it does not come under the law, in our opinion, and therefore on all the grounds, the [defendant] will be acquitted and discharged.
>
> We leave that publication to the good judgment of this City of New York and their fellows in the newspaper world. The question, as far as this Court is concerned, is not a violation of the law . . .

In response to the Court's ruling that public opinion and not the courts should judge a newspaper, Joseph Schultz lashed out at John Sumner. "Mr. Sumner should take a hint from that and leave to whom it properly belongs the right to pass upon the merits or demerits of what they read."

Undaunted by the court's decision, Sumner, in comments directed to news reporters who had gathered outside his offices upon release of the opinion, maintained that public sentiment was clearly on his side. Ninety percent of the people, according to his statistics, were against the *Graphic* and its vulgar publications. In a chilling parting comment, Sumner warned that though the state had no right of appeal in this case, the penal code statute still stood and that if the *Graphic* or any other publication chose to circulate material that he believed violated that statute, they would find themselves right back in court.

John Sumner would be watching.

'Peaches' Struts Her Stuff

—Photo by P. & A.

"PEACHES" BROWNING   LESLIE COUILLARD

"PEACHES," possibly the best-known girl in the United States, famed for her marriage to "Daddy" Browning and the subsequent suit for separation, made her debut to theatricals in a Chicago cabaret. Although she had been

Des O New Mar 2, 192

PEACHES GETS JOB

NEW YORK, March 26 — (A P)—Peaches says she has signed a $100,000 contract for appearance twice a day in independent vaudeville for six months. This figures out about $3,700 more per week than her lost alimony.

COSHOCTON O TRIBUNE Mar 27, 1927

MILLION DOLLAR
RAINBO
CLARK ST. at LAWRENCE AVE

FRED MANN Presents

"PEACHES" BROWNING

Reservations Ardmore 3700

"Peaches" Signs to Appear in Vaudeville; Attorney at Trial "Thru with Her," He Declares

NEW YORK, March 26.—"Peaches" Heenan Browning, whose wealthy middle aged husband Edward W. Browning recently obtained a separation, has become a vaudeville headliner, having signed a contract for $100,000.

She signed up with Arnold Stoltz, producer, to appear in vaudeville and picture theatres. Her first public appearance—outside of a courtroom—will take place April 18 in a little town in her native Ohio. d she's going to do a song and tour will take her as far

west as Chicago and in each theatre she will be on the stage 20 minutes.

"Ma" Heenan will be with her. And she's going to walk right out on the stage with her daughter, and prove to people that even tho Peaches may be "on the stage," she is quite properly chaperoned.

Special scenery is being made for "Peaches'" act.

A dancing team will perform and there will be two pianists.

"Peaches" will play in Cleveland and in Chicago, her agent stated,

(Continued on Page Two)

PROFUNDO! PEACHES!

VERSE

Girls, if you're thinking
of marrying,
Some one much older than
you.
Don't do the same thing
that I did
Or you'll be lonesome and
blue.

CHORUS

When Flaming Youth marries Old Age
Oh what regrets, bitter
regrets.
What good is being in
castles of gold
If your golden castles are
icy and cold?
I've learned a lesson I'll
remember for years,
And I have paid for it
with bitter tears.
When Flaming Youth marries Old Age—
Oh what regrets, wh

DETROIT MICH TIMES
APRIL 18, 1927

DANCING IN CHICAGO CAFE

CHICAGO ILL EXAMINER
MAY 20, 1927

'Peaches,' Bidding City Adieu, to Be Feted

Frances ("Peaches") Browning, saying farewell to Chicago, will appear at the Midway Gardens tomorrow night. She will be a feature of an elaborate "party" George O'Hare has scheduled.

DULUTH, MINN. HERALD

MAY 28

"Peaches" in Picture House.

Chicago, May 28.—"Peaches" Browning will play the Congress beginning June 5 for the first half of the week.

The Congress engagement will l "Peaches'" first in a picture hous The girl has worked about thing else in town, including ville, cabarets and ballroom

CHAPTER XXVII

POST PEACHES
AND DADDY

REPORTER: *Were you in love with him?*

PEACHES: *Not at all.*

REPORTER: *Why did you marry him?*

PEACHES: *I haven't the faintest idea. How can you account for the actions of a 15-year-old?*

—PEACHES BROWNING, 1954

DADDY BROWNING BASKED IN THE GLOW OF HIS VICTORY. JUDGE SEEGER'S decision had provided not only the complete legal vindication that he sought, but also personal rehabilitation for his tarnished reputation. He read with delight the bags of congratulatory letters and telegrams that poured into his office. When he met with the reporters who had swarmed through his doors as news of the decision broke, Browning turned to the blank space on his desk where Peaches' picture had stood and offered for the record, "I don't want to be uncharitable, but she'll never squeeze another cent out of me!" The prediction was, perhaps, premature.

❖

To a gathering of reporters outside of her apartment, an indignant Carolyn Heenan publicly lambasted Seeger's decision as one-sided and cruel. "The verdict was rough on me and my daughter," she said. To make matters worse, Browning's pre-trial alimony obligation of $300 per week was voided with Seeger's order.

Even as Peaches and her mother lamented their future, Henry Epstein began the arduous task of appeal. Though Judge Seeger had dealt Peaches an absolute defeat, he did grant an order for Browning to pay Epstein an additional $4,300 in accumulated legal fees and expenses. As

Epstein petitioned the court for the enforcement of that order and others, however, his efforts were immediately faced with resistance from Browning and his legal team. To his mounting frustration, every order of the court was argued, delayed, or appealed in some fashion or another, and with each required measure or response, Peaches' financial obligations only rose. Browning twice appealed that portion of the decision requiring him to pay Peaches' prior legal fees, and he vigorously objected to her claim for the future expenses of appeal.

Though Epstein did believe that he had at least some viable grounds to assert an appeal to Seeger's decision, Peaches steadfastly maintained that she lacked the funds with which to prosecute it to conclusion. Unless Epstein could secure an order to force Browning to pay his client's expenses of appeal, Judge Seeger's decision would remain forever undisturbed.

❖

Within days of her devastating defeat, Peaches Browning launched a new career. "I have undertaken the only means of earning a livelihood which was afforded me when my husband's allowances were stopped and when I was cast out into the world without any means whatsoever," she would write.

In the wake of the nationwide notoriety that she had gained during the separation trial, Peaches had been heavily pursued by theatre and show business concerns anxious to capitalize on the fame she had already generated. On March 27, 1927, Peaches Browning signed a contract with a producer and a booking agent for a career in vaudeville that would, in the coming years, take her to theatres and cafes from Chicago to Atlantic City and earn her the label of the "Most Talked of Girl in All the World."

Peaches traveled across the country with a troupe of cabaret entertainers and her mother in tow, and unflinchingly entertained huge audiences, not the least bit unsettled by the grueling schedule or the glaring eye of the spotlight. She performed in venues with names such as Rainbo Gardens, Rivoli Theatre, and the RenDezvous, but wherever the name Peaches Browning appeared in news bills or on theatre marquees, huge and curious crowds turned out eager to see the infamous child-bride and her roving hippodrome.

On a typical night, her act would consist of the singing of a song or two, a dance with a partner or burlesque group, and a short monologue jesting about her life with Daddy Browning and bestowing her tidbits of wisdom gained from the experience. In a droll effort at a Tin Pan Alley production, Peaches was credited with writing a song entitled "When Flaming Youth Marries Old Age," which she often performed during her act:

> Girls, if you're thinking of marrying,
> Someone much older than you,
> Don't do the same thing that I did,
> Or you'll be lonesome and blue.
> When Flaming Youth marries Old Age,
> Oh what regrets, bitter regrets.
> What good is being in castles of gold,
> If your golden castles are icy and cold?
> I've learned a lesson I'll remember for years,
> And I have paid for it with bitter tears.
> When Flaming Youth marries Old Age—
> Oh what regrets, what bitter regrets!

In the early months of her vaudeville career, the topic of how much money Peaches was earning was of great curiosity in the press, and Daddy Browning's legal team took notice. By the early summer of 1927, evidence, in the form of affidavits from Peaches' booking agent and promoter (with whom she was already butting heads) suggested that she had a yearly earning potential of nearly $100,000 and was booked for events well into the future.

Predictably, Peaches denied those claims and argued that her expenses were almost as great as what she was earning. When the matter ultimately came before Judge Seeger, however, he once again ruled in favor of Daddy Browning and refused to award Peaches her expenses of appeal. For all practical purposes, the ruling sounded the death-knell for a further challenge of Seeger's trial judgment.

Other difficulties having nothing to do with her separation seemed to plague the early months of Peaches' budding career. She seemed to travel under a cloud of bad feelings and bad luck. In Pittsburgh, the manager of a nightclub where the young actress was scheduled for appearance cancelled the show, claiming city authorities felt that "the public has had enough of her." Shortly thereafter, the Motion Picture Theatre Owner's Association of several states barred her from appearing in any of its four hundred affiliated facilities because she had not "earned by hard work and ability the right to appear."

On April 19, 1927, Peaches was arrested in Chicago on a charge of disorderly conduct when she volubly protested a traffic officer's charge of speeding for a vehicle in which she rode as a passenger, and on July 10, burglars broke into an Atlantic City apartment where Peaches and her mother were staying and made off with fur coats and other clothing. In the coming months Peaches would find herself embroiled in the divorce litigation of her new booking agent, Edgar Allen, whose wife had accused him of having an affair with the young performer. In early December, 1928, Ruth Shepley, the star of the theatrical production *The Squealer* walked off the set upon hearing that Peaches Browning would be entering the show with primary billing.

Peaches was persuaded by her handlers to have reconstructive surgery for the scars left by the acid burns. The surgery was performed by a plastic surgeon who was later banned from practice for negligently disfiguring a patient. While traveling between engagements in Ohio, she and her mother were injured when an automobile they were riding in swerved off the road to avoid another machine.

Her perils were at times pathetic and even comical, but she was not yet prepared to let Daddy Browning go. If she was to remain his wife legally, she was determined that he would pay for the privilege. At the end of her road to appeal, it seemed that Peaches had had enough of Henry Epstein—and the feelings were manifestly mutual. As the two parted company, Peaches found another attorney to handle matters with her estranged and wealthy husband. In Peaches' mind, those matters were only just beginning.

Henry Epstein quickly put the matter of Peaches and Daddy Browning behind him. In the coming years he would become active in state and municipal government serving as the Solicitor General of New York as well as Deputy Mayor under Mayor Robert Wagner. In 1955, Epstein was elected to the New York Supreme Court where he gained a staunch reputation for protecting the rights of religious organizations. Peaches Browning would become a curious footnote in an otherwise well respected and untarnished legal career.

❖

Legally exonerated and emotionally invigorated, Daddy Browning pressed forward with his real estate and philanthropic efforts. He attended charitable functions and contributed to civic endeavors—as always, with a full bevy of news cameras and reporters in tow. With his credibility restored as a result of Judge Seeger's trial verdict, many of Browning's prior legal problems seemed to have dissolved.

Immediately following the trial, Browning actively sought to allay any remaining suspicions that Vincent Pisarra and the Children's Society may have harbored regarding his relations with Dorothy Sunshine. He worked cordially and aggressively with Pisarra, answering whatever questions remained after Seeger's exculpation. He asked the Society not to punish his daughter for how they might have felt about him. To Daddy Browning's relief, Vincent Pisarra quietly ceased his investigation and forever closed his file on the matter within a few weeks of the trial.

Browning then turned his attentions to the Renee Shapiro lawsuit, and by the end of 1927 had settled the matter for a tiny percentage of the $100,000 demanded. That part of his life Browning was ready to let go. Mary Spas, however, was a different matter altogether.

❖

On the day that Daddy Browning's adoption of Mary Spas was annulled by the Queens County Surrogate's Court, the paper that Mary so vehemently protested signing was in fact a retraction and release of all claims with regard to the matters of her adoption. After certain cajoling by both Browning and her parents, Mary had ultimately signed the document, and now Browning used it in his defense. For five long years, Daddy Browning would keep the Spas case alive, peppering the girl with costly motions and petitions. Finally, in October of 1931, as the case came up for trial, Browning made an offer of settlement that was roughly equivalent to what she had expended in legal fees through the years. A year earlier Mary had eloped—with a dentist—and now she and her husband both just wanted the matter behind them. The offer was accepted and the last of Daddy Browning's embarrassing legal entanglements was over.

❖

By the summer of 1928, however, Peaches Browning and her new attorney, Daniel Cohalan, the politically well-connected former New York Supreme Court Justice, were focused on Browning's intricate real estate maneuvers. As Browning began buying, selling, leasing, and exchanging multiple forms of property, he was prominent, as always, in the newspapers and in social circles. Cohalan began searching the public records of Browning's past real estate transactions, and was astonished to learn of the series of transfers that Browning had made to his corporation Edbro Realty Company, Inc., on the very morning of his wedding to Peaches. The value of that property, Cohalan learned, was somewhere near one million dollars. Since the marriage, Browning had transferred to the corporation additional property valued at $300,000.

In a series of lawsuits filed against Daddy Browning from 1928 through 1930, Peaches sought to establish her one-third-dower interest in all property either transferred to or originally purchased under the name of Edbro Realty Company. Browning, Peaches alleged, had used the corporation as a dummy or a sham for the express purpose of defeating her legally required dower rights, and she claimed that justice required she be given a full interest in and to those properties. For good measure, Cohalan successfully placed *Lis Pendens*, or liens, pending trial, on the earlier transferred pieces of property. Browning would be effectively restrained from further conveying them without payment to his estranged wife.

❖

As the brisk real estate market of the 1920s began to mature, Daddy Browning saw troubling signs on the horizon where few others did. Beginning in the spring of 1929, he began selling his holdings not encumbered by Peaches' claims and converting the proceeds to cash. In a highly publicized and much anticipated public auction held at Madison Square Garden on June 17, 1929, Daddy Browning divested himself of fifteen parcels of real estate valued at over 2.6 million dollars. Then he hunkered in for what he knew would be a rough ride. Browning had foreseen the Great Depression and to a great degree had salvaged his imperiled fortune.

In August 1929, Browning settled Peaches' dower claim in an effort to free up the remaining properties and to allow their sale. In the next several months, as Browning liquidated the Edbro holdings that he had attempted to place beyond Peaches' grasp on his wedding day, Peaches received a dower interest totaling $189,000.

Several months later, in an unabashed stroke of legal creativity, Cohalan again sued Daddy Browning on behalf of Peaches. Recognizing that the bulk of Browning's real estate fortune was still held by Edbro Realty Company, he sought to establish his client's dower rights in all the rest of the property owned by the corporation, regardless of when or how that property had been originally procured. This time, Cohalan's theory relied upon Peaches' allegation that in contemplation of their marriage, Browning had promised that she would have a wife's dower interest in *all* property that he owned in the name of his alter-ego corporation. In its most basic form, the case was simply one of breach of contract. The theory, however, failed. The court rejected the case on the absence of any written agreement on Browning's part to share this property with his wife. Peaches' last hope for untold wealth was gone.

❖

On August 26, 1930, as an exclamation point to his separation from Peaches, Daddy Browning executed a codicil to his 1912 Last Will and Testament. In essence, the codicil left in place the main charitable provisions of his original will and also provided a yearly income of $10,000 to Dorothy Sunshine, to be increased to $25,000 per year upon her 21st birthday. Then, in an angry parting shot, Browning disinherited his wife to the full extent that the law of New York allowed:

> Whereas I have heretofore married Frances Heenan Browning, and whereas our marital relationship has been unhappy, and she having left me and by her acts caused me to lose all my love and affection for her and causing me great mental distress and worries, and the said Frances Heenan Browning having also caused me humiliation, embarrassment and unwarranted and unnecessary expense of money in the defense and prosecution of legal actions caused through the conduct of my said wife, Frances Heenan Browning; and whereas after a protracted trial of the issues in the Supreme Court of Westchester County New York, I was fully vindicated by the decision entirely in my favor because of my said wife's abandonment of me, it is now my wish that my said wife shall not share in any of my personalty or other estate; and because of her conduct as herein described toward me, I disinherit her from any of the benefits of my estate, except such interest as the law provides for her at the date of this Codicil.

Though the Great Depression enveloped the nation like a deadly fog, Daddy Browning had found relaxation for the first time in months. Finally, he thought, the last chapter of the saga of Peaches and Daddy had been written.

He couldn't have been more mistaken.

Edward Browning, surrounded by his team of attorneys, heads into the courts of New York once again.

CHAPTER XXVIII

MONEY, MONEY, EASY MONEY

"I have been frequently warned that attempts would be made to 'frame' me . . ."

—DADDY BROWNING

As Peaches Browning came of age, the albatross of a marriage-in-form-only began to weigh heavily on her mind. Not quite twenty years old, she found herself legally bound to a man who was nearly three times her age, and the result was the loss of what should have been the best years of her life. She felt constricted and fearful of creating any enduring relationships with men, and she saw little hope for the future. With the close of the "Lawless Decade" of the 1920s, it became clear to Peaches that she could no longer live her life in the interminable wait for the death of her estranged husband.

Having already established whatever dower rights in Browning's property that she legally could and after lengthy deliberations with her mother and Daniel Cohalan, Peaches realized that whatever rights she might give up with a termination of her marriage could be made up with the intangible benefits of freedom—and alimony. It was time for a divorce. The question, however, was how.

The same matrimonial laws that prevented Peaches and Daddy from ending their marriage in 1927 still prevailed in New York three years later. Without proof of adultery, no divorce could be granted and no financial orders could be sought. In order for Peaches to now successfully prosecute her suit for divorce, she would be required to obtain evidence of Browning's infidelity. She was sure of his nature—his proclivity for young women, his odd sexual practices that she swore to in the separa-tion trial, and his utter need to be seen in public—and she remained con-fident that, in time, his indiscretions would lead her to the evidence she required. As the winter of 1929 to 1930 bore down on the City of New York, Daddy Browning was blissfully unaware that private detectives engaged by Daniel Cohalan and his desperate client were tracking his every move.

❖

"The answer to the whole case is MONEY, MONEY, EASY MONEY!" protested Daddy Browning. The formal statement came in response to Peaches' divorce suit and had been distributed to his friends at the news-papers, who had already seen the complaint and were readying the story for the morning editions. By Christmas of 1930, Peaches, it seemed, had obtained her evidence, and another holiday season would find Daddy Browning embroiled in fierce litigation with his young wife.

For a period of several months, Peaches' private investigators had observed Browning as he cruised about New York in his distinctive Rolls Royce in the company of two young women. John S. Guishaw, Browning's chauffer (who, by early 1930, was feuding with his boss), had been contacted by Peaches' detectives and persuaded to swear out an affidavit as to his observations. With little more than Guishaw's statement and his promise to testify at trial, Daniel Colahan filed suit on behalf of his client.

Immediately, Colahan sought and was awarded $10,000 in counsel fees—about $125,000 today—from Browning to enable Peaches to prosecute her case. The primary objective of the suit aside from the obvious dissolution of the marriage was, of course, an order for the pay-ment of alimony, but the amount and form of that alimony would be left to the final determination of the judge at trial.

Throughout the pre-trial process, Daddy Browning maintained that Guishaw's claims were false and slanderous. He promised a vigorous defense to the case. Browning again felt that his character and his repu-tation had been impugned and regardless of the monetary consequences principle compelled his staunch refutation of the charges.

❖

Within a year after Peaches' case was filed, the parties once again found themselves hurling barbs at one another in a New York courtroom. Though a gathering of the curious greeted the wary litigants as they arrived, the trial began with little of the fanfare that had accompanied their earlier legal tussles. Peaches herself would offer no sensational testimony in these proceedings, opting instead to remain silent and solemn in the back of the gallery while her case unfolded through the testimony of others.

John Guishaw testified that he was retained as Daddy Browning's chauffer from March of 1924 to March of 1930 and that in the latter part of the relationship he kept a small notebook of his experiences. As he now nervously thumbed through the book, Guishaw recounted a series of long rides through Westchester County, or to and from nightclubs, during which he had chauffeured Daddy Browning in the company of two young sisters, whom he identified as Evelyn and Marion Jenis. When asked to point out the girls in the courtroom, Guishaw pointed his finger in the direction of the gallery. Upon command of the court, the sisters both gracelessly rose for the purpose of identification.

Instantly laughter swept through the gallery as the spectators beheld the Jenis sisters. Appearing to be in their early to mid-twenties and looking very much like impish twins, the two were dressed in identical blue suits, each with peroxide blonde hair set in matching bobbed styles. They looked about the room and smiled witlessly as Judge Walsh, the presiding justice, chided the spectators and threatened to clear the court.

With the resumption of testimony, Guishaw stated that on various occasions he had observed Browning and the Jenis girls engaged in what he described as "petting parties," and that he heard feminine squeals of laughter and amusement coming from the rear seat of the Rolls Royce such as, "Oh . . . Ah" and "Don't do that!" and "Let go my leg!" Upon the occasional glance into the windshield mirror, Guishaw said that he observed on more than one instance one or the other of the sisters sitting on Browning's lap and cooing with mischievous delight. After each tryst, Guishaw had to clean the rear of the car, which was always covered with peanut shells and smears of candy.

In defense of Guishaw's allegations, Browning's attorney, James Murray, called Marion Jenis as his first witness. Marion fluttered to the stand, her shoulders windmilling proudly. Browning looked on at the girl with beguiled admiration.

"Daddy Browning was a perfect gentleman at all times," squeaked

Marion. She denied that Browning had ever done anything inappropriate to them, and she protested as untrue any allegation that either she
or her sister had ever sat on his lap. "Mr. Browning always sat in the
center and my sister and I on either side."

"Were you or your sister guilty of any improprieties?" asked
Murray.

"No."

Marion went on to testify that the purpose of their repeated rides
with Daddy Browning, despite the ongoing speculation, was nothing
more than to discus the matter of dietetics. Marion, it seemed, was suffering at the time from an extended case of indigestion, and Browning,
by now a raw food enthusiast, was bestowing his knowledge and wisdom of the subject upon the sisters.

In the back of the courtroom, Peaches Browning rolled her eyes.

❖

In the four years since he had last offered testimony against his
wife—and despite his alleged attention to dietary matters—Daddy
Browning had begun to show the grind of his years. His hair had
whitened and receded, and his cheeks drooped in heavy bags, as did
the puffy darkness beneath his eyes. His voice, though strong when
he was angry, seemed at times resigned and muted. Browning ambled
to the witness box, and once again he swore to tell nothing but the
truth.

"You've got me," stammered Browning when asked in the preliminary phase of questioning what his age was. He leaned back in the
chair, turned his eyes upward, and began counting on his fingers. "I
think I'm 56 or 57." He could only begrudgingly recall the date of his
marriage to Peaches when reminded of such by a copy of his marriage
certificate.

On the matters alleged by Guishaw, Browning testified that he had
met the Jenis sisters through a hostess at a very exclusive establishment
called the Crescent Social Club, and that his relationship with the girls
was nothing but an innocent friendship. He denied even the hint of
impropriety in their long rides in his limousine and he insisted that
much of the conversation between them was focused on matters of a
dietary nature, as Marion Jenis had said. Browning then lectured the
courtroom on the importance of a diet filled with uncooked foods as the
key to good health and contentment.

"Were *both* young ladies suffering from stomach trouble?" asked Cohalan during cross-examination.

"No, but they were interested in dietetics," came the response. "I've read about 50 books on raw food."

"What else did you talk about with these young girls?"

"Books—they were very well read," answered Browning. "Music and all the nice, clean topics that all the nice clean girls talk about. Why these girls were just like Mother!" Browning then leaned forward and regarded the barrister. "And you nor no one else will dispute my mother with me."

Cohalan ignored the challenge. "Did you ever talk to these young ladies about their bodies?"

Browning flushed to near purple. "That's a dirty thought!" he roared. "Why don't you come out and say what you mean? *I* have a clean mind!"

"Were they always perfect young ladies?" asked Cohalan.

"Yes. I would be glad to have them for my own sisters or daughters and you would be too!"

Cohalan then queried whether it would be possible for a person in a passing car to see a girl sitting on a man's lap in the rear compartment of a Rolls Royce.

"I'm not a good authority on lap sitting."

"Isn't it a fact that your car was especially built for lap sitting?

"Absolutely not!"

With the close of Browning's defense, Cohalan rose to call his first rebuttal witness. Abruptly, however, Judge Walsh instructed the lawyer to take his seat.

"The court has listened attentively to all the testimony in this case," began Walsh. I don't think it needs any more testimony . . . for nothing can change its conclusion."

Browning leaned forward and watched with fixed and narrowed eyes.

"In ruling on a matter of fact this court finds that in all the allegations made in the complaint and in the bill of particulars not sufficient evidence has been brought to support the charges."

Amidst gasps of surprise throughout the courtroom, Cohalan pleaded with Judge Walsh to withhold judgment until given an opportunity to file briefs on the case. With a rap of the gavel, however, Cohalan's request was denied and the court was adjourned.

Peaches rose angrily and stormed from the courtroom amongst a bevy of news reporters.

"Have you anything to say about the court's judgment?" she was asked.

"No!" she shouted, and stomped her foot. "Not a word."

❖

As Daddy Browning shook hands with his lawyer and strolled blithely from the courthouse, he wondered whether his court battles with Peaches were finally at an end. In fact, they were. Peaches never sued him again, and she remained, until the day he died, the wife of Daddy Browning.

"Are you going to bring suit for divorce?" shouted the reporters.

"Don't bother me about that now," he said with a wince. "Christmas is coming and I've got to think about the children. I'm through with women. I'm going to devote my life to looking after kids—to making them happy wherever I find them." Then he paused and, as if in deep reflection, he added, "Honesty is the best policy. Truth wins. If you don't get your reward in this world you will in the next."

With a doff of the hat, Daddy Browning bid the reporters a good day and he walked out of the courthouse for the last time.

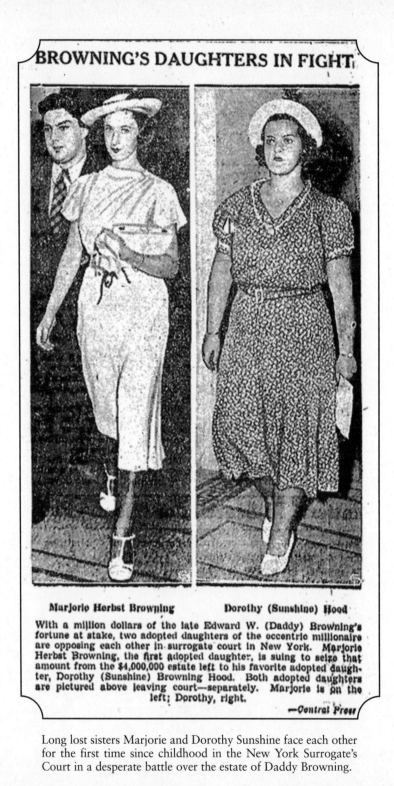

BROWNING'S DAUGHTERS IN FIGHT

Marjorie Herbst Browning   **Dorothy (Sunshine) Hood**

With a million dollars of the late Edward W. (Daddy) Browning's fortune at stake, two adopted daughters of the eccentric millionaire are opposing each other in surrogate court in New York. Marjorie Herbst Browning, the first adopted daughter, is suing to seize that amount from the $4,000,000 estate left to his favorite adopted daughter, Dorothy (Sunshine) Browning Hood. Both adopted daughters are pictured above leaving court—separately. Marjorie is on the left; Dorothy, right.

—Central Press

Long lost sisters Marjorie and Dorothy Sunshine face each other for the first time since childhood in the New York Surrogate's Court in a desperate battle over the estate of Daddy Browning.

THE BROWNING PRIZES

"Don't let it end like this. Tell them I said something."

—Last words of PANCHO VILLA, 1923

IT HAS BEEN SAID THAT "MEN ARE APT TO PREFER A PROSPEROUS ERROR TO an afflicted truth." The last days of Daddy Browning's life were marked by betrayal and greed on the part of those who surrounded him. The shear breadth of Browning's pending estate proved too much of a temptation for those who were charged with tending to his final needs.

Despite a medical pronouncement of mental incompetence by his treating physicians, as Browning lay near death in the rented home in Scarsdale he was persuaded by a newly retained business attorney, Victor K. Ross, and Edbro office manager, Harry Hackman, to execute a Second Codicil to his will, disposing of nearly $300,000. During Browning's final illness, Ross and Hackman had taken control of Edbro Realty Company, removed Browning from the Board of Directors for mental incompetence, and dramatically raised their own salaries. Throughout their tenure, they took complete control of Browning's business and personal affairs, and denied access to the friends and acquaintances that sought to see and speak with the man prior to his death.

The codicil, which was drawn by Ross, gave certain bequests to the hospital where Browning received care, two of his doctors, his two attending nurses, his chauffeur, his sister, his son-in-law, and several others. More importantly, however, it also gifted $10,000 to Harry Hackman, who was named as co-executor of the estate, and provided further:

> In appreciation of the loyal, devoted and competent services now being rendered and heretofore rendered to me by my personal attorney and general counsel, Victor K. D. Ross, of the City of New York, for which he has not been adequately compensated by me, I hereby order and direct that after my decease he shall remain and be retained as the sole and exclusive general attorney and counsel of and for my estate . . .

With a stroke of the pen, Ross had guaranteed himself a steady stream of legal fees for years to come.

In good health and in prior years the signature of Edward West Browning projected the same ebullient force as his imposing financial position suggested. The thick letters rose high above the lines and stretched exaggeratingly far across the page in an almost gothic announcement of confidence and resolution. The codicil now foisted on the stricken Browning, however, was signed with a few shaky lines that barely constituted his feeble mark on the document. The hand that had penned massive real estate transactions in the heart of Manhattan and romantic love notes to teenage girls had faltered. The stalwart figure that had once captured the imagination of an eager public was fading.

Shortly after the burial of Edward "Daddy" Browning, the attorney for the estate arranged a luncheon during which the Last Will and Testament was read to the named beneficiaries. The event was highly anticipated by Browning's relations and the public alike. Uncomfortable glances and raised eyebrows amongst those in the room punctuated each provision of the reading and hinted of rancor to come.

Browning's will left nearly all of his property to six charitable endeavors to fund the so-called "Browning Prizes," to be awarded for the best results achieved in each of six categories:

a . The prevention of cruelty to children or animals, or the promotion of peace and international harmony.

b. The spreading of the Gospel under Protestant auspices, either by distinguished example, effective teaching or exceptional personal service.

c. The uplifting of the moral condition of the world, either by some direct and positive service or example to that end, or by the introduction or furtherance of methods most successful in decreasing vice, gambling, intemperance, or dishonesty and corruption in government and politics.

d. The production of the most serviceable or useful discovery; or architectural improvement in fireproofing and sanitation or otherwise; or the most important work of art in painting, sculpture or literature.

e. The most widely beneficial discovery of new methods in medicine, surgery or in the prevention of disease.

f. The increased production of improvement of fish, birds or animals; the conservation of forests; the irrigation of arid lands; the increase or improvement of crops, flowers or plants.

With the 1930 codicil that disinherited Peaches except for any forced marital dower share, the only beneficiary that should have been in the room was Dorothy Sunshine. At the reading, however, the *second* codicil, which Browning had executed only days before his death, was proffered and immediately the tinge of suspicion suffused the air.

At the time of Browning's death estimates as to the value of his estate ranged anywhere from six to ten million dollars. Though he had divested himself of some real estate holdings in 1929, through the years of the Great Depression he added greatly to his worth by creatively and intelligently purchasing properties at bargain prices. With the legal uncertainties created by the second codicil and the acrimony generated by Browning's unusual charitable bequests, it was inevitable that the will would be contested. The magnitude of the estate demanded it.

❖

After a lengthy inquiry, the New York County Surrogate's Court refused to allow probate of the Second Codicil. At the inquest, Victor Ross testified that he read the document to Browning, and the court found this to be true, but also found that Browning was asleep at the time. Doctors testified that Browning suffered from an exaggerated ego and experienced delusions. The integrity of the inquest itself came into question when charges of attempts to influence witnesses were levied and investigated by District Attorney, William C. Dodge. A hospital orderly who cared for Browning testified that he had placed his signature on the codicil as witness eight days after it was actually signed by Browning, and that he did so at the behest of Victor Ross. He was promised $500 for his services from Harry Hackman.

In a written opinion, the Surrogate's Court judge concluded that provision had been made in the codicil for "everyone who could give any information as to the actual condition of the deceased during the last four weeks of his life." The court found that the codicil had been left carelessly lying about Browning's room in plain view of his attendees and observed, "It must have been tempting bait to nurses and doctors to find themselves named for substantial bequests in a paper which could be signed only if deceased could be shown to have regained the mental and physical capacity which he lacked . . ." The opinion was also a harsh indictment of Victor Ross, who would "stand to profit very largely . . . because of the fees he might earn—fees wholly out of keeping with the modest pay he was receiving while deceased was competent." It was a convenient mutiny and those closest to Browning as his death approached were at the helm of the pirate ship.

❖

Within several weeks of Browning's death, claims were also filed against the estate by Nellie Adele and Marjorie Browning, Dorothy Sunshine, who was now married and living in North Carolina, and Peaches Browning, all of whom sought distributive shares on the basis that Browning's charitable bequests were vague and against public policy. The rancorous and often painful ensuing litigation resulted in decades of intense and personal clashes with the courts and with one another and required years of petitions, hearings, trials, appeals, and further appeals. As administrative costs, legal fees, taxes, and simple depreciation whittled away at the value of the estate, the ultimate reward remained an elusive and ever changing web of confusion.

Early in the process, the courts determined that Browning's Paris divorce of Nellie Adele in 1924 was valid and that she was, accordingly, excluded from his estate by virtue of the final divorce agreement. Likewise, Peaches was also excluded by virtue of the 1930 codicil that disinherited her, with the exception of her one-third-dower interest, which remained intact. The battle over Browning's estate would, therefore, ultimately come down to a heartbreaking collision of long-lost sisters.

❖

Years earlier, little Marjorie and Dorothy Sunshine Browning had lovingly played in the carefree Gardens of Babylon atop their parent's lavish Central Park penthouse. With the subsequent divorce of their parents, however, and their cruel abrupt separation from one another, the happy years of their youth were but a memory. As the years went by, each knew that the other existed but their worlds remained as separate as the lingering anger of their estranged parents.

In the years following the breakup of Browning's first marriage, Marjorie remained with Nellie Adele in New York. Though she was sent to boarding schools and grew up feeling somewhat estranged from her mother, she did feel a kinship to Daddy Browning. Whatever early memories she had of her life in the apartment with the rooftop gardens were happy ones shrouded with the love of a doting father. With the death of Daddy Browning, however, Marjorie learned a painful secret that had been withheld from her for her entire life. Browning was neither her legal nor biological father. Though there had been no contact with the man throughout her life, she had at least assumed that she knew who her father was, and upon his death she believed that she was entitled to at least some benefit of his estate.

In August of 1937, Marjorie Browning, now a twenty-two-year-old student at Barnard College, took up swords against Dorothy Sunshine Browning in a highly anticipated and nationally followed New York Surrogate's Court proceeding. The essence of Marjorie's claim was that although she was neither fathered nor legally adopted by Edward Browning, he had made a promise to support, educate, and name her as his heir. She now sought to enforce that promise as a legal and binding obligation.

Witnesses for Marjorie testified to the circumstances of her original adoption by Nellie Adele and maintained that Browning's failure to join in that adoption was formality only—that he fully intended to treat the child as his own with full rights to his fortune. At a heart-wrenching and emotional point of the proceedings, Marjorie's biological parents, Jacob and Minnie Herbst, whom Marjorie had not seen in nineteen years, appeared and testified on behalf of their child. Tears welled in the eyes of all in the courtroom as a sobbing Mrs. Herbst told of how she and her husband had answered Browning's adoption advertisement and ultimately given up their child, promising never to have contact with her again.

In a twice-appealed decision, the Surrogate's Court failed to find any express or implied contract on the part of Edward Browning to care for the estranged Marjorie, and it accordingly denied her claim. The long-lost sisters would never speak again.

By 1940, Dorothy Sunshine remained as the sole heiress to whatever was left of Daddy Browning's estate, to be shared, however, with the Charitable Trusts that Browning had created in his 1912 will. Through the years Peaches had established and collected her dower interest and had finally exited the proceedings. Likewise, exhaustive appeals finally adjudicated the validity of the charitable gifts that Browning had made in his will, leaving only the complex task of determining the relative shares to each beneficiary. Without the management and manipulation of its creator, however, the value of Browning's vast fortune continued to be eaten by endless claims, taxes, and administrative costs. In the end only a small percentage of the original fortune ever found its way to Dorothy Sunshine or to the charitable awards that Browning had so nobly envisioned so many years before.

❖

On August 23, 1956, Carolyn Heenan heard an alarming sound in the bathroom of the New York apartment that she shared with Peaches. When she went to investigate, she found her forty-six-year-old daughter sprawled on the floor dressed in a nightgown and bleeding from a large contusion above the ear. She never regained consciousness. Though the exact circumstances of the fall were not determined, an autopsy revealed that Peaches suffered from liver disease reportedly caused by alcoholism. At her death her name was Frances Belle Heenan Browning Hynes Civelli Wilson, but her obituary in the *New York Times* simply called her "Peaches Browning . . . Child-Bride Symbol of Twenties."

"It's so easy to get married," she had said. "I don't understand girls who can't get married." She lived true to her word. Several weeks after Daddy Browning's death in 1934, Peaches announced her engagement to the wealthy New York theatre manager Bernard Hynes. Within the next twelve years she would divorce twice and marry twice more, and in the meantime carry on a several-month tryst with Milton Berle. "She was fun and easy to be with," wrote Berle in his autobiography. "We just enjoyed each other every way a man and woman can."

Through it all, Peaches never mothered a child of her own. Carolyn Heenan, however, had nothing but praise for her daughter. After Peaches' marriage in 1946 to her fourth husband, Ralph Wilson, Carolyn referred to Peaches as "the wisest of all the girls who made the headlines in the 20's. Most of the other girls of that period are broke now, but Frances has all of her money in real estate."

❖

In 1969, thirty-five years after the death of Edward West Browning, his estate was finally closed. The final value of his once staggering fortune had been reduced to a mere $648,000. The stark accounting of the Surrogate's Court spoke nothing, however, of the man who had endured the advent of the Great Depression and forever changed the city skyline of New York.

Though the memory of Edward "Daddy" Browning has long ago faded into the nostalgic archives of an ever-changing nation, his legacy of success despite radical nonconformity survives to this day. His char-

Peaches Browning, child-bride icon of the 1920s.

itable intentions did take wing, and in 1971, a few years after the death of his daughter Dorothy Sunshine, the first five recipients of the Browning Achievement Awards were distributed. True to Browning's wishes, these prizes were conferred upon individuals who had demonstrated preeminent results in their particular fields of environmental conservation, improvement of food sources, disease prevention, alleviation of addiction, and the spreading of the Christian gospel. Awards in Browning's name continue to this very day.

❖

With the final settlement of Daddy Browning's estate, the Clerk of the New York Surrogate's Court stamped the file "closed" and marked it for storage in the courthouse file depository. He lifted the last of the heavy boxes that contained the wearisome chronicle and almost didn't notice as a solitary paper tore loose from one of the files and wafted to the ground. As he picked up the paper he noticed that it was a small death announcement, and he curiously began to read:

> New York. Oct. 16.—(AP)—Three thousand orchids covered the casket at the funeral service of Edward West "Daddy" Browning today. The services were held at Campbell's on Broadway. There were 150 mourners but Frances Heenan, the "Peaches" of one of Daddy's romances, was not among them.

With a shrug, the clerk placed the paper back into the file and transported the "Matter of Edward West Browning" to its dusty grave in the bowels of the courthouse.

NOTES

Page 12   *preside over a happy home*   "Cinderella Wife Spends Day Purchasing Feminine Apparel," *The Harve Daily News,* Apr. 16, 1926; 1.

Page 12   *mid-life sentimental frolics*   "Rich Mr. Browning's Romantic Search for the 'Fair Helen'", W.B. Seabrook; Fresno Bee, May 23, 1926: 29.

Page 13   *I've kissed a dozen men*   F. Scott Fitzgerald, *This Side of Paradise* (Scribner, 1920), 165.

Page 13   *the allegations in a family newspaper*   Damon Runyon, *Trials & Other Tribulations* (Dorset Press, 1946), 108.

Page 13   *drop coverage of the case altogether*   "Editorial," *Boston Traveler,* Jan. 31, 1927: 1.

Page 13   *reading the paper in those days*   Robert Ruark, "Nostalgia Takes Ruark Back to Peaches Browning Period," *Oshkosh Daily Northwestern,* Sept. 12, 1956: 7.

Page 14   *hatred only causes hatred*   Michael S. Leif, H. Mitchell Caldwell and Benjamin Bycel, *Ladies and Gentlemen of the Jury, Great Closing Arguments in Modern Law* (Scribner, 1998), 181.

Page 15   *Year of the Big Shriek*   Allen Churchill, *The Year the World Went Mad* (Thomas Y. Crowell Company, 1960).

Page 15   *encounter he had with Edward Browning*   Jack Lait, "Walter Winchell On Broadway," *The Daily Mirror,* July 30, 1946.

Page 16   *the most maniacal publicity hound*   Ibid.

Page 16   *single letter to the editor*   Oliver H.P. Garrett, "The Gods Confused," *American Mercury Magazine,* Sept.-Dec. 1927: 328.

Page 19   *a case of love at first sight*   Stanley Walker, *Mrs. Astor's Horse,* Frederick A. Stokes Company, 1935: 208.

Page 19   *the largest hotel in New York*   "Streetscapes: The McAlpin Marine Grill; The Fate of a Polychrome Grotto Hangs in Balance," *The New York Times;* nytimes.com; July 23,1989.

Page 20   *he dearly loves the spotlight*   Stanley Walker, *Mrs. Astor's Horse,* Frederick A. Stokes Company, 1935: 201.

Page 20   *chucking chins, pinching cheeks*   Allen Churchill, *The Year the World Went Mad* (Thomas Y. Crowell Company, 1960), 30.

Page 21   *intoxication of rouge*   Frederick Lewis Allen *Only Yesterday, An Informal History of the Nineteen-Twenties,* (Harper Row, 1931), 89, quoting Dorothy Speare, *Dancers in the Dark,* George H. Doran Company, 1922.

Page 21   *a thick Bowery accent*   Damon Runyon, *Trials & Other Tribulations* (Dorset Press, 1946), 129.

Page 21   *resentment among some of the sisters*   Allen Churchill, *The Year the World Went Mad* (Thomas Y. Crowell Company, 1960), 30.

Page 21   *capable of lighting up a room*   Ibid., 32.

Page 21   *pos-i-tive-ly* Ibid., 45.

Page 21   *mysterious something called It* Ibid., 31-32.

Page 22   *going to call you Peaches* Ibid., 31.

Page 25   *moans of anguish* Accounts of the final days of Edward Browning are based upon records of a New York Surrogate Court inquiry into Browning's competence to execute a second codicil to his will, and are found in *First Revelations of the Fantastic Last Days of Incredible "Daddy" Browning*, King Feature Syndicate, Inc. 1936.

Page 26   *and you'll get back to health* "E.W. Browning Dies in Scarsdale at 59," *New York Times*, Oct. 13, 1934: 13.

Page 26   *if there is a gardener in Heaven* "Funeral Rites Held for E.W. Browning," *New York Times*, Oct. 16, 1934: 24.

Page 26   *sweet mind of a child* Ibid.

Page 26   *proceeds of the auction sale* "E.W. Browning Dies in Scarsdale at 59," *New York Times*, Oct. 13, 1934: 13.

Page 27   *hire Madison Square Garden* "Browning Has Exciting Day Playing Santa," *The Syracuse Herald*, Dec. 23, 1928: 8.

Page 27   *swimming pool for children* "E.W. Browning Dies in Scarsdale at 59," *New York Times*, Oct. 13, 1934: 13. Thought plans were drawn, the City declined the offer.

Page 29   *counting, drooling, gloating* Jack Lait, "Walter Winchell On Broadway," *The Daily Mirror*, July 30, 1946.

Page 31   *great progress and great instability* http://www.livingcityarchive.org/htm /decades/1870.htm

Page 31   *London in 1618* Ibid., 13-14.

Page 32   *the name Browning, King & Co.* The business was begun under the name of Hanford & Browning. The name was changed in 1861 to William C. Browning & Co. when it merged with a concern of Henry W. King. *Genealogy of the Brownings in American from 1621 to 1908*, Edward Franklin Browning A.M., Newburg, NY 1908, pg. 66. Also see *Outfitter's End*, Time Magazine, May 21, 1934.

Page 32   *outfitted the gold rush* "Outfitters' End," *Time Magazine*, May 21, 1934.

Page 33   *became a presidential elector* Ibid.

Page 33   *until his death of fever at Nashville, Tenn.* "Genealogy of the Brownings in America from 1621 to 1908," Edward Franklin Browning, A.M., Newburg, N.Y. 1908, pp. 13-14.

Page 34   *humorous sketches and with legerdemain* Ibid., 144.

Page 34   *prospered and owns many fine buildings* Ibid.

Page 34   *favorite of the social world* Ibid. Curiously, Edward Franklin mentions very little of his son in *Genealogy of the Brownings in America from 1621 to 1908*. While page upon page of detailed research is devoted to Browning's ancestors, only several short paragraphs, with limited detail, are written of his only son who worked close with him at the time. One can only speculate as to the reason.

Page 35   *in August they ballooned and ruptured* Erik Larson, *The Devil in the White City* (Vintage Books, 2003), 28.

Page 35   *improvements made to his properties* www.raken.com/American_Wealth /realtors/Landlords_NewYorkCity1.asp

Page 36   *a narrow twelve-story apartment building* Christopher Gray, "Streetscapes/

Notes ❖ 325

42 West 72nd Street and 126 West 73rd Street; 3 Identical Buildings, With a "Daddy" as Their Father," *New York Times*, Mar. 15, 1998.

Page 36   *Browning's odd building*   Office for Metropolitan History "Manhattan NB Database 1900-1986," Accessed June 22, 2007, http:// www.MetroHistory.Com.

Page 36   *cloud-cathedrals of the religion*   Lloyd Morris, *Incredible New York, High Life and Low Life of the Last Hundred Years* (Random House, 1951), 287.

Page 37   *resembled an illusion conjured up by poets*   Ibid.

Page 37   *communication center of the nation*   Oliver E. Allen, *New York, New York, A History of the World's Most Exhilarating & Challenging City* (Atheneum Macmillan Publishing Company, 1990), 246.

Page 37   *birth of the electric elevator*   Ibid.

Page 37   *limited by the thickness of the walls*   Ibid.

Page 37   *modern renaissance style of terra cotta*   "In the Real Estate Field," *New York Times*, Dec. 21, 1910.

Page 38   *a notable addition*   Ibid.

Page 38   *tallest office building ever built*   Sarah Bradfor Landau and Carl W. Condit, *The Rise of the Skyscraper, 1865-1913* (Yale University Press, 1996), 395.

Page 38   *window frames of golden bronze*   "Trading is Brisk In Realty Market," *New York Times*, Apr. 2, 1929: 2.

Page 38   *invisible population*   Christopher Gray, "An 1880's West Side Block With Many Changes," *New York Times*, Oct. 19, 2003.

Page 38   *erect apartment houses on the now empty lots*   "Building Mystery in 72d Street," *New York Times*, June 14, 1914.

Page 39   *policy of erecting tower-like structures*   "Tall Apartment Hotels," *New York Times*, Sept. 6, 1914.

Page 39   *ornamental facades of brick and terra cotta*   "The Real Estate Field," *New York Times*, June 17, 1914.

Page 39   *accentuate the New York skyline*   Christopher Gray, "Streetscapes/42 West 72nd Street and 126 West 73rd Street; 3 Identical Buildings, With a "Daddy" as Their Father," *New York Times*, Mar. 15, 1998.

Page 39   *quatrefoil form in cartouches*   Ibid.

Page 39   *approximately 30,000,000 cubic feet*   "Browning to Sell Most of His Realty," *New York Times*, May 18, 1929, p. 11. These figures have been extrapolated from this article.

Page 40   *show a client the sunny rooms first*   Jay Robert Nash, *Zanies, The World's Greatest Eccentrics* (New Century Publishers, Inc., 1982), 47.

Page 40   *ownership of certain gas ranges*   "Suit Over Brokaw Auto. Buyer Says it Did Not Come Up to the Promises," *New York Times*, Mar. 9, 1906, p. 2, and "An Interesting Decision," *New York Times*, March 26, 1911, p. XXI.

Page 40   *advancement of learning*   "Funds of Millions To Aid Research," *New York Times*, Sept. 4, 1912.

Page 40   *monument to his memory*   Affidavit of Joseph V. McKee, Attorney for Title Guarantee and Trust Company, In Re: Edward W. Browning, Surrogate's; New York County, dated August 4, 1937.

Page 40   *leading businessmen, philanthropists, and educators*   "Fund of Millions to Aid Research," *New York Times*, Sept. 4, 1912, 1.

Page 40   *how it could have leaked out*   Ibid.

Page 40   *ignorant of his appointment*   Ibid.

Page 41   *registration of the Selective Service Act*   During World War I there were three registrations. The first, on June 4, 1917, was for all men between the ages of 21 and 31. The second, on June 5, 1918, registered those who attained the age of 21 after June 5, 1917. The third registration took place on September 12, 1918. http://www.Archives.gov/genealogy/military/ww1/draft-registration/. Accessed June 23, 2007.

Page 41   *dropping bombs from an airship*   www.firstworldwar.com/airwar/summary .htm

Page 41   *key element of battle plans*   Ibid.

Page 42   *enthusiast for preparedness*   "Wants to Bombard Times Sq. From Aero," *New York Times*, Feb. 18, 1916: 7.

Page 421   *dropping dummy bombs*   Ibid.

Page 42   *circle the tower and drop imitation bombs*   Ibid.

Page 43   *practical to build a hanger*   Ibid.

Page 45   *disciplined in the modern wife*   "Why Rich Mr. Browning is 'Through With Women,'" *Ogden Standard Examiner*, July 13, 1924: 11.

Page 46   *the pain of ordinary living*   Ibid.

Page 46   *the couple's marital home*   "Bridal Pair's Roof Garden," *New York Times*, Apr. 16, 1915: 13.

Page 46   *furnishings that would typify my inward love*   "Why Rich Mr. Browning is 'Through With Women,'" *Ogden Standard Examiner*, July 13, 1924: 11.

Page 46   *combined magnificent opulence*   "First Revelations of the Fantastic Last Days of Incredible 'Daddy' Browning," *King Feature Syndicate, Inc.* 1936.

Page 47   *elephants and combating lions*   "Eastern Treasures in Browning Sale," *New York Times*, May 7, 1924: 14.

Page 47   *bearing Italian coats of arms*   Ibid.

Page 47-48 *the gown she is wearing*   "Why Rich Mr. Browning is 'Through With Women,'" *Ogden Standard Examiner*, July 13, 1924: 11.

Page 48   *fill up our hearts and time*   Ibid.

Page 48   *surrendering parents*   The Adoption History Project, http://www.uoregon .edu/~adoption/topics/birthparents.htm, Accessed June 25, 2007.

Page 48-49 *finest product of civilization*   The Adoption History Project, http://www .uoregon.edu/~adoption/topics/placingout.htm, Accessed June 25, 2007.

Page 49   *prominent wealthy old New York family*   "Public Notices," *New York Times*, Apr. 14, 1918: Page RE 1.

Page 50   *technically she was not his child*   At the time of the adoption, Section 110 of the New York Domestic Relations Law allowed "An adult unmarried person, *or an adult husband or wife,* or an adult husband and his adult wife together" to adopt a child. Emphasis added. On May 30, 1920, Section 110 was amended to omit the words, "or an adult husband or wife." New York Acts of 1920, Chapter 433.

Page 51   *bills were in one-dollar denominations*   "Browning Agrees To Give Up Girl, Who Is 17 or Older," *New York Times*, Aug. 8, 1925: 1

Page 51   *boat in the miniature lake*   "Browning Tots Rival 'Alice in Wonderland'; Are Idolized By All Little Kiddies in Land," *The Charleston Daily Mail*, June 20, 1920. N.E.A. Staff Correspondent, Lorry Jacobs, 12.

Page 53-54 *woman love to be browbeaten*   "Why Rich Mr. Browning is 'Through With Women,'" *Ogden Standard Examiner*, July 13, 1924: 11.

Page 55   *nothing short of 'hypnotic'*   "Most Outrageous Dentist's Bill a Husband Ever Paid?" *Ogden Standard Examiner*, Aug. 12, 1923, Sunday Feature Section.

Page 55   *engaged to marry Wilen*   Ibid.

Page 59   *having the appearance of a student*   "Says Mrs. Browning Fled With Dentist," *New York Times*, July 21, 1923: 7

Page 60   *if they should return to America*   Ibid.

Page 60   *he still loves his wife*   Ibid.

Page 61   *it ruins one good dentist*   "Dr. C.H. Wilen Denies Elopement Charges," *New York Times*, July 23, 1923: 15.

Page 61   *a quiet divorce in Paris*   Ibid.

Page 61   *my wife is as though she were dead*   "Most Outrageous Dentist's Bill a Husband Ever Paid?" *Ogden Standard Examiner*, Aug. 12, 1923, Sunday Feature Section.

Page 61   *eloped with Mrs. Browning*   "Paves Way For Wife to Marry Dentist 'Sheik,'" *The Modesto Evening News*, Aug. 3, 1923, 11.

Page 61   *boast of my ability to hate*   Ibid.

Page 61   *the two diamond rings she gave him*   "Cuts Off The Trust Fund of Eloping Wife," *The Davenport Democrat and Leader*, July 25, 1923.

Page 61   *has made a fool out of me*   Ibid.

Page 63   *sensible woman fall in love with a dentist*   Allen Churchill, *The Year the World Went Mad* (Thomas Y. Crowell Company, 1960).

Page 63   *already my husband*   "How Come?" *The Helena Daily Independent*, Mar. 10, 1926: 1.

Page 64   *entire sumptuous furnishings*   Display Ad, *New York Times*, May 4, 1924.

Page 64   *End of a Beautiful Romance*   Ibid.

Page 64   *largest and most important apartment sale*   "Browning Sale Totals $51,250," *New York Times*, May 9, 1924: 20.

Page 64-65 *shall not marry again*   "Why Rich Mr. Browning is 'Through With Women,'" *Ogden Standard Examiner*, July 13, 1924, 11.

Page 65   *other women very much younger*   Ibid.

Page 67   *meanest piece of publicity*   "Coler Investigates Browning Adoption; Tells of Protests," *New York Times*, Aug. 7, 1925: 1.

Page 68   *pretty refined girl*   "Public Notices," *New York Times*, July 6, 1925: 3.

Page 69   *opened up the gates of fairyland*   "Girls Vie To Win Offer Of Rich Home," *New York Times*, July 7, 1925: 1.

Page 71   *a contest among New York orphans*   "Riches for Poor Girl," *New York Daily Mirror*, July 23, 1925.

Page 72   *tears streamed from her eyes*   "Girls Vie To Win Offer Of Rich Home," *New York Times*, July 7, 1925: 1.

Page 72   *kind and fatherly*   Ibid.

Page 72   *playing the violin for you*   Ibid.

Page 73   *in need of some ready money*   "Siegal Boy's Story of Beating Untrue," *New York Times*, July 21, 1925, 4.

Page 75-76 *small service for a stranger*   "Queer Turns in Case of Boy Blackmailer," *New York Times*, July 20, 1925: 3.

Page 76   *and be murdered for it*   "Bail cut to $7,500, Siegal Boy is Freed," *New York Times*, July 22, 1925: 7.

Page 77   *on the question of bail*   "Siegal Bail Raised; Pleads Not Guilty," *New York Times*, July 25, 1925: 2.

Page 78   *syndicated expose entitled* "The Smile That Upset All Rich Mr. Browning's Plan," *The Galveston Daily New,* Aug. 30, 1925, 14.

Page 78   *obedient slave* Ibid.

Page 78   *not unlike hypnotic influence* "Mary is Hypnotist Says Browning Aid," *New York Times,* Aug. 13, 1925: 7.

Page 80   *father is a superintendent* "Browning's 'Poor Lassie' 21 and Nearly Engaged," *New York Daily Mirror,* Aug. 6, 1925: 2.

Page 81   *didn't spend all I had* "Browning's Adoption of Girl May Be Subject of Investigation," *Middleton Daily Herald,* Aug. 6, 1925.

Page 81   *preliminary shopping trip* Ibid.

Page 81   *I love my new daddy* "Cinderella Baby, Millionaire Pet, Bared as Actress 21 and Heiress," *Oakland Tribune,* Aug. 5, 1925: 1.

Page 83-84 *Browning's teeth on edge* "Browning's 'Poor Lassie' 21 and Nearly Engaged," *New York Daily Mirror,* Aug. 6, 1925: 2.

Page 84   *absolute faith in Mary Louise* Ibid.

Page 84   *her sixteenth birthday* "Browning and Girl Deny She Is Over 16," *New York Times,* Aug. 6, 1925: 1.

Page 84   *that she is an only child* Ibid.

Page 84   *Cinderella enough for me* "Browning's 'Poor Lassie' 21 and Nearly Engaged," *New York Daily Mirror,* Aug. 6, 1925: 2.

Page 84   *accentuated by the long golden brown curls* "Browning and Girl Deny She Is Over 16," *New York Times,* Aug. 6, 1925: 1.

Page 85   *the boys in Astoria* "Coler Investigates Browning Adoption; Tells of Protests," *New York Times,* Aug. 7, 1925: 1.

Page 85   *boyfriends or gentlemen friends* "Browning's 'Poor Lassie' 21 and Nearly Engaged," *New York Daily Mirror,* Aug. 6, 1925: 2.

Page 85   *papa and mama came to America from Prague* Ibid.

Page 85   *they say she is sixteen* "Browning and Girl Deny She Is Over 16," *New York Times,* Aug. 6, 1925: 1.

Page 85   *down to Kew Gardens tonight alone* Ibid.

Page 86   *highly unmoral transaction* "Coler Investigates Browning Adoption; Tells of Protests," *New York Times,* Aug. 7, 1925: 1.

Page 86   *statute that a parent cannot sell a child* "Attack Browning Adoption," *The Davenport Democrat,* Aug. 6, 1925:1.

Page 86   *praiseworthy and philanthropic act* "Coler Investigates Browning Adoption; Tells of Protests," *New York Times,* Aug. 7, 1925: 1.

Page 86   *have a clear conscience* "Attack Browning Adoption," *The Davenport Democrat,* Aug. 6, 1925:1.

Page 87   *offered myself for adoption* "Coler Investigates Browning Adoption; Tells of Protests," *New York Times,* Aug. 7, 1925: 1.

Page 87   *Bird Coler received a letter* "Begs Coler Aid in Recover of Sunshine Girl," *New York Daily Mirror,* Aug. 8, 1925: 3.

Page 88   *will be a sure-enough Cinderella* "New Episode in Adoption," *The Republican Press,* Aug. 7, 1925: 1.

Page 88   *the Mullen girl was in my office yesterday* Ibid.

Page 89-90 *the nasty things Mr. Coler has been saying* "New York 'Cinderella' Tries Suicide," *Wisconsin Rapids Daily Tribune,* Aug. 8, 1925: 1.

Page 90   *It's all past now*   "Browning Girl is 21, He Sends Her Away; Will End Adoption," *New York Times*, Aug. 9, 1925: 1.

Page 91   *because I want to be sixteen*   Ibid.

Page 92   *I will fight him*   "Browning Sorry; But Not Ashamed," *The Fitchburg Sentinel*, Aug. 10, 1925: 1.

Page 92   *Cinderella Wants Revenge*   "Cinderella Wants Revenge Against Browning," *New York Daily Mirror*, Aug. 11, 1925: 3.

Page 92   *capitalize on her notoriety*   "Cinderella Turns on Foster-Father," *New York Times*, Aug. 11, 1925: 16.

Page 93   *disgraceful ostentation of wealth*   Ibid.

Page 93   *the bulwarks of the American home*   Ibid.

Page 95   *honorable man on earth*   "Spas Girl Still Likes Limelight," *The Helena Daily Independent*, Aug. 13, 1925, 2.

Page 95   *trying to do good for people*   "Browning Sorry; But Not Ashamed," *The Fitchburg Sentinel*, Aug. 10, 1925: 1.

Page 97   *affairs at men's colleges*   Ellen Welles Page, "A Flapper's Appeal to Parents," *Outlook Magazine*, Dec. 6, 1922, 607.

Page 97   *one disillusioned young man*   Frederick Lewis Allen, *Only Yesterday, An Informal History of the Nineteen-Twenties*, (Harper Row, 1931), 95.

Page 98   *well Rosalind has still to meet the man*   F. Scott Fitzgerald, *This Side of Paradise* (Scribner, 1920), 159-160.

Page 98   *you simply had to or all life went punk*   Etahn Mordden, *That Jazz! An Idiosyncratic Social History of the American Twenties* (G.P. Putnam's Sons, 1978), 53.

Page 99   *large and blonde*   Damon Runyon, *Trials & Other Tribulations* (Dorset Press, 1991), 103.

Page 99   *she has stout legs*   Ibid.

Page 99   *buxom child*   Allen Churchill, *The Year the World Went Mad* (Thomas Y. Crowell Company, 1960).

Page 99   *with an overdeveloped body*   Jay Robert Nash, *Zanies, The World's Greatest Eccentrics* (New Century Publishers, Inc., 1982), 50.

Page 100   *cute and a little on the plump side*   Milton Berle and Haskle Frankel, *Milton Berle An Autobiography* (Delacorte Press, 1974), 116.

Page 101   *syncopated embrace*   Frederick Lewis Allen, *Only Yesterday, An Informal History of the Nineteen-Twenties*, (Harper Row, 1931), 90.

Page 101   *the female only half dressed*   Ibid.

Page 101   *a nice girl who petted*   "The Jazz Age's Favorite Scandal, The Perils of Peaches and Daddy," Suburbia Today, Bill Falk, *Gannett Westchester Rockland Newspapers*, Jan. 24, 1986: 6.

Page 103   *her best chance in life was to marry a millionaire*   Allen Churchill, *The Year the World Went Mad* (Thomas Y. Crowell Company, 1960).

Page 105   *opportunity for healthy entertainment*   "Browning, Erstwhile Fairy Godfather, Has Cinderella," *The Daily Messenger*, Apr. 1, 1926, 1.

Page 106   *the Cinderella of my heart*   "'I Was Her Slave' – Browning," *New York Daily Mirror*, Oct. 5, 1926: 4.

Page 107   *his savoir faire*   Allen Churchill, *The Year the World Went Mad* (Thomas Y. Crowell Company, 1960).

Page 109   *a kind and honorable gentleman*   "Browning May Wed New Cinderella, 15," *New York Times*, Apr. 1, 1926: 26.

Page 110   *the finest engagement ring*   "15-Year High School Girl New Cinderella," *The Bee, Danville, VA,* Apr. 1, 1926: 3.

Page 113   *curly but cut short, you know*   "Browning, Erstwhile Fairy Godfather, Has Cinderella," *The Daily Messenger,* Apr. 1, 1926.

Page 113   *whether or not we will marry*   "New Cinderella Picked as Bride For Browning," *Oakland Tribune,* Apr. 1, 1926: 8.

Page 113   *erstwhile fairy godfather*   "Browning, Erstwhile Fairy Godfather, Has Cinderella," *The Daily Messenger,* Apr. 1, 1926.

Page 113   *girl to marry millionaire in June*   "Assert 15 Year Old High School Girl to Marry Millionaire in June," *The Lancaster Daily Eagle,* Apr. 1, 1926: 1.

Page 113   *role of godfather to Cinderella*   "Realtor Is In the Role of Godfather to Cinderella," *The Portsmouth Daily Times,* Apr. 1, 1926: 1.

Page 113   *described in weights and measures*   "Browning's New Cinderella to Keep Beauty," *New York Daily Mirror,* Apr. 1, 1926: 4.

Page 113   *Browning jinx*   "Browning Jinx," *The Morning Herald,* Apr. 5, 1926: 5.

Page 115   *kept away from young girls*   "Plans Court Action In 'Cinderella' Case," *New York Times,* Apr. 6, 1926: 31.

Page 116   *greatest police effect in the history*   "Entire City Force Hunts Kidnappers," *New York Times,* Mar. 3, 1932: 9.

Page 116   *vicious outrage*   Ibid.

Page 116   *rides, reels and rum*   "Vincent Pisarra S.P.C.C. Head, Dies," *New York Times,* June 11, 1939: 44.

Page 117   *to rescue little children*   "The New York Society for the Prevention of Cruelty to Children 125th Anniversary 1875-2000," http://www.nyspcc .org/beta_history/index_history.htm. Accessed Sept. 10, 2007.

Page 117   *conviction rate of 94%*   "The NYSPCC Story," http://www.nyspcc.org /beta_history/index_history.htm. Accessed Sept. 10, 2007.

Page 118   *just as soon as I get well*   "Browning Wins 'Cinderella,'" *Chester Times,* Apr. 3, 1926: 1.

Page 118   *misinterpreted his kindness*   "Tells of Romance," *Edwardsville Intelligencer,* Apr. 3, 1926:1.

Page 118   *correct the impression*   Ibid.

Page 118   *discuss serious things for hours*   Ibid.

Page 119   *founding a girls' sorority*   "Children's Society in Browning Case," *New York Times,* Apr. 2, 1926: 3.

Page 119   *what is it that induces a man*   Ibid.

Page 119   *night rides in a Rolls-Royce*   "'Fairy Prince' Faces Three Probes As Result of Latest Interest in New Cinderella," *The Portsmouth Daily News,* Apr. 2, 1926: 3.

Page 121   *crave any of his publicity*   "Plans Court Action In 'Cinderella' Case," *New York Times,* Apr. 6, 1926: 31.

Page 122   *done with remarkable accuracy*   "Browning v. Browning," 220 N.Y.S., 129 Misc. Rep. 137, 1927, Page 653.

Page 122   *inflicted the injury herself*   "Thinks Acid Attack on Girl Was A Fake," *New York Times,* Apr. 4, 1926: 16.

Page 122   *spoiled her hefty good looks*   Allen Churchill, *The Year the World Went Mad* (Thomas Y. Crowell Company, 1960).

Page 124   *a separate Children's Court*   "Hoyte for Choate," *Time Magazine,* Sept. 30, 1935.

Page 124   *Bad Boy's Friend*   Mildred Adams, "Trail Blazer in Courts For Childen," *New York Times*, July 9, 1933: Page SM12.

Page 126   *consent of a Supreme Court Justice*   "Heenan Girl Too Ill To Appear in Court," *New York Times*, Apr. 9, 1926: 6.

Page 126   *old enough to be her grandfather*   "'Bunny' – 'Peaches' Program Strikes New Snag in Bill," *New York Daily Mirror*, Apr. 9, 1926: 3.

Page 127   *strategic wartime maps*   Emile Gauvreau, *Hot News* (The MaCaulay Company, 1931), 16.

Page 127   *a fox within a fox*   Lester Cohen, *The New York Graphic, The World's Zaniest Newspaper* (Chilton Books, 1964), 50.

Page 129   *magnet attracts iron filings*   "Dictionary of American Biography, Emile Henry Gauvreau," Supplement 6, 1956-1960, American Council of Learned Societies, 1980.

Page 130   *slammed the story*   Emile Gauvreau, *My Last Million Readers* (E.P. Dutton & Co., Inc., 1941), 90.

Page 130   *since Johannes Gutenberg*   Ibid., 103.

Page 131   *World's Zaniest Newspaper*   Lester Cohen, *The New York Graphic, The World's Zaniest Newspaper* (Chilton Books, 1964).

Page 131   *worst form of debauchery*   Simon Michael Bessie, *Jazz Journalism, The Story of the Tabloid Newspapers* (Russell & Russell, 1969), 184.

Page 131   *the new fungus with gentle compassion*   Oliver H.P. Garrett, "The Gods Confused," *American Mercury Magazine*, Sept.-Dec. 1927, 327.

Page 132   *genuine and full-fledged Menace*   Simon Michael Bessie, *Jazz Journalism, The Story of the Tabloid Newspapers* (Russell & Russell, 1969), 184.

Page 132   *an unholy blot*   Ibid., 19.

Page 132   *perversion of journalism*   John D. Stevens, *Sensationalism and the New York Press* (Columbia University Press, 1991), 128.

Page 132   *process of fastening a camera lens*   Simon Michael Bessie, *Jazz Journalism, The Story of the Tabloid Newspapers* (Russell & Russell, 1969), 19.

Page 134   *treatment for heart disease*   Lester Cohen, *The New York Graphic, The World's Zaniest Newspaper* (Chilton Books, 1964), 212, 215.

Page 134   *bacteria of a vile disease*   Ibid., 214.

Page 134   *mystery, secrecy, ignorance, superstition*   American Newspaper Journalists, 1901-1925, *Dictionary of Literary Biography*, Edited by Perry J. Ashley, Bruccoli Clark, Vol. 25, Page 182.

Page 134   *classical nude poses*   Ibid.

Page 135   *taxi drivers and store clerks*   American Newspaper Journalists, 1901-1925, *Dictionary of Literary Biography*, Edited by Perry J. Ashley, Bruccoli Clark, Vol. 25, Page 182.

Page 135   *limb swingers into a furious temp*   Emile Gauvreau, *My Last Million Readers* (E.P. Dutton & Co., Inc., 1941), 102-103.

Page 136   *the editor's diminutive bicep*   Ibid., 105.

Page 136   *my message into their brains*   Emile Gauvreau, *Hot News* (The MaCaulay Company, 1931), 31.

Page 136   *blackest day in the history*   John D. Stevens, *Sensationalism and the New York Press* (Columbia University Press, 1991), 136. Quoting Robert L. Taylor, "Physical Culture," *The New Yorker*, Oct. 14-28, 1950: 26, 33-35.

Page 137   *keyhole journalism*   Lester Cohen, *The New York Graphic, The World's Zaniest Newspaper* (Chilton Books, 1964), 30.

Page 139   *he'll go places*   Lester Cohen, *The New York Graphic, The World's Zaniest Newspaper* (Chilton Books, 1964), 159.

Page 140   *for the benefit of circulation*   Emile Gauvreau, *Hot News* (The MaCaulay Company, 1931), 58.

Page 140   *polluted palate craved*   Ibid.

Page 140   *scent rich copy*   Ibid., 60.

Page 151   *no power on earth*   "Browning Marriage Victory for Girl's Mother," *New York Daily Mirror*, Apr. 12, 1927: 3.

Page 151   *you don't know my Frances*   Ibid.

Page 154   *been married for a week*   "$1,000 A Day Provided For Mrs. Browning," *Logansport Pharos-Tribune*, Apr. 17, 1926: 1.

Page 154   *Daddy wants me to spend*   "'Peaches' Browning Engulfed by Curious New York Crowd," *Atlanta Constitution*, Apr. 18, 1926: 12.

Page 155   *Peaches for life for me now*   "Sure Sugar Daddy," *Olean Evening Times*, Apr. 17, 1926: 1.

Page 156   *to his head like synthetic gin*   Emile Gauvreau, *Hot News* (The MaCaulay Company, 1931), 61. Though *Hot News* was thinly veiled as a fictional novel, it has been universally constructed as Gauvreau's autobiographical work. In writing of Peaches and Daddy, Gauvreau refers to "Uncle Cocoa" and "Sugar Plum," in an apparent attempt to protect himself from liability.

Page 156   *Mephistopheles to his Faust*   Ibid.

Page 157   *servants are a great problem*   "Peaches Browning Buys Gowns, Hats As 'Daddy' Proudly Supplies The Money," *The Lima News and Times-Democrat*, May 21, 1926: 2.

Page 157   *the web of their destiny*   Emile Gauvreau, *Hot News* (The MaCaulay Company, 1931), 65.

Page 157   *a new journalistic technique*   Ibid., 64.

Page 157   *the size of our bed*   "Why I Left Daddy Browning," *New York Evening Graphic*, Oct. 6, 1926.

Page 157   *eaten up like a strawberry sundae*   Emile Gauvreau, *Hot News* (The MaCaulay Company, 1931), 66.

Page 162   *elderly vulgarian and his bride*   Ibid., 69.

Page 164   *the legendary United States Congressman*   Adam Clayton Powell, Jr., *Adam by Adam: The Autobiography of Adam Clayton Powell, Jr.* (Kensington Publishing Corp., 1971), 33.

Page 168   *cheered by a letter of encouragement*   "Valentino Is Worse; Physicians Alarmed As Pleurisy Sets In," *New York Times*, Aug. 22, 1926: 1.

Page 168   *hysterical outburst and occasional convulsions*   Affidavit of Carolyn M. Heenan in Support of Motion for Alimony and Counsel Fee, Edward W. Browning, New York Supreme Court, Case No: 3/44.

Page 169   *money isn't everything*   Allen Churchill, *The Year the World Went Mad* (Thomas Y. Crowell Company, 1960), 38.

Page 169   *the bottom of my heart*   "Peaches In A $30,000 Cleanup," *New York Daily News*, Oct. 6, 1926: 3.

Page 169   *the varnish on the floors*   "Rich Cleanup By Peaches," *New York Daily News*, Oct. 6, 1926: 1.

Page 170   *My dream of love*   "Why I left Daddy Browning," *New York Evening Graphic*, as reprinted in *This Fabulous Century, 1920-1930* (Time-Life Books, New York, 1969), 192.

Page 171   *My dream of happiness*   "Peaches Tells Her Story," *The San Antonio Light*, Oct. 12, 1926: 1.

Page 171   *the costly things he promised*   Ibid., 12.

Page 171   *I really did love him then*   "Wanted Baby, But It Was Denied Her, Peaches Declares," *The Bridgeport Telegram*, Oct. 14, 1926: 10.

Page 171   *a very different girl now*   "Why I left Daddy Browning," *New York Evening Graphic*, as reprinted in *This Fabulous Century, 1920-1930* (Time-Life Books, New York, 1969), 192.

Page 171   *overwhelming obsession with him*   Ibid.

Page 171   *cage was not so gilded*   "Peaches Tells Her Story," *The San Antonio Light*, Oct. 12, 1926: 1.

Page 172   *marriage was in name only*   "Why I left Daddy Browning," *New York Evening Graphic*, as reprinted in *This Fabulous Century, 1920-1930* (Time-Life Books, New York, 1969), 193.

Page 172   *from the very first night*   Ibid.

Page 172   *no dove of peace*   Ibid.

Page 172   *potent as a youth of 20*   Ibid.

Page 173   *a child of my own*   Ibid.

Page 173   *in cash for paste diamonds*   "Peaches Like Ice, Says Browning," *New York Daily Mirror*, Oct. 12, 1926: 2.

Page 173   *my wife weighed 135 pounds*   "Browning Asserts Love For His Bride," *New York Times*, Oct. 10, 1926: 30.

Page 173   *both of us day and night*   "Peaches Like Ice, Says Browning," *New York Daily Mirror*, Oct. 12, 1926: 2.

Page 173   *she took her daughter away*   "Browning Blames His Mother-In-Law," *New York Times*, Oct. 12, 1926: 23.

Page 173   *murdering of the goose that laid the golden eggs*   "Peaches Still Aloof But Sends Bill For Clothes," *The Chicago Tribune*, Oct. 7, 1926: 3.

Page 173   *Peaches like ice*   "Peaches Like Ice, Says Browning," *New York Daily Mirror*, Oct. 12, 1926: 2.

Page 173   *Peaches pans her Daddy*   "Peaches Pans Her Daddy," *New York Daily News*, Oct. 9, 1926: 1.

Page 173   *Daddy rails at Peaches*   Ibid., 2.

Page 173   *night clubs, not babies*   "Night Clubs, Not Babies, All Peaches Wanted," *New York Daily Mirror,* Oct. 12, 1926: 4.

Page 174   *Browning blames his mother-in-law*   "Browning Blames His Mother-In-Law," *New York Times*, Oct. 12, 1926: 23.

Page 175   *tearing the guts out of the press*   Stanley Walker, *City Editor*, Frederick A. Stokes Company, 1934. Reprinted by Johns Hopkins University Press, 1999, Page 72.

Page 177   *barred the news photographers*   Frank Mallen, *Sauce For The Gander, The Amazing Story of a Fabulous Newspaper* (Baldwin Books, 1954), 29.

Page 178   *confession in the caption*   Ibid.

Page 179   *the most amazing thing that ever appeared*   Ibid.

Page 179   *a new chapter in the history of tabloid journalism* Emile Gauvreau, *Hot News* (The MaCaulay Company, 1931), 40.

Page 179   *employing the human figure itself* Ibid.

Page 180   *bastard art form* Stanley Walker, *City Editor*, Frederick A. Stokes Company, 1934. Reprinted by Johns Hopkins University Press, 1999, Page 72.

Page 183   *if a person cares for any one* "Starts Suit to Separate from Peaches," *Chicago Tribune*, Oct. 17, 1926: 1

Page 184   *remedy of legal separation* The remedy of Annulment would theoretically have also been available to the Brownings though there was never any such claim made by the parties.

Page 184   *cruel and inhuman treatment* New York Civil Practice Act, Section 1161.

Page 185   *since their marriage the defendant* Complaint, Edward W. Browning vs. Frances Heenan Browning, New York Supreme Court No. 3/44.

Page 185   *full of surprises lately* "Browning's Charge Angers Young Wife," *New York Times*, Oct. 18, 1926: 16.

Page 187   *to her life and limb* Counter claim, Edward W. Browning vs. Frances Heenan Browning, New York Supreme Court, Cause No. 3/44.

Page 187   *an hysterical, nervous condition* Ibid., Paragraph 12.

Page 187   *a form of sexual abnormality* Ibid., Paragraph 15.

Page 190   *decadent influence of Browning* "Browning May Lose Sunshine Girl," *New York Daily Mirror*, Oct. 30, 1926: 2.

Page 190   *to the Editor of The New York Times* "Mr. Will Rogers Wants a Divorce From the Browning Case," *New York Times*, Oct. 20, 1926: 27.

Page 190   *pendente lite* Meaning pending the outcome of the litigation.

Page 191   *I do solemnly appeal* Notice of Motion and Affidavits in Support of Motion, Edward W. Browning vs. Frances Heenan Browning, New York Supreme Court, Case No. 3/44.

Page 191   *Heaven knows all* "Daddy Browning Proves That Papa Pays and Pays," *The Times Recorder*, Nov. 2, 1926: 2.

Page 191   *a great joke to give taxi drivers* Ibid.

Page 192   *no new hats, new coats, nor new dresses* "'Peaches' Must Put Off Shopping Feast For Time," *Chicago Tribune*, Nov. 12, 1926: 34.

Page 192   *confidante of both of the parties* Affidavit and Order to Show Cause, Edward W. Browning vs. Frances Heenan Browning, New York Supreme Court, Cause 3/44.

Page 193   *no fish, after being stranded* Emile Gauvreau, *Hot News* (The MaCaulay Company, 1931), 87.

Page 195   *Carmel is a fine little town* "Puts Ban On 'Slush' In Browning Suits," *New York Times*, Dec. 19, 1926: 18.

Page 195   *violently laid hands upon* "Win If I Live, Says Browning," *New York Daily Mirror*, Dec. 17, 1926: 3.

Page 195   *fight this suit to the bitter end* "Mary Spas Sues Daddy Browning For Half Million," *Olean Evening Times*, Dec. 16, 1926: 1.

Page 197   *discouraged with life* Ibid., 4.

Page 197   *money means nothing to me* Ibid.

Page 197   *maybe people will believe me now* "Mary Spas Sues Daddy Browning For Half Million," *Olean Evening Times*, Dec. 16, 1926: 1.

Page 198   *doctored liquor* "City Welcomes New Year With Lavish Celebration; Gay Paraders Brave Rain," *New York Times*, Jan. 1, 1927: 1.

Page 198   *greatest outturnings*   Ibid.

Page 198   *The Year the World Went Mad*   Allen Churchill, *The Year the World Went Mad* (Thomas Y. Crowell Company, 1960).

Page 198   *dabbled in the law*   "John Mack Dies; Ex-State Justice," *New York Times*, Feb. 25,1959: 19.

Page 200   *relations with the little girl members*   "Browning's Cult," *New York Daily Mirror*, Jan. 3, 1927: 3.

Page 200   *back of his Rolls Royce*   Ibid.

Page 201   *sharing his caresses apparently without jealousy*   Ibid.

Page 201   *to your absence sir*   "Little Stories of Fact and Fancy, It Paid to be Truthful," *New York Times,* Sept. 21, 1913, Page SM8.

Page 202   *no taxes on beauty*   "Beauty Contest In Court," *New York Times,* Aug. 30, 1924: 9.

Page 202   *ridiculous attempt to gain sentiment*   "Browning Denies Charge," *New York Times,* Jan. 20, 1927: 16.

Page 203   *tuned in to the Queen's taste*   Damon Runyon, *Trials & Other Tribulations* (Dorset Press, 1991), 100.

Page 203   *many a large city*   "Browning Suit Opens; Adjourns Until Tuesday," *The Chester Times,* Jan. 24, 1927: 2.

Page 206   *no effort to avoid publicity*   Ibid.

Page 206   *stage of the game*   "Maimed by Bunny, Is Peaches' Plea," *The New York Daily Mirror,* Jan. 25, 1927: 3.

Page 207   *the great American Public*   "Damon Runyon, *Trials & Other Tribulations* (Dorset Press, 1991), 107.

Page 207   *man of peculiar character*   Browning v. Browning, 220 N.Y.S. 651, 1927, at 655.

Page 209   *Your correspondent's manly cheeks*   Damon Runyon, *Trials & Other Tribulations* (Dorset Press, 1991), 107.

Page 209   *surplus flesh* "Throngs Cheer Browning as Peaches Weeps," *The New York Daily Mirror,* Jan. 25, 1927: 4.

Page 209   *tenement girl bride*   The Best in *The World*, A Selection of New and Feature Stories, Editorials, Humor, Poems, and Reviews from 1921 to 1928. The Viking Press, 1973, Page 362. (Quoting from news article of January 26, 1927).

Page 209   *intimate relations with soap and water*   "Writer Hails 'Daddy as Peer of All Modern Publicity Engineers," *The Davenport Democrat,* Jan. 27, 1927: 1.

Page 210   *New York Journalism*   "Shadow of Censorship Menaces Press; Many Editors Revolt at Browning Smut," *Editor & Publisher,* Feb. 5, 1927: 1.

Page 210   *birthplace of New York State*   "Dr. Graham and the County Seat," *White Plains Times,* June 29, 2006.

Page 211   *gray-haired old wowser*   Damon Runyon, *Trials & Other Tribulations* (Dorset Press, 1991), 99.

Page 211   *made known to the world*   The Best in *The World*, A Selection of New and Feature Stories, Editorials, Humor, Poems, and Reviews from 1921 to 1928. The Viking Press, 1973, Page 362. (Quoting from news article of January 26, 1927).

Page 211   *open to the public*   Ibid.

Page 212   *young girls shall not be permitted*   Ibid.

Page 213   *health, safety, and peace of mind*   Browning v. Browning, 220 N.Y.S. 651, 1927, at 652.

Page 214 *Her English was good* "Browning's Wife Tells Her Story," *New York Times*, Jan. 26, 1927: 3.

Page 217 *so terribly funny* "Ibid.

Page 218 *hot-tempered and querulous* Affidavit of Frances Heenan Browning in Support of Motion for Alimony and Counsel Fee, Edward W. Browning vs. Frances Heenan Browning, New York Supreme Court, Case No. 3/44.

Page 242 *my daughter's husband is sexually abnormal* Affidavit of Carolyn M. Heenan in Support of Motion for Alimony and Counsel Fee, Edward W. Browning vs. Frances Heenan Browning, New York Supreme Court, Case No. 3/44.

Page 244 *retrieve your memory* "She's Not So Innocent, Says Daddy," *New York Daily Mirror*, Jan. 27, 1927: 4.

Page 247 *kindly ministrations of the psychopath* "Editorial," *Editor & Publisher*, Feb. 5, 1927: 34.

Page 248 *the bird has been through enough* "Browning to Tell His Story in Court Monday; Declares There Will Be No Reconciliation," *New York Times*, Jan. 28, 1927: 3.

Page 249 *childish defiance* "Emile Gauvreau, *Hot News* (The MaCaulay Company, 1931), 75.

Page 249 *boxed his ears* Ibid.

Page 249 *House of Usher* New York Evening Graphic, Jan. 28,1927: 1.

Page 250 *Nothing more sensational or fantastic* Frank Mallen, *Sauce For The Gander, The Amazing Story of a Fabulous Newspaper* (Baldwin Books, 1954), 120.

Page 250 *decision for publicity* "Sumner Vice Head, Raps at Seeger," *New York Daily Mirror*, Jan. 27, 1927: 3.

Page 250 *editorial revulsion* "Shadow of Censorship Menaces Press; Many Editors Revolt at Browning Smut," *Editor & Publisher*, Feb. 5, 1927: 1.

Page 251 *sanitary measure* "Won't Print Browning Story," *New York Times*, Jan. 27, 1927: 3.

Page 251 *morals of the community* "Editorial," *Boston Traveler*, Jan. 31, 1927: 3.

Page 251 *beyond the line of decency* "Shadow of Censorship Menaces Press; Many Editors Revolt at Browning Smut," *Editor & Publisher*, Feb. 5, 1927: 1. (Quoting New York Daily News, Jan. 31, 1927).

Page 251 *flagrant pictorial and news debauch* "Assails Publicity In Browning Suit," *New York Times* Jan. 31, 1927: 20.

Page 251 *peaches, mush, and applesauce* "Will Rogers Fed Up On 'Peaches' And Mush," *New York Times*, Jan. 28, 1927: 3.

Page 251 *the finer instincts* "Don't Want Her," *The Zanesville Signal*, Jan. 28, 1927: 1.

Page 253 *Who Picked Peaches* Allen Churchill, *The Year the World Went Mad* (Thomas Y. Crowell Company, 1960), 41.

Page 253 *You Are Old* Henry M. Paynter, "You Are Old," *New York Daily Mirror*, Jan. 27, 1927: 3.

Page 254 *Yo-do-dee-o-DO* Thomas J. Creswell, JSTOR, American Speech: Vol. 37, No. 1, 1962, Page 32-33. See also, Allen Churchill, *The Year the World Went Mad* (Thomas Y. Crowell Company, 1960), 41-42. *Crazy Words, Crazy Tune*, music by Milton Ager, lyrics by Jack Yellen, 1927.

Page 254 *I ordered Peaches* Lester Cohen, *The New York Graphic, The World's Zaniest Newspaper* (Chilton Books, 1964), 128-129.

Page 254 *marry Siamese twins* "Bunny-Peaches Wisecracks Pay Well," *The New York Daily Mirror*, Jan. 28, 1927: 2.

Page 254-5 *like a tiny amphitheatre* "Court Bars Attacks On Browning's Wife," *New York Times*, Feb. 1, 1927: 3.

Page 256, *how it happened* Ibid.

Page 249, *never opened his mouth* Ibid.

Page 257, *a black, beetled brow* Damon Runyon, *Trials & Other Tribulations* (Dorset Press, 1991), 118.

Page 259, *non payment of kisses* Coined by Columnist for I.N.S., James L. Kilgallen, Jan. 24, 1927. See, "Browning's Separation Suit Against 'Peaches" His Child Bride Begins." *The Bee*, January 24, 1927, 1.

Page 264, *an air of welcome expectancy* "Browning Testifies As Wife's Suit Ends," *New York Times*, Feb. 2, 1927: 3.

Page 264, *Fulton fish market* Lester Cohen, *The New York Graphic, The World's Zaniest Newspaper* (Chilton Books, 1964), 128-129.

Page 277 *constitutional guarantee* "Editorial," *Editor & Publisher*, Feb. 5, 1927: 34.

Page 278 *license of filth* "Vice Society Hales N.Y. Graphic To Court," *Editor & Publisher*, Feb. 12, 1927: 5.

Page 279 *circulation of obscene literature* 63rd Annual Report of the New York Society for the Suppression of Vice, 1936, Page 19.

Page 279 *berserk lion of purity* "Noncensorship," *Time Magazine*, Feb. 21, 1927.

Page 281 *Plead guilty* Emile Gauvreau, *My Last Million Readers* (E.P. Dutton & Co., Inc., 1941), 112.

Page 281 *a strain of dangerous filth* "Vice Society Hales N.Y. Graphic To Court," *Editor & Publisher*, Feb. 12, 1927: 5.

Page 282 *Comstockism and Somnerism* Ibid. quoting New York Graphic, Feb. 9, 1927.

Page 282 *privilege of splitting fifty-fifty* "Vice Foe Sues Graphic," *New York Times*, Feb. 11, 1927: 2.

Page 282 *never before read a tabloid* "Graphic Editor Held In $100 Bail For Trial," *New York Times*, Apr. 26, 1927: 31.

Page 285 *The fair name of White Plains* Bill Falk, *The Perils of Peaches and Daddy*, Suburbia Today, Gannet Westchester Rockland Newspapers, Jan. 24, 1982, 6.

Page 286 *for what they are worth* "Assails Mixon Testimony," *New York Times*, Feb. 13, 1927: 2.

Page 286 *ninety-nine chances* "Peaches Thinks She Will Win Her Case; Daddy Also," *The Bee*, Feb. 3, 1927: 8.

Page 286 *pitch through the window* "Justice Seeger Hot Over Browning Story," *Burlington Daily Times*, Mar. 15, 1927: 1.

Page 287 *careful consideration of the testimony* Browning v. Browning, 220 N.Y.S. 651, 652 (1927)

Page 288 *the greatest care* Ibid., 653.

Page 288 *charges of alleged cruelty* Ibid.

Page 288 *abnormal and unnatural acts and practices* Ibid., 654.

Page 288 *The weight of evidence* Ibid.

Page 288 *false charges of penuriousness* Ibid., at 653.

Page 288 *furnishing defendant's mother with rooms* Ibid., at 654.

Page 289 *gained 20 pounds in weight* Ibid., at 655.

Page 289 *the plaintiff locked defendant* Ibid.

Page 289 *encouraged by her mother* Ibid.

Page 289   *unbelievable that the acid burns*   Ibid.

Page 289   *an investigation made by the police*   Ibid., 652-653.

Page 289   *She copied her diary*   Ibid., 655.

Page 290   *conspired to compel the plaintiff*   Ibid., 654-655.

Page 290   *been disregarded entirely*   Ibid., 655.

Page 290   *witnesses should be prosecuted*   Ibid.

Page 290   *a man of peculiar character*   Ibid., 655-656

Page 291   *an annulment of the marriage*   Ibid., 656.

Page 293   *famous remark of Voltaire*   "New York Graphic Was 'Within The Law,'" *Editor & Publisher,* July 9, 1927: 11.

Page 294   *find the defendant guilty*   Ibid.

Page 294   *the good judgment of this City of New York*   Ibid.

Page 296   *merits or demerits*   Ibid.

Page 297   *the actions of a 15-year-old*   Jay Robert Nash, *Zanies, The World's Greatest Eccentrics* (New Century Publishers, Inc., 1982), 57.

Page 297   *squeeze another cent*   "Peaches May Go on Stage; Daddy in a Jolly Humor," *New York Daily Mirror,* Mar. 22, 1927.

Page 297   *the verdict was rough*   Ibid.

Page 298   *only means of earning a livelihood*   Affidavit of Frances Heenan Browning, June 27, 1927.

Page 298   *Most Talked of Girl in All the World*   "Peaches Browning, Entertainer," *South Town Economist,* May 20, 1927.

Page 299   *public has had enough*   "Café Cancels Peaches' Date," *Oakland Tribune,* Mar. 30, 1927: 1.

Page 299   *earned by hard work*   "Stage Bars Mrs. Browning," *New York Times,* Apr. 1, 1927: 27.

Page 305   *I have been frequently warned*   "Sues Browning for Divorce Here," *New York Times,* Dec. 28, 1930: 28.

Page 310   *Not a word*   "'Peaches' Browning Loses Suit for Absolute Divorce," *The Charleston Gazette,* Dec. 19, 1931: 1.

Page 310   *Honesty is the best policy*   Ibid.

Page 313   *prefer a prosperous error*   Jeremy Taylor, a 17th century clergyman in the Church of England.

Page 314   *probate of the Second Codicil*   According to New York law at the time, an inquest is mandatory where a testamentary document is executed within 30 days of death.

Page 316   *actual condition of the deceased*   "Browning Codicil Rejected By Court," *New York Times,* July 18, 1935.

Page 316   *physical capacity which he lacked*   Ibid.

Page 316   *stand to profit very largely*   Ibid. A request to the Grievance Committee of the New York Association of the Bar was made regarding Victor Ross's involvement in the Browning codicil. "$75,000 Settlement on Browning Codicil," *New York Times,* June 8, 1937.

Page 318   *so easy to get married*   "New Romance For 'Peaches,'" *The San Mateo Times,* June 5, 1950: 7.

Page 318   *fun and easy to be with*   Milton Berle and Haskle Frankel, *Milton Berle An Autobiography* (Delacorte Press, 1974), 118.

Page 318-9 *the wisest of all the girls*   "Honeymoon Diary," *San Antonio Light,* Nov. 10, 1946.

AUTHOR'S NOTE ON SOURCES

The story of Peaches and Daddy is true, though truth is often a matter of perspective. The relationships described in this book were highly contentious and each person's version of the facts differed in almost every respect. As with any legal proceeding, the court papers and journalistic accounts are replete with inconsistent and contested statements. Where there is corroboration as to facts, I have relied on the prevailing view. Where unresolved conflicts leave no alternative, I have presented multiple views. Where there are simply no facts as to specific points of a minor nature, I have taken creative license and supplemented the record based on the history of the parties, the views of the day, and common sense.

The primary characters of this story are no longer with us. Their experiences have survived, however, in the form of newspaper stories, books, magazines, and portions of the court record. I have relied on all of these, wherever available, in compiling the story of Peaches and Daddy. Though I was provided access to some of the court files of the separation trial, a large portion of that file has been lost, stolen, or destroyed. The only known source for the actual trial testimony is contained in a pamphlet housed at the University of Minnesota Law Library entitled, *Peaches - Browning, The most sensational Divorce Case in History: A Complete Story of the Trial at White Plains Word By Word From the Official Court Record*, which I have relied upon for most of the quoted testimony found in this book. The content of much of that testimony has been corroborated by eyewitness accounts of the trial as recorded in many newspapers of the day.

BIBLIOGRAPHY

BOOKS

Allen, Frederick Lewis. *Only Yesterday, An Informal History of the Nineteen-Twenties*. Harper Row, 1931.

Allen, Oliver E. *New York, New York, A History of the World's Most Exhilarating & Challenging City*. Atheneum Macmillan Publishing Company, 1990.

Ashley, Perry J. (Edited by). *American Newspaper Journalists, 1901-1925, Dictionary of Literary Biography*. Volume 25. Bruccoli Clark, Gale Research Company, 1984.

Berle, Milton and Frankel, Haskle. *Milton Berle An Autobiography*. Delacorte Press, 1974.

Bessie, Simon Michael. *Jazz Journalism, The Story of the Tabloid Newspapers*. Russell & Russell, 1969.

Browning, Edward Franklin. *Genealogy of the Brownings in America from 1621 to 1908*. A.M., Newburg, N.Y., 1908.

Churchill, Allen. *The Year the World Went Mad*. Thomas Y. Crowell Company, 1960.

Cohen, Lester. *The New York Graphic, The World's Zaniest Newspaper*. Chilton Books, 1964.

Dictionary of American Biography, Emile Henry Gauvreau, Supplement 6, 1956-1960, American Council of Learned Societies, 1980.

Fitzgerald, F. Scott. *This Side of Paradise*. Scribner, 1920.

Gauvreau, Emile. *Hot News*. The Macaulay Company, 1931.

Gauvreau, Emile. *My Last Million Readers*. E.P. Dutton & Co., Inc. 1941.

Landau, Sarah Bradford and Condit, Carl W. *The Rise of the New York Skyscraper, 1865-1913*. Yale University Press, 1996.

Larson, Erik. *The Devil in the White City*. Vintage Books, 2003.

Leif, Michael S., Caldwell, Mitchell H., and Bycel, Benjamin. *Ladies and Gentlemen of the Jury, Great Closing Arguments in Modern Law*. Scribner, 1998.

Mallen, Frank. *Sauce For The Gander, The Amazing Story of a Fabulous Newspaper*. Baldwin Books, 1954.

Mordden, Ethan. *That Jazz! An Idiosyncratic Social History of the American Twenties*. G.P. Putnam's Sons, 1978.

Morris, Lloyd. *Incredible New York, High Life and Low Life of the Last Hundred Years*. Random House, 1951.

Nash, Jay Robert. *Zanies, The World's Greatest Eccentrics*. New Century Publishers, Inc., 1982.

Powell, Jr., Adam Clayton. *Adam by Adam: The Autobiography of Adam Clayton Powell, Jr.* Kensington Publishing Corp., 1971.

Runyon, Damon. *Trials & Other Tribulations*. Dorset Press, 1946.

This Fabulous Century, 1920-1930. Time-Life Books, New York, 1969.

Stevens, John D. *Sensationalism and the New York Press*. Columbia University Press, 1991.

The Best in The World, A Selection of New and Feature Stories, Editorials, Humor, Poems, and Reviews from 1921 to 1928, The Viking Press, 1973.

Walker, Stanley. *Mrs. Astor's Horse*. Frederick A. Stokes Company, 1935.

MAGAZINES AND PAMPHLETS

Creswell, Thomas J. *What Did Peaches Browning Say?* JSTOR, American Speech: Vol. 37, No. 1, 1962.

Garrett, Oliver H.P. *The Gods Confused*. American Mercury Magazine, September-December 1927.

Hoyte for Choate. Time Magazine. September 30, 1935.

Outfitters' End. Time Magazine, May 21, 1934.

Page, Ellen Welles. *A Flapper's Appeal to Parents*. Outlook Magazine, December 6, 1922.

Peaches - Browning, The most sensational Divorce Case in History: A Complete Story of the Trial at White Plains Word By Word From the Official Court Record. Author: unknown. Publisher: unknown. (Housed at University of Minnesota Law Library), 1927.

Noncensorship, Time Magazine, February 21, 1927.

ACKNOWLEDGMENTS

In the course of conducting the research for this book, Peaches and Daddy revealed themselves to me through a great many people and offices, all of whom I owe a debt of gratitude. The wonderful assistance and many courtesies extended to me were vital to the telling of this story, and are deeply appreciated.

I would foremost like to thank Thomas James Kearney, Jr., Surya-Patricia Lane Hood, and Dorothy Ann Hood Zembruski, the children of Dorothy Sunshine Browning, for providing me with insights into the personality of Daddy Browning that no written source could ever provide. The open and forthright input of the entire family was integral to the project and vital to an accurate portrayal of the characters. Sadly, Dorothy Ann Hood Zembruski passed away just weeks after our initial conversation. My sympathies go out to her family. I am also grateful for the kind assistance of Ellie Krajewski, the daughter of Marjorie Browning, and to Marie Gauvreau, the daughter-in-law of Emile Gauvreau.

Research for any book begins at the library and with a competent and patient librarian. In my case, Peaches and Daddy could never have taken shape without the kind assistance and guidance of David Smith of the New York Public Library—affectionately hailed as the "Librarian to the Stars." I am greatly indebted to him for an endless amount of information—and encouragement—that proved vital at every stage of this project.

The names of every person who provided help in assembling the nuts-and-bolts of this book could fill as many pages as the book itself. I do wish to thank, however, the following people for providing special assistance and information critical to the research of Peaches and Daddy:

Jaime Studley, Professor Bob Stepno, Attorney Robert E. Nowak, Reginald White of the Putnam County Historians office, Elaine Massena of the White Plains City Archives, Attorneys J. Joseph McGowan and Phillip Shatz of the law firm McCabe & Mack, LLP, Natalie Marshall, Lewis Wyman of the Prints and Photographs Division of the Library of Congress, Gary Schieferstin of Blake & Blake Genealogists, Peter and Daniel Cohen, Dr. Marc Garden, Eric Paisner, and Carol March.

A special thank you to David Reuter, who provided that jolt of encouragement when all seemed lost. Funny how a simple compliment can get a person right back on track.

For proofreading, guidance, and just plain inspiration, I wish to thank my entire family and, of course, Cousin Phil Chait. They supported me and endured me throughout the writing of this book.

Finally, I wish to thank my agent, Greg Daniel, and my editor, Juliet Grames, for allowing me the privilege of bringing Peaches and Daddy to life. Of an author's plight, Stephen King once wrote, "Writing is a lonely job. Having someone who believes in you makes a lot of difference."

INDEX